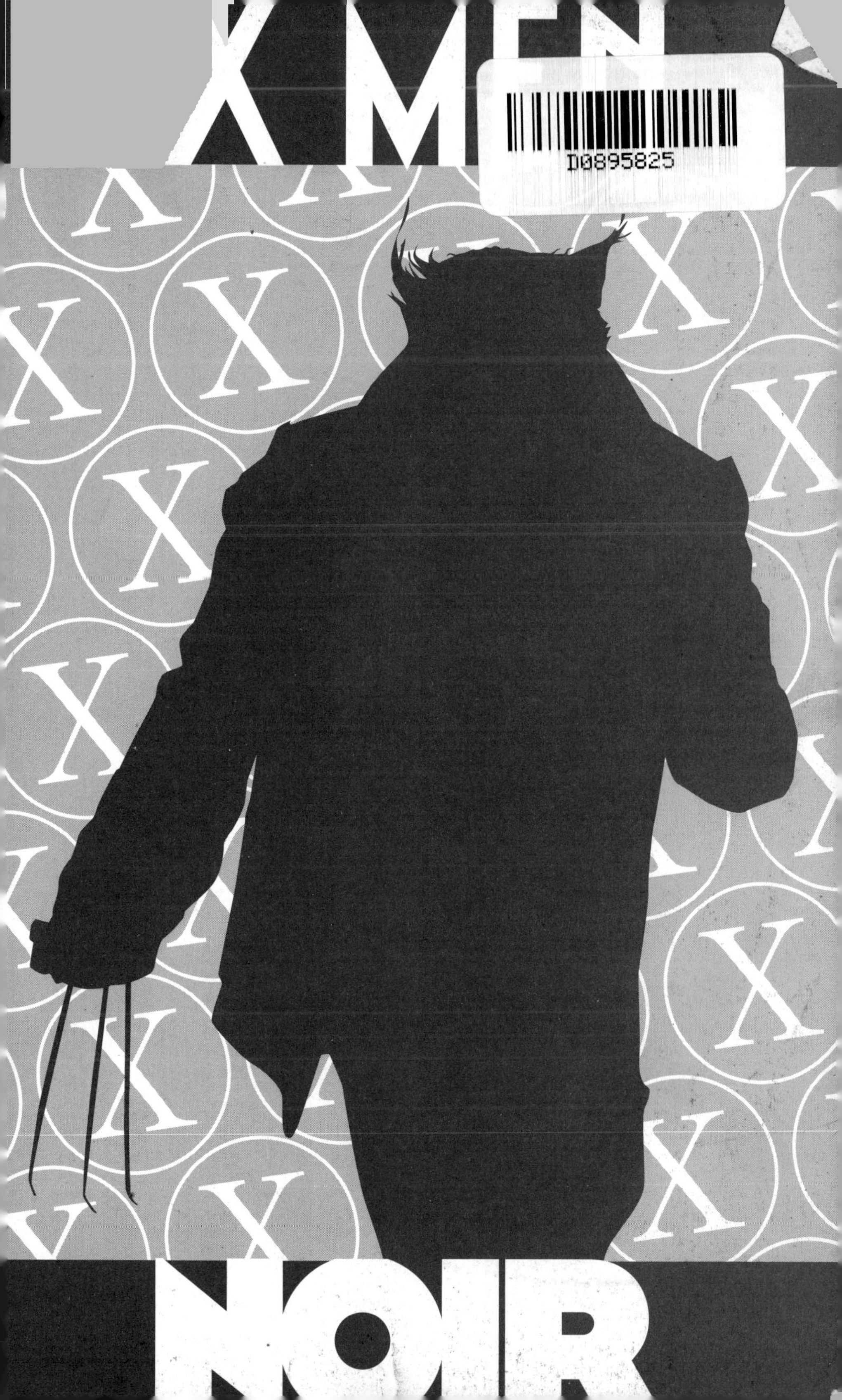
NOIR

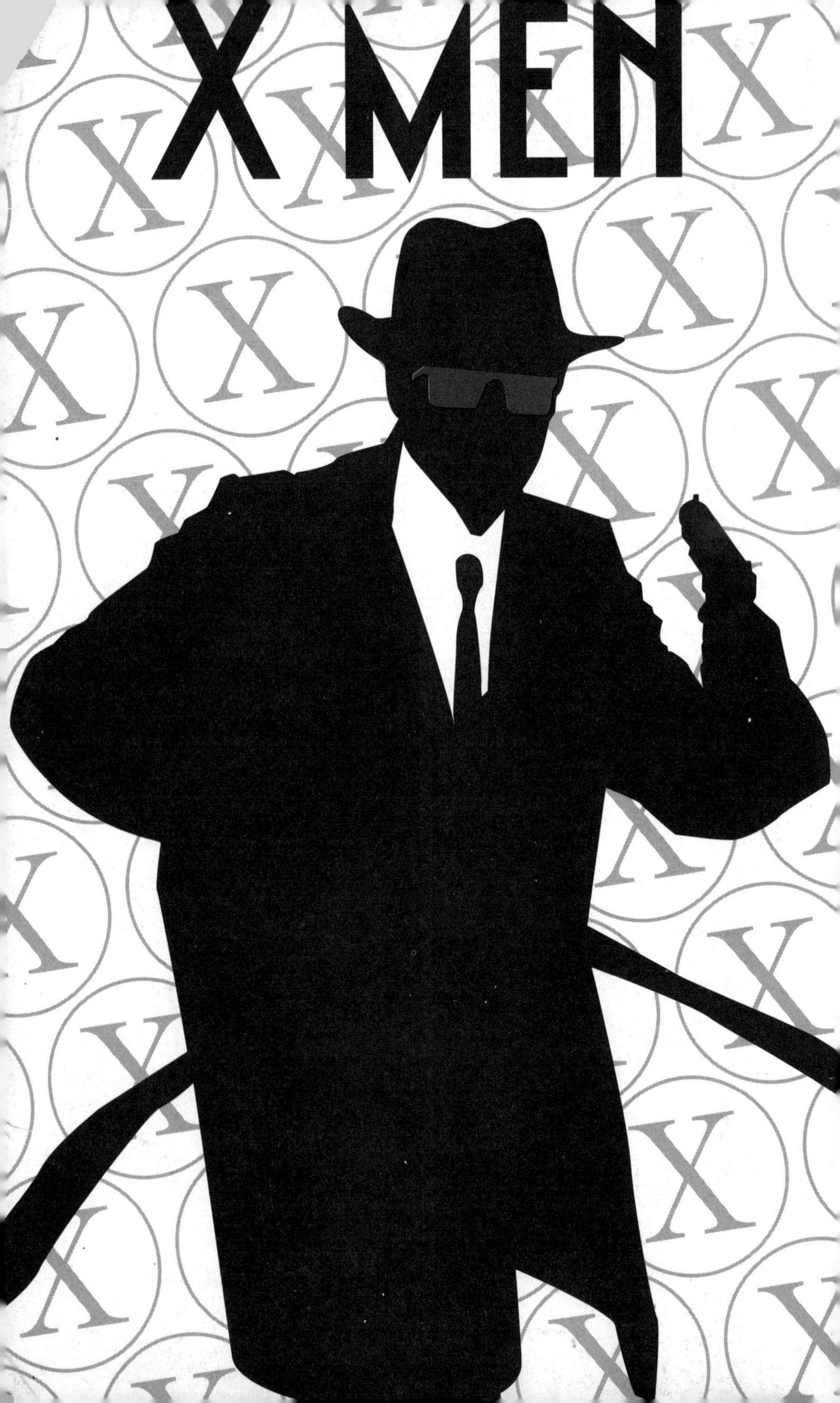
X MEN

WRITER
FRED VAN LENTE

ART
DENNIS CALERO

LETTERS
BLAMBOT'S
NATE PIEKOS

CONSULTING EDITORS
MARK PANICCIA &
RALPH MACCHIO

EDITOR
NATHAN COSBY

COLLECTION EDITOR
JENNIFER GRÜNWALD
ASSISTANT EDITORS
ALEX STARBUCK & JOHN DENNING
EDITOR, SPECIAL PROJECTS
MARK D. BEAZLEY
SENIOR EDITOR, SPECIAL PROJECTS
JEFF YOUNGQUIST
SENIOR VICE PRESIDENT OF SALES
DAVID GABRIEL
BOOK DESIGNER
JEFF POWELL

EDITOR IN CHIEF
JOE QUESADA
PUBLISHER
DAN BUCKLEY
EXECUTIVE PRODUCER
ALAN FINE

X-MEN NOIR. Contains material originally published in magazine form as X-MEN NOIR #1-4. First printing 2009. ISBN# 978-0-7851-3183-0. Published by MARVEL PUBLISHING, INC., a subsidiary of MARVEL ENTERTAINMENT, INC. OFFICE OF PUBLICATION: 417 5th Avenue, New York, NY 10016. Copyright © 2008 and 2009 Marvel Characters, Inc. All rights reserved. $14.99 per copy in the U.S. (GST #R127032852); Canadian Agreement #40668537. All characters featured in this issue and the distinctive names and likenesses thereof, and all related indicia are trademarks of Marvel Characters, Inc. No similarity between any of the names, characters, persons, and/or institutions in this magazine with those of any living or dead person or institution is intended, and any such similarity which may exist is purely coincidental. **Printed in the U.S.A.** ALAN FINE, EVP - Office Of The Chief Executive Marvel Entertainment, Inc. & CMO Marvel Characters B.V.; DAN BUCKLEY, Chief Executive Officer and Publisher - Print, Animation & Digital Media; JIM SOKOLOWSKI, Chief Operating Officer; DAVID GABRIEL, SVP of Publishing Sales & Circulation; DAVID BOGART, SVP of Business Affairs & Talent Management; MICHAEL PASCIULLO, VP Merchandising & Communications; JIM O'KEEFE, VP of Operations & Logistics; DAN CARR, Executive Director of Publishing Technology; JUSTIN F. GABRIE, Director of Publishing & Editorial Operations; SUSAN CRESPI, Editorial Operations Manager; ALEX MORALES, Publishing Operations Manager; STAN LEE, Chairman Emeritus. For information regarding advertising in Marvel Comics or on Marvel.com, please contact Mitch Dane, Advertising Director, at mdane@marvel.com. For Marvel subscription inquiries, please call 800-217-9158. **Manufactured between 9/4/09 and 9/23/09 by R. R. DONNELLEY, CRAWFORDSVILLE, IN, USA.**

10 9 8 7 6 5 4 3 2 1

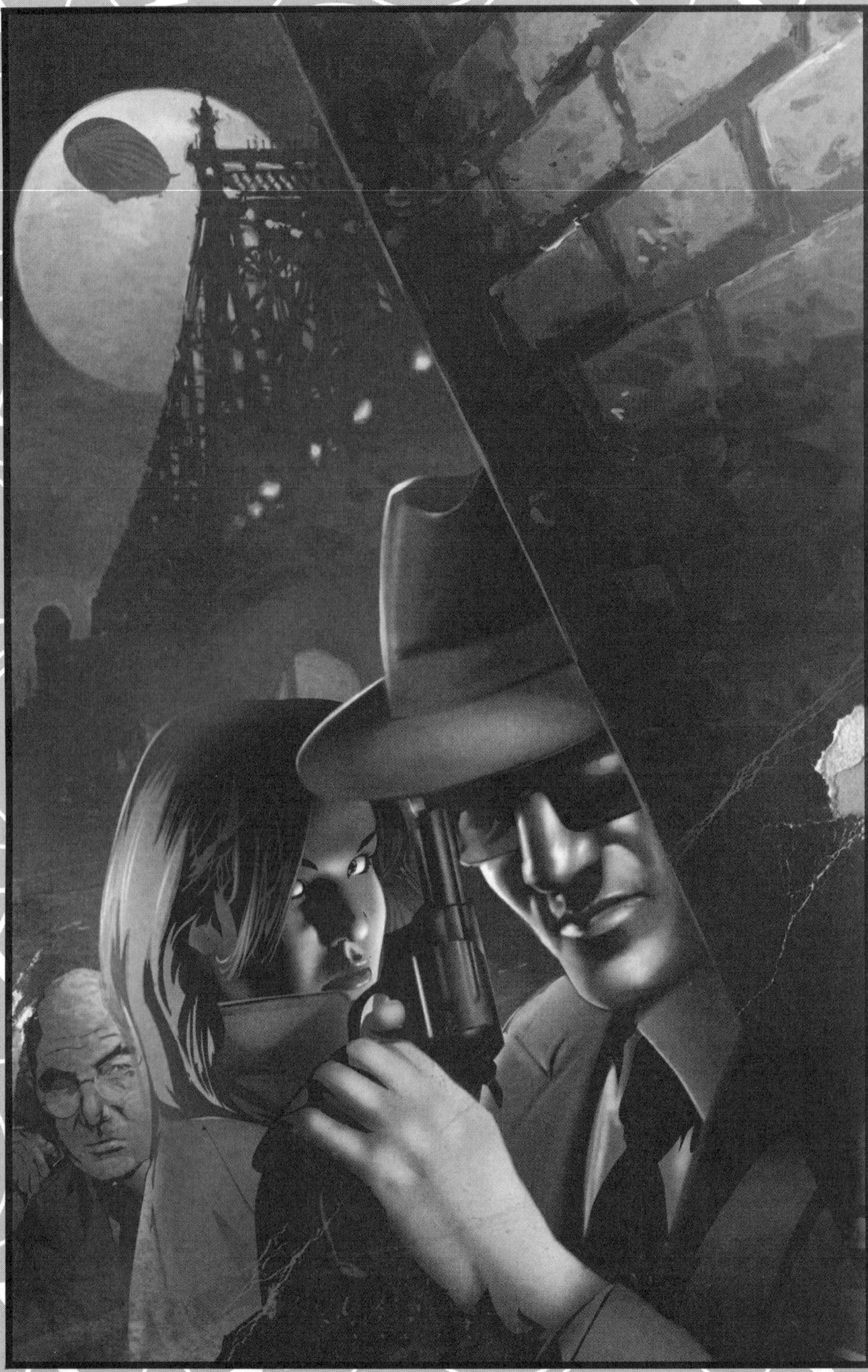

ONE

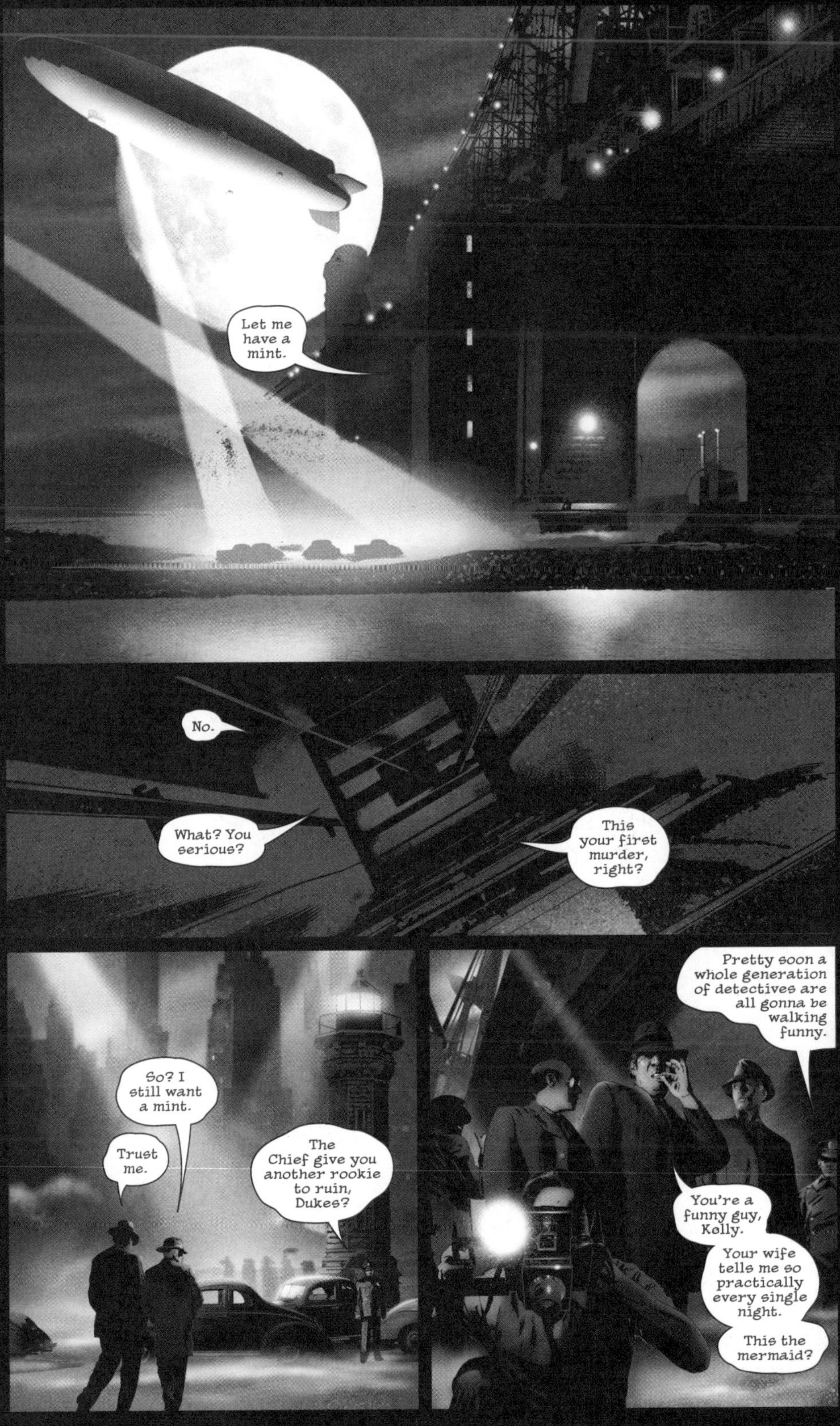
Let me have a mint.
No.
What? You serious?
This your first murder, right?
So? I still want a mint.
Trust me.
The Chief give you another rookie to ruin, Dukes?
Pretty soon a whole generation of detectives are all gonna be walking funny.
You're a funny guy, Kelly.
Your wife tells me so practically every single night.
This the mermaid?

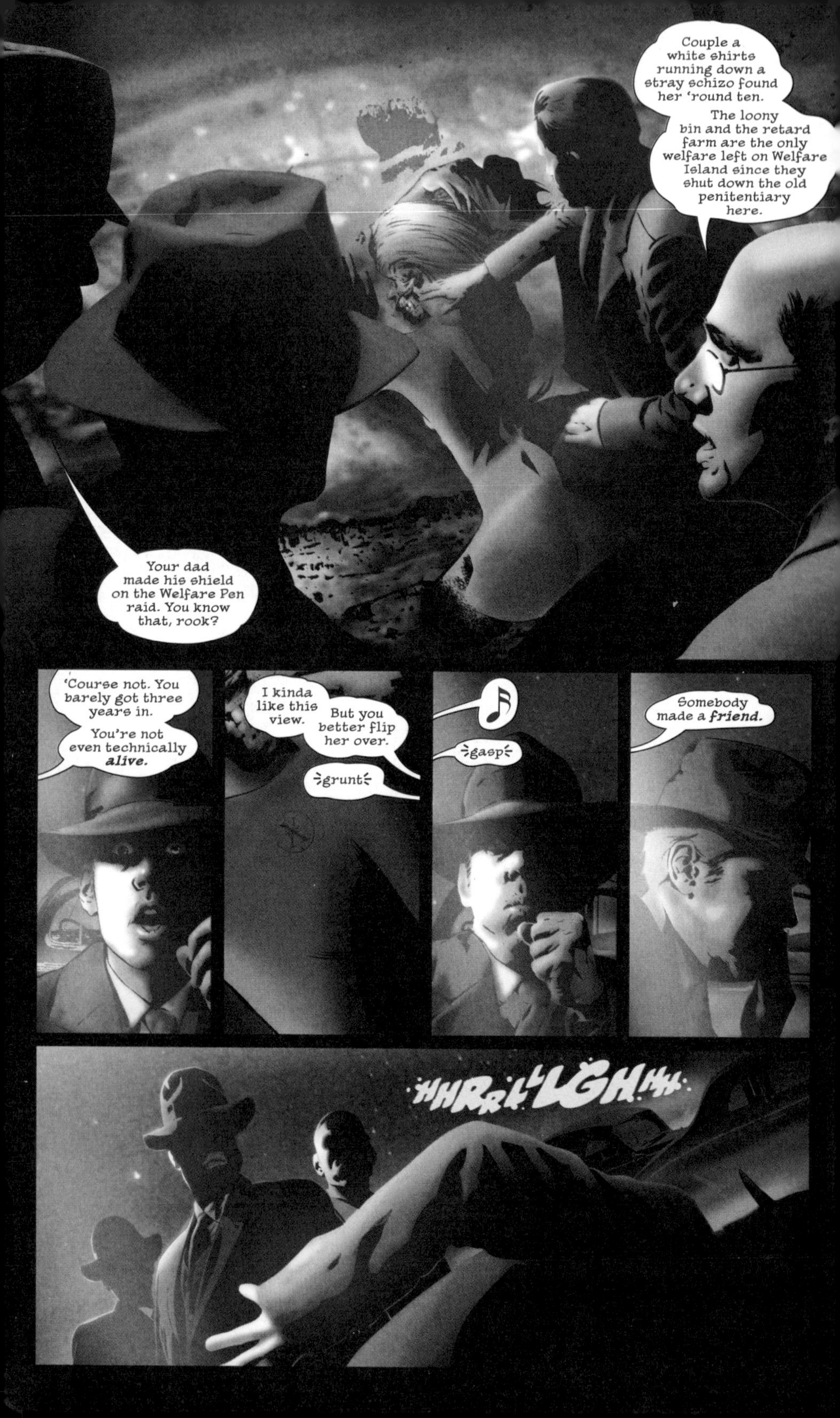
Couple a white shirts running down a stray schizo found her 'round ten.
The loony bin and the retard farm are the only welfare left on Welfare Island since they shut down the old penitentiary here.
Your dad made his shield on the Welfare Pen raid. You know that, rook?
'Course not. You barely got three years in.
You're not even technically *alive.*
I kinda like this view.
But you better flip her over.
grunt
♬
gasp
Somebody made a *friend.*
HHRRLLLGH!HH

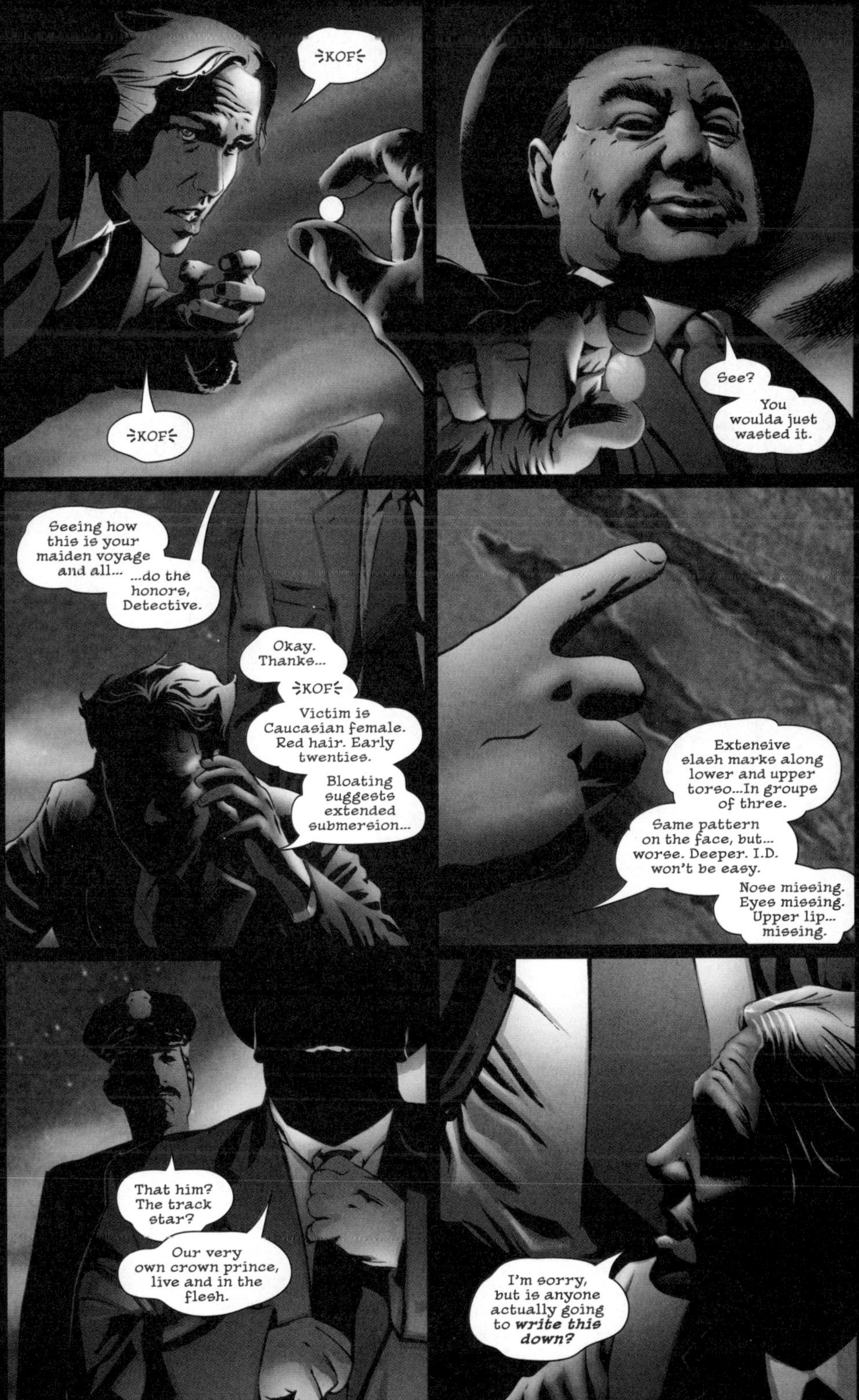

KOF
KOF
See?
You woulda just wasted it.
Seeing how this is your maiden voyage and all...
...do the honors, Detective.
Okay. Thanks...
KOF
Victim is Caucasian female. Red hair. Early twenties.
Bloating suggests extended submersion...
Extensive slash marks along lower and upper torso...In groups of three.
Same pattern on the face, but... worse. Deeper. I.D. won't be easy.
Nose missing. Eyes missing. Upper lip... missing.
That him? The track star?
Our very own crown prince, live and in the flesh.
I'm sorry, but is anyone actually going to *write this down?*

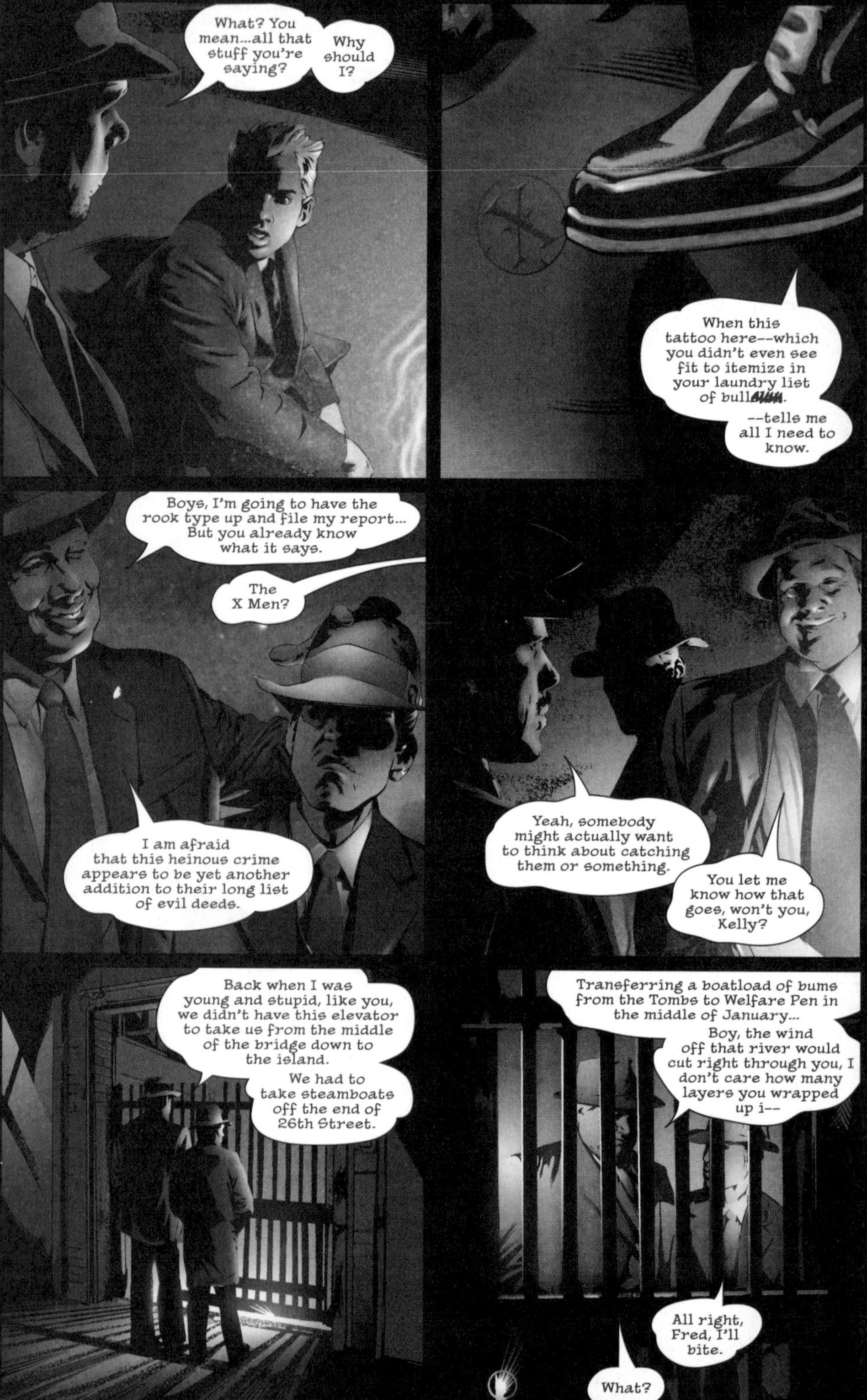
What? You mean...all that stuff you're saying?
Why should I?
When this tattoo here--which you didn't even see fit to itemize in your laundry list of bull[redacted].
--tells me all I need to know.
Boys, I'm going to have the rook type up and file my report... But you already know what it says.
The X Men?
I am afraid that this heinous crime appears to be yet another addition to their long list of evil deeds.
Yeah, somebody might actually want to think about catching them or something.
You let me know how that goes, won't you, Kelly?
Back when I was young and stupid, like you, we didn't have this elevator to take us from the middle of the bridge down to the island.
We had to take steamboats off the end of 26th Street.
Transferring a boatload of bums from the Tombs to Welfare Pen in the middle of January...
Boy, the wind off that river would cut right through you, I don't care how many layers you wrapped up i--
All right, Fred, I'll bite.
What?

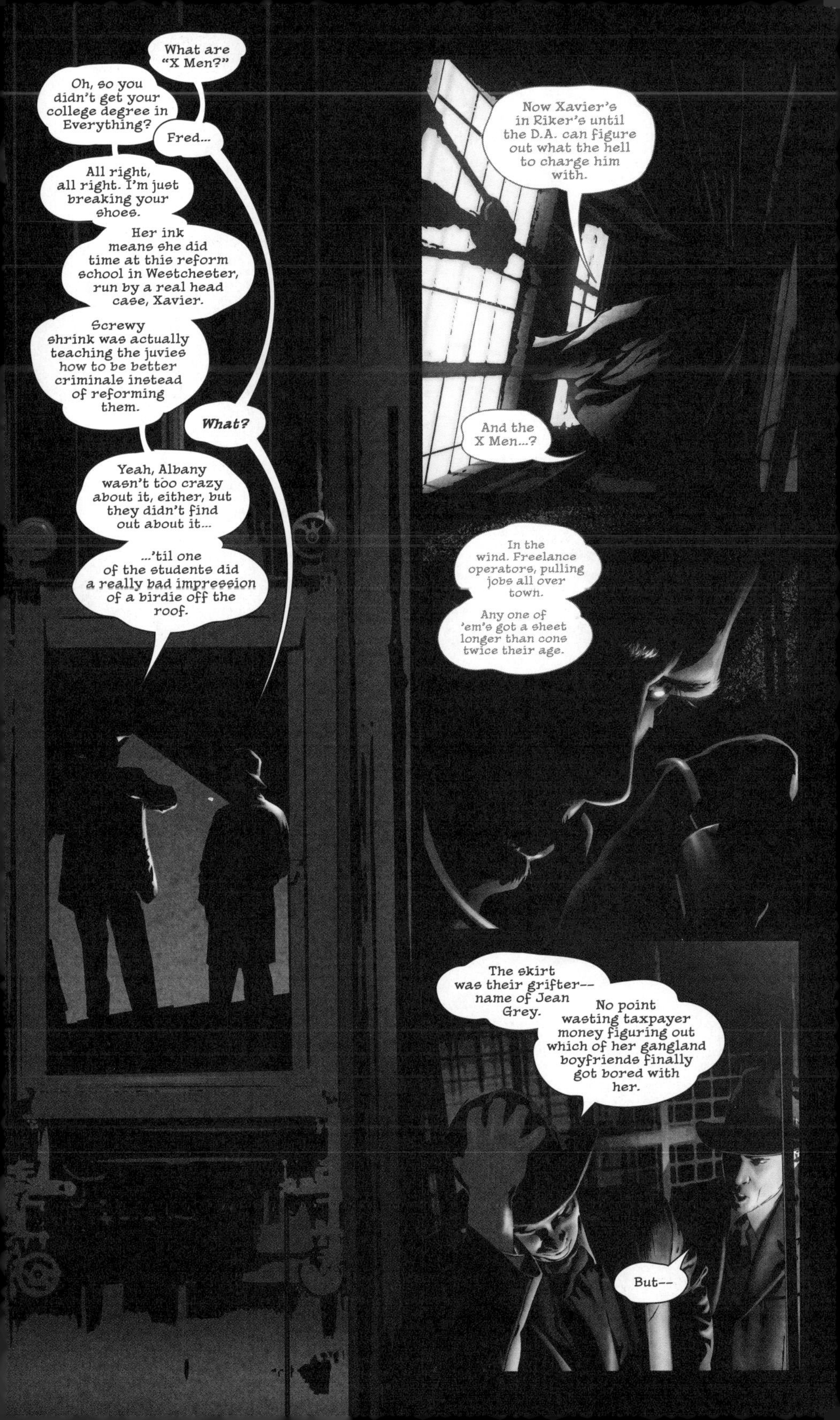
What are "X Men?"
Oh, so you didn't get your college degree in Everything?
Fred...
All right, all right. I'm just breaking your shoes.
Her ink means she did time at this reform school in Westchester, run by a real head case, Xavier.
Screwy shrink was actually teaching the juvies how to be better criminals instead of reforming them.
What?
Yeah, Albany wasn't too crazy about it, either, but they didn't find out about it...
...'til one of the students did a really bad impression of a birdie off the roof.
Now Xavier's in Riker's until the D.A. can figure out what the hell to charge him with.
And the X Men...?
In the wind. Freelance operators, pulling jobs all over town.
Any one of 'em's got a sheet longer than cons twice their age.
The skirt was their grifter-- name of Jean Grey.
No point wasting taxpayer money figuring out which of her gangland boyfriends finally got bored with her.
But--

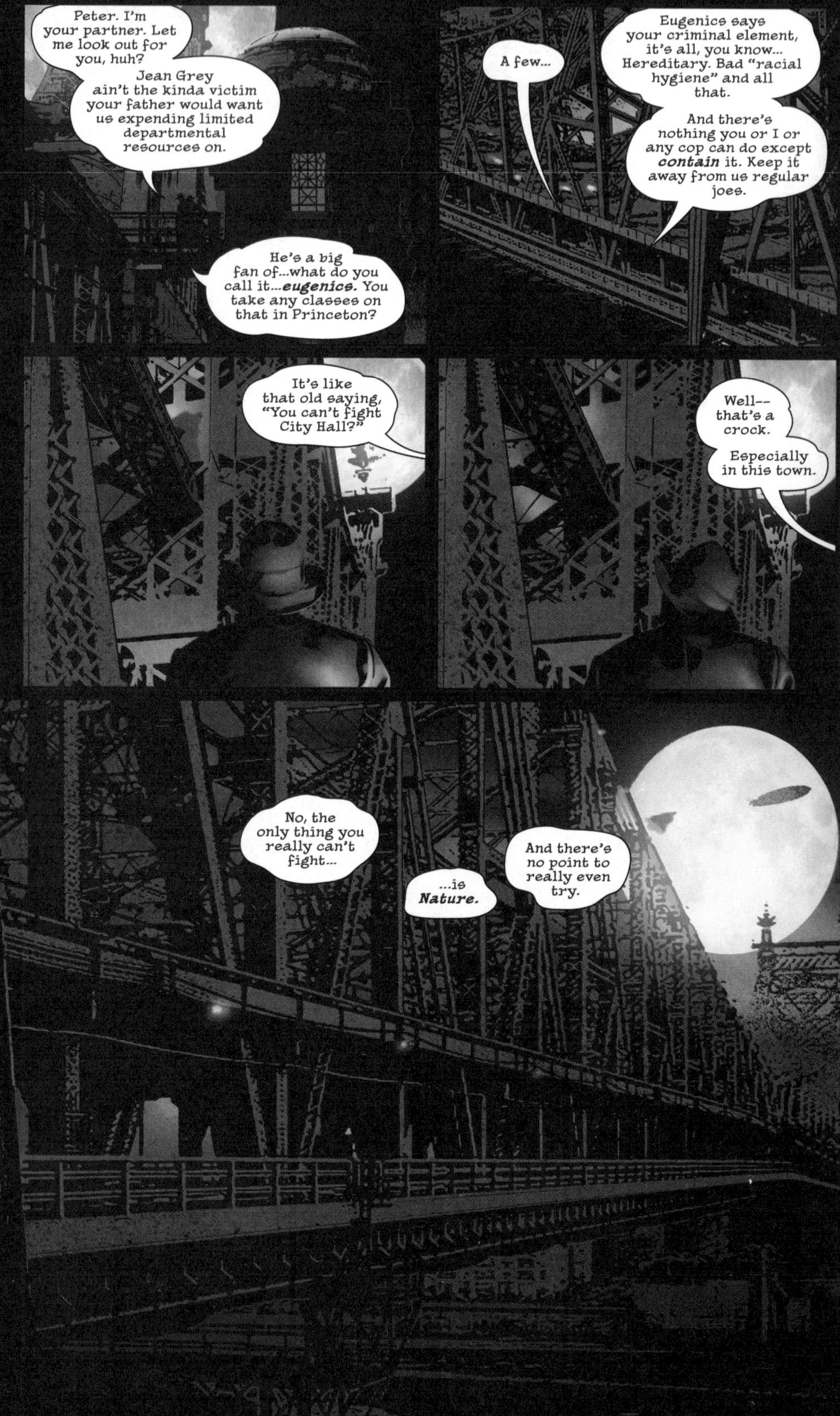
Peter. I'm your partner. Let me look out for you, huh?
Jean Grey ain't the kinda victim your father would want us expending limited departmental resources on.
He's a big fan of...what do you call it...**eugenics.** You take any classes on that in Princeton?
A few...
Eugenics says your criminal element, it's all, you know... Hereditary. Bad "racial hygiene" and all that.
And there's nothing you or I or any cop can do except **contain** it. Keep it away from us regular joes.
It's like that old saying, "You can't fight City Hall?"
Well-- that's a crock.
Especially in this town.
No, the only thing you really can't fight...
...is **Nature.**
And there's no point to really even try.

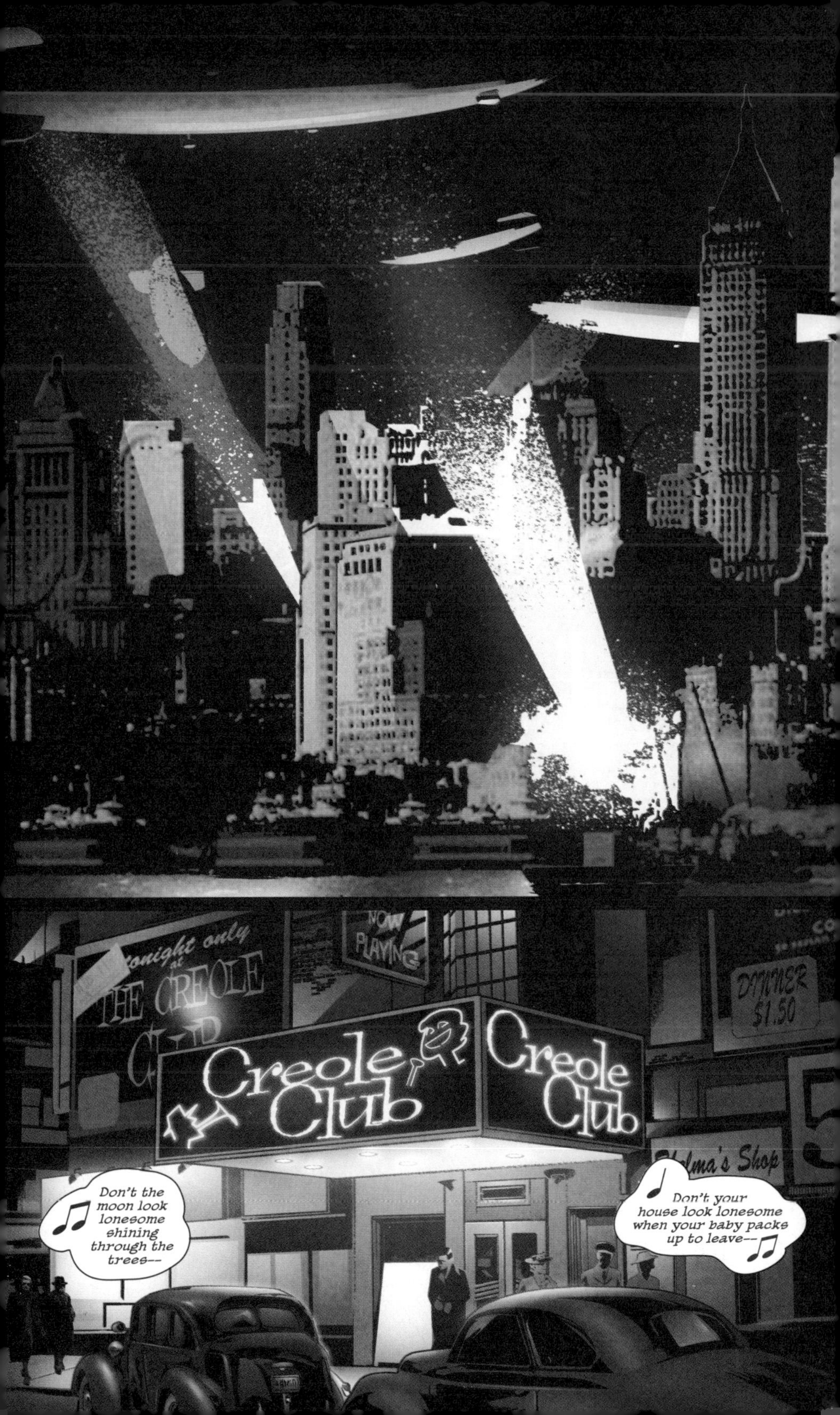
tonight only at
THE CREOLE
NOW PLAYING
Creole Club
Creole Club
DINNER $1.50
Don't the moon look lonesome shining through the trees--
Don't your house look lonesome when your baby packs up to leave--

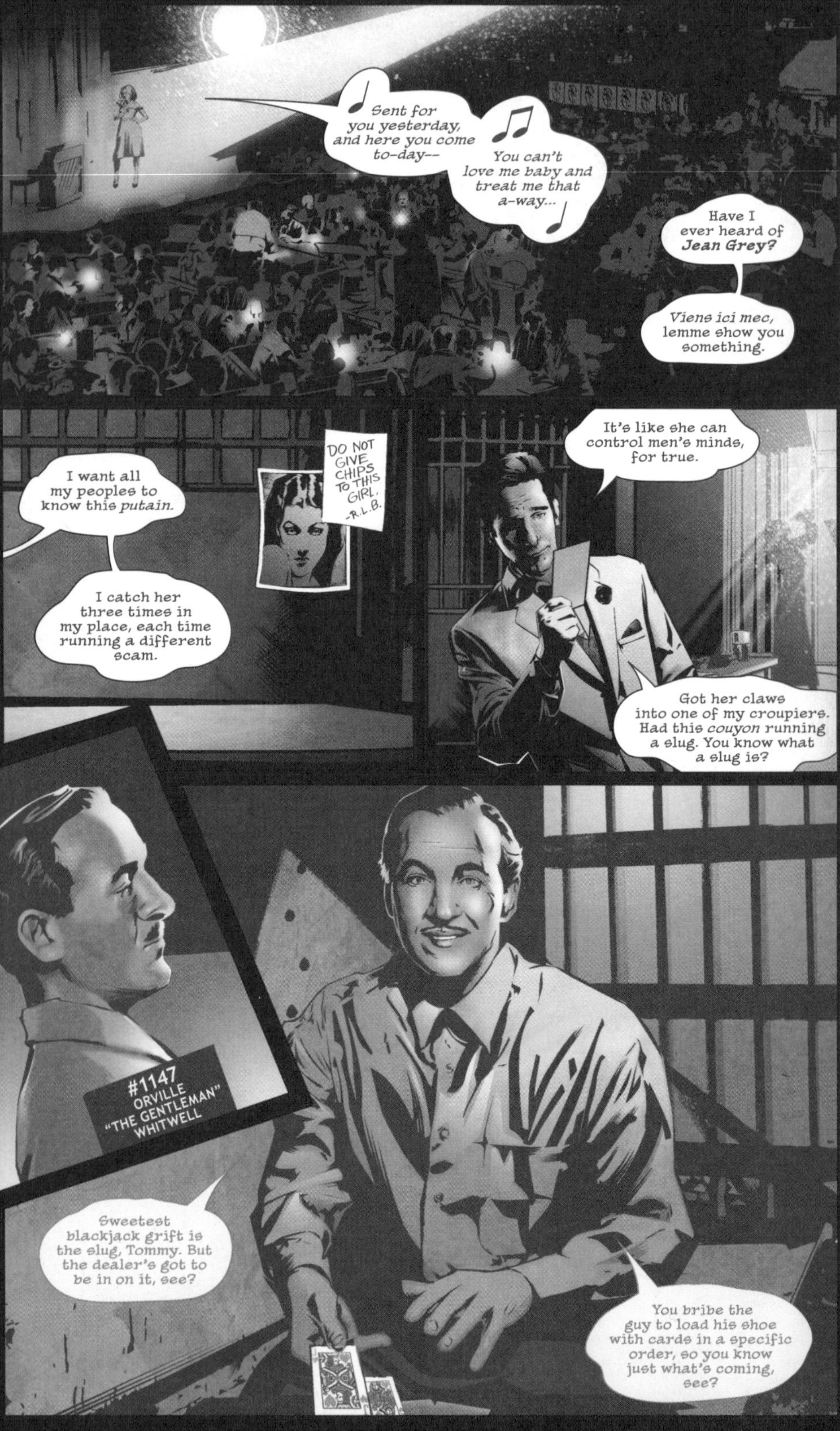
Sent for you yesterday, and here you come to-day--
You can't love me baby and treat me that a-way...
Have I ever heard of Jean Grey?
Viens ici mec, lemme show you something.
I want all my peoples to know this putain.
I catch her three times in my place, each time running a different scam.
DO NOT GIVE CHIPS TO THIS GIRL. -R.L.B.
It's like she can control men's minds, for true.
Got her claws into one of my croupiers. Had this couyon running a slug. You know what a slug is?
#1147 ORVILLE "THE GENTLEMAN" WHITWELL
Sweetest blackjack grift is the slug, Tommy. But the dealer's got to be in on it, see?
You bribe the guy to load his shoe with cards in a specific order, so you know just what's coming, see?

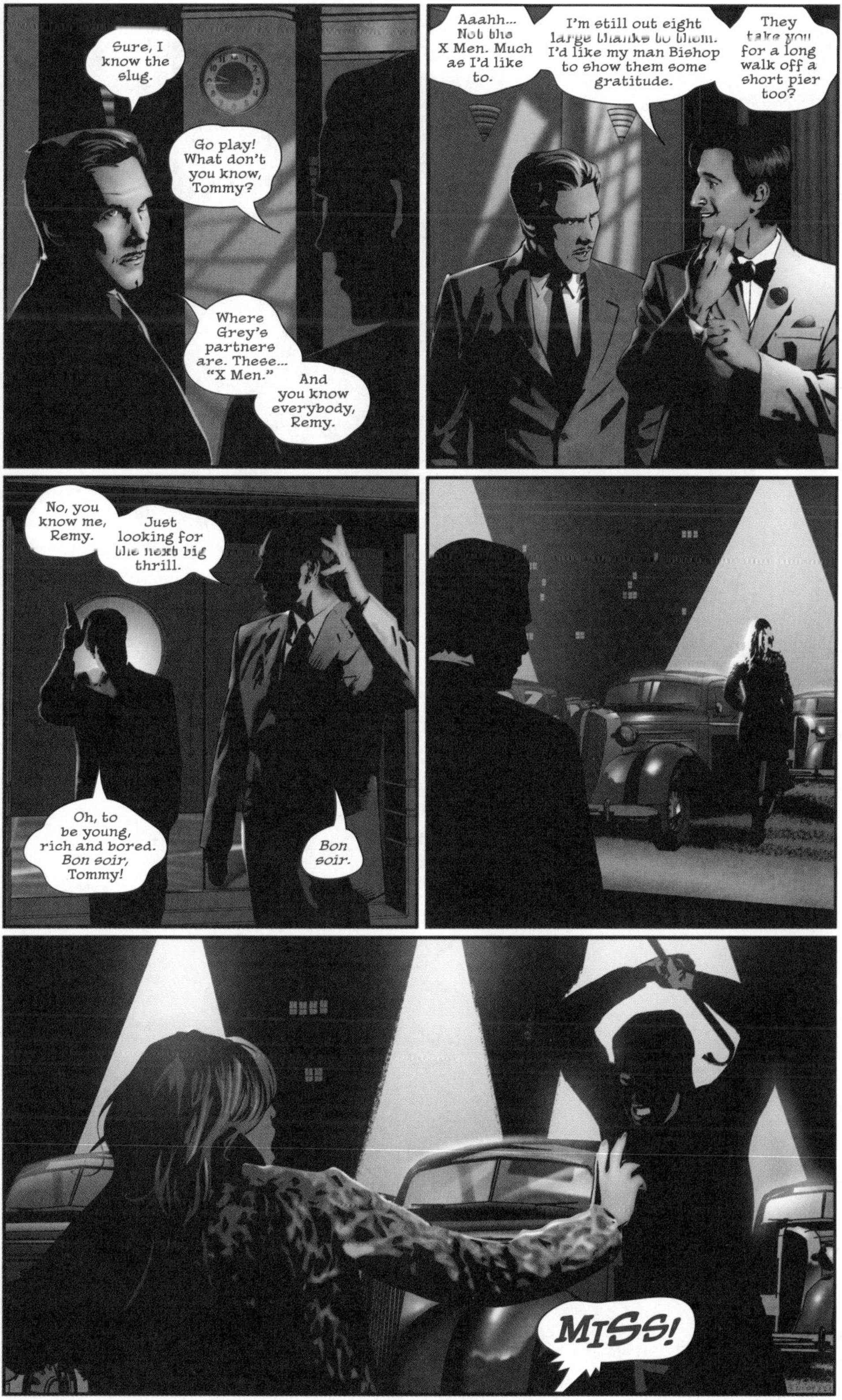
Sure, I know the slug.
Go play! What don't you know, Tommy?
Where Grey's partners are. These... "X Men."
And you know everybody, Remy.
Aaahh... Not the X Men. Much as I'd like to.
I'm still out eight large thanks to them. I'd like my man Bishop to show them some gratitude.
They take you for a long walk off a short pier too?
No, you know me, Remy.
Just looking for the next big thrill.
Oh, to be young, rich and bored. *Bon soir,* Tommy!
Bon soir.
MISS!

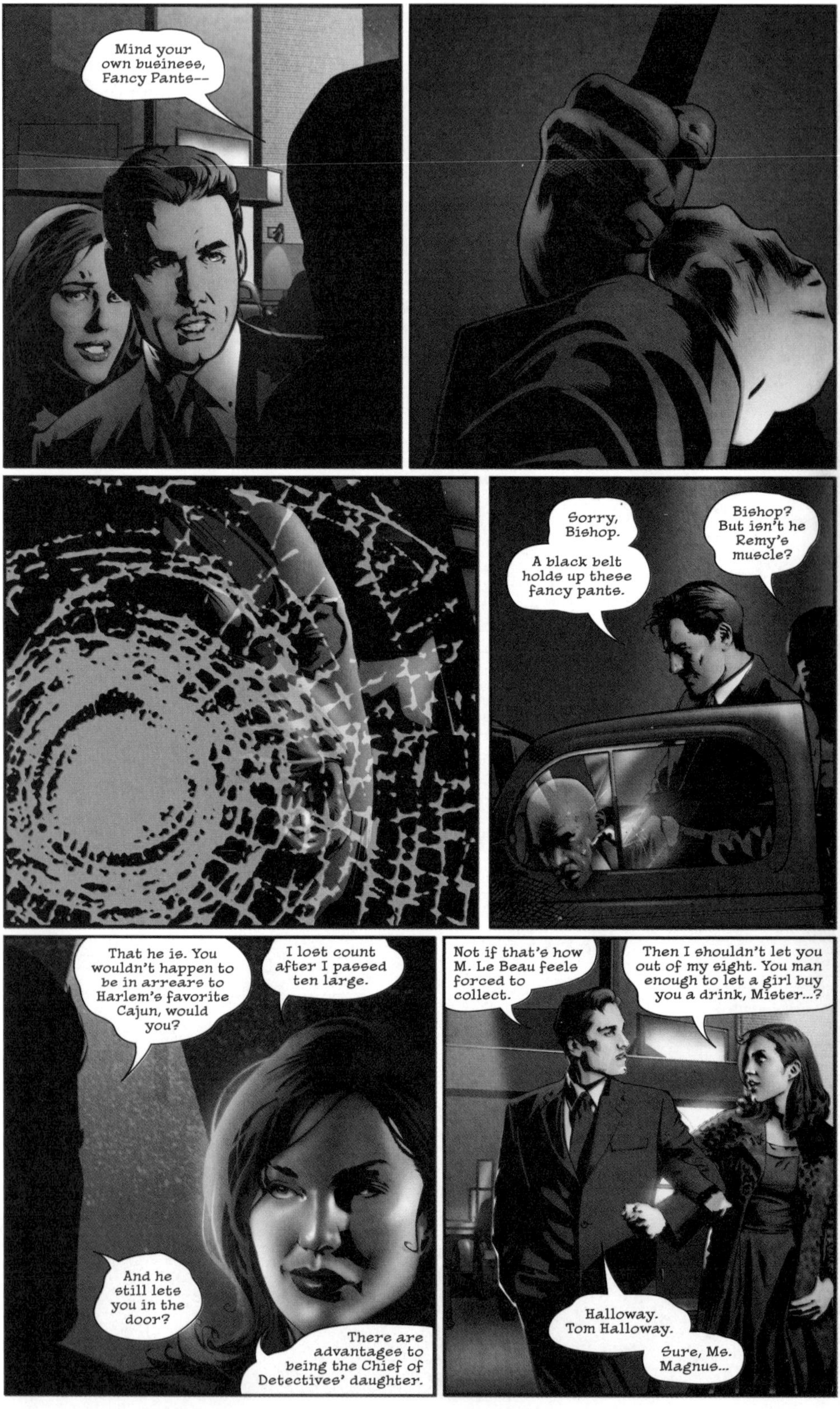
Mind your own business, Fancy Pants--
Sorry, Bishop.
A black belt holds up these fancy pants.
Bishop? But isn't he Remy's muscle?
That he is. You wouldn't happen to be in arrears to Harlem's favorite Cajun, would you?
I lost count after I passed ten large.
And he still lets you in the door?
There are advantages to being the Chief of Detectives' daughter.
Not if that's how M. Le Beau feels forced to collect.
Then I shouldn't let you out of my sight. You man enough to let a girl buy you a drink, Mister...?
Halloway. Tom Halloway.
Sure, Ms. Magnus...

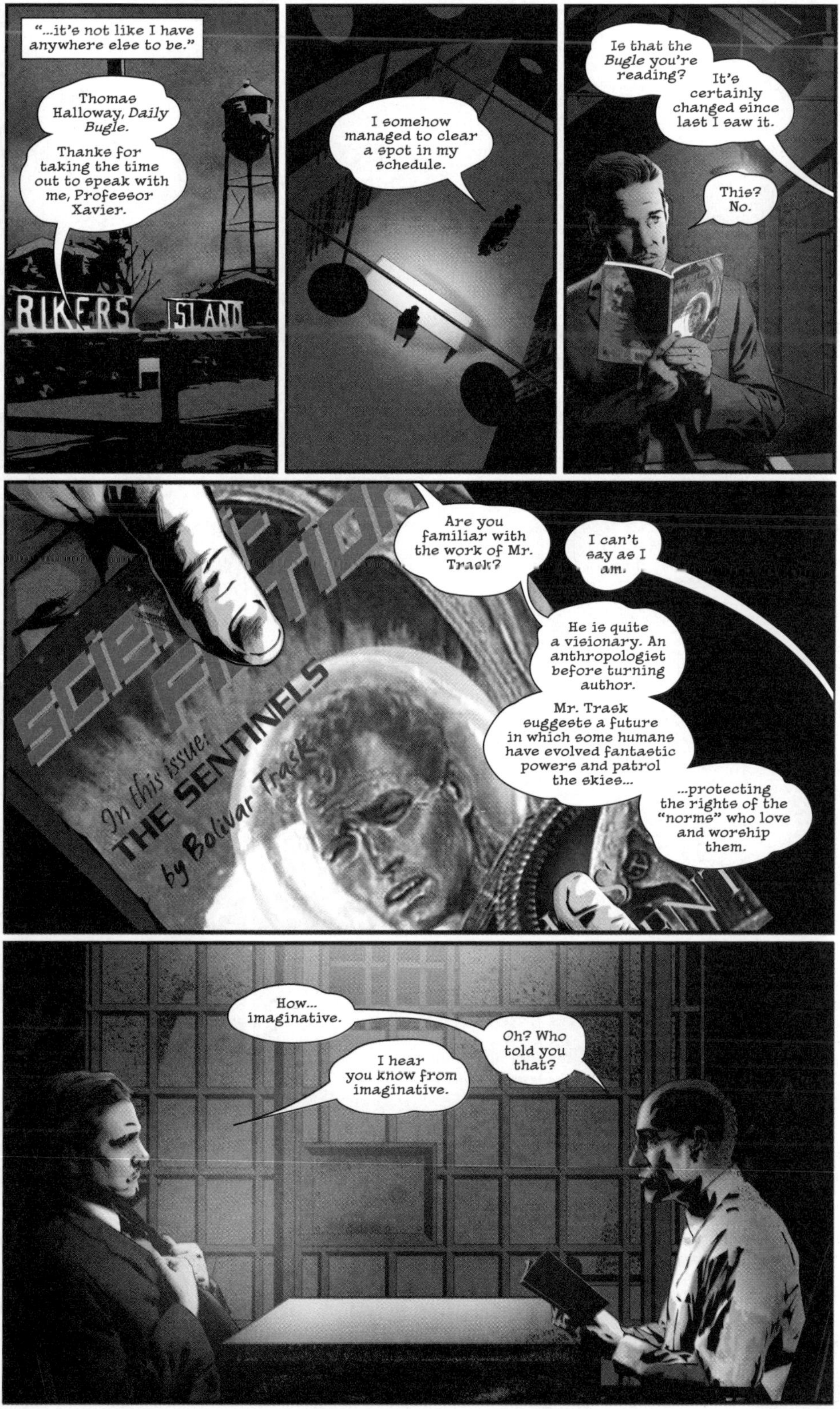
"...it's not like I have anywhere else to be."
RIKERS ISLAND
Thomas Halloway, *Daily Bugle.*
Thanks for taking the time out to speak with me, Professor Xavier.
I somehow managed to clear a spot in my schedule.
Is that the *Bugle* you're reading?
It's certainly changed since last I saw it.
This? No.
Science Fiction
In this issue: THE SENTINELS by Bolivar Trask
Are you familiar with the work of Mr. Trask?
I can't say as I am.
He is quite a visionary. An anthropologist before turning author.
Mr. Trask suggests a future in which some humans have evolved fantastic powers and patrol the skies...
...protecting the rights of the "norms" who love and worship them.
How... imaginative.
Oh? Who told you that?
I hear you know from imaginative.

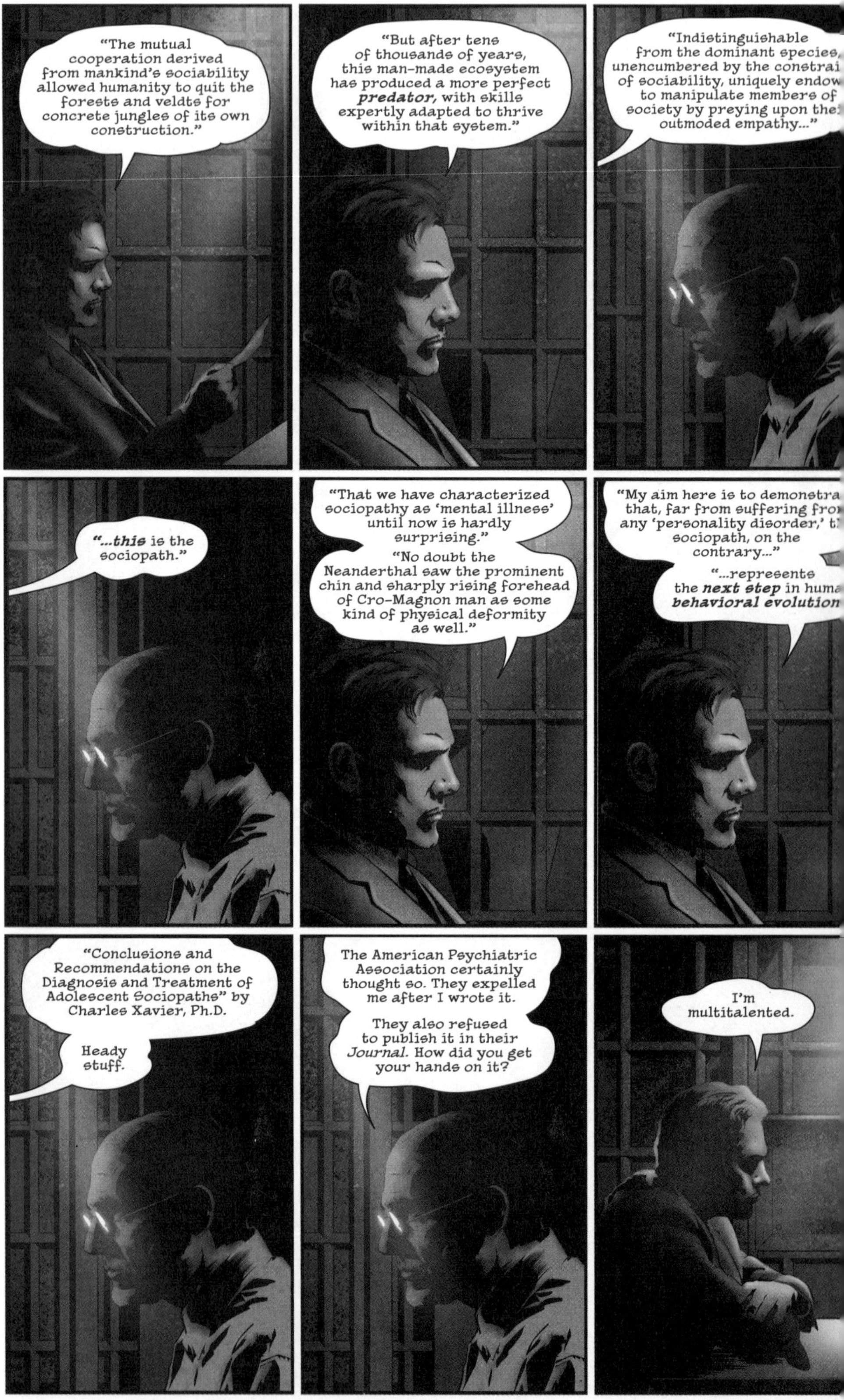
"The mutual cooperation derived from mankind's sociability allowed humanity to quit the forests and veldts for concrete jungles of its own construction."
"But after tens of thousands of years, this man-made ecosystem has produced a more perfect ***predator,*** with skills expertly adapted to thrive within that system."
"Indistinguishable from the dominant species, unencumbered by the constrai of sociability, uniquely endow to manipulate members of society by preying upon the outmoded empathy..."
"...***this*** is the sociopath."
"That we have characterized sociopathy as 'mental illness' until now is hardly surprising."
"No doubt the Neanderthal saw the prominent chin and sharply rising forehead of Cro-Magnon man as some kind of physical deformity as well."
"My aim here is to demonstra that, far from suffering fro any 'personality disorder,' t sociopath, on the contrary..."
"...represents the ***next step*** in huma ***behavioral evolution***
"Conclusions and Recommendations on the Diagnosis and Treatment of Adolescent Sociopaths" by Charles Xavier, Ph.D.
Heady stuff.
The American Psychiatric Association certainly thought so. They expelled me after I wrote it.
They also refused to publish it in their *Journal.* How did you get your hands on it?
I'm multitalented.

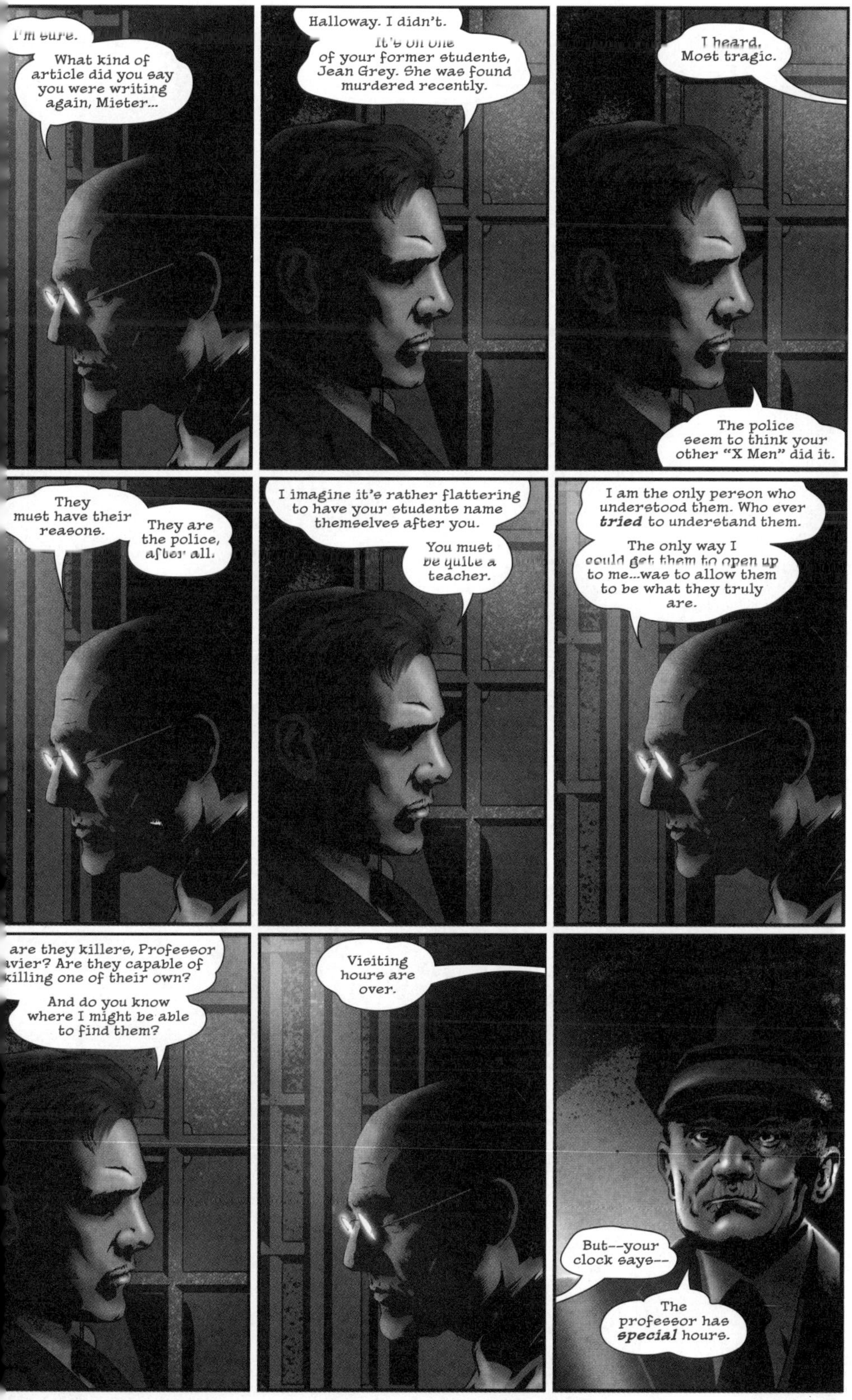
I'm sure.
What kind of article did you say you were writing again, Mister...
Halloway. I didn't.
It's on one of your former students, Jean Grey. She was found murdered recently.
I heard. Most tragic.
The police seem to think your other "X Men" did it.
They must have their reasons.
They are the police, after all.
I imagine it's rather flattering to have your students name themselves after you.
You must be quite a teacher.
I am the only person who understood them. Who ever *tried* to understand them.
The only way I could get them to open up to me...was to allow them to be what they truly are.
are they killers, Professor avier? Are they capable of killing one of their own?
And do you know where I might be able to find them?
Visiting hours are over.
But--your clock says--
The professor has *special* hours.

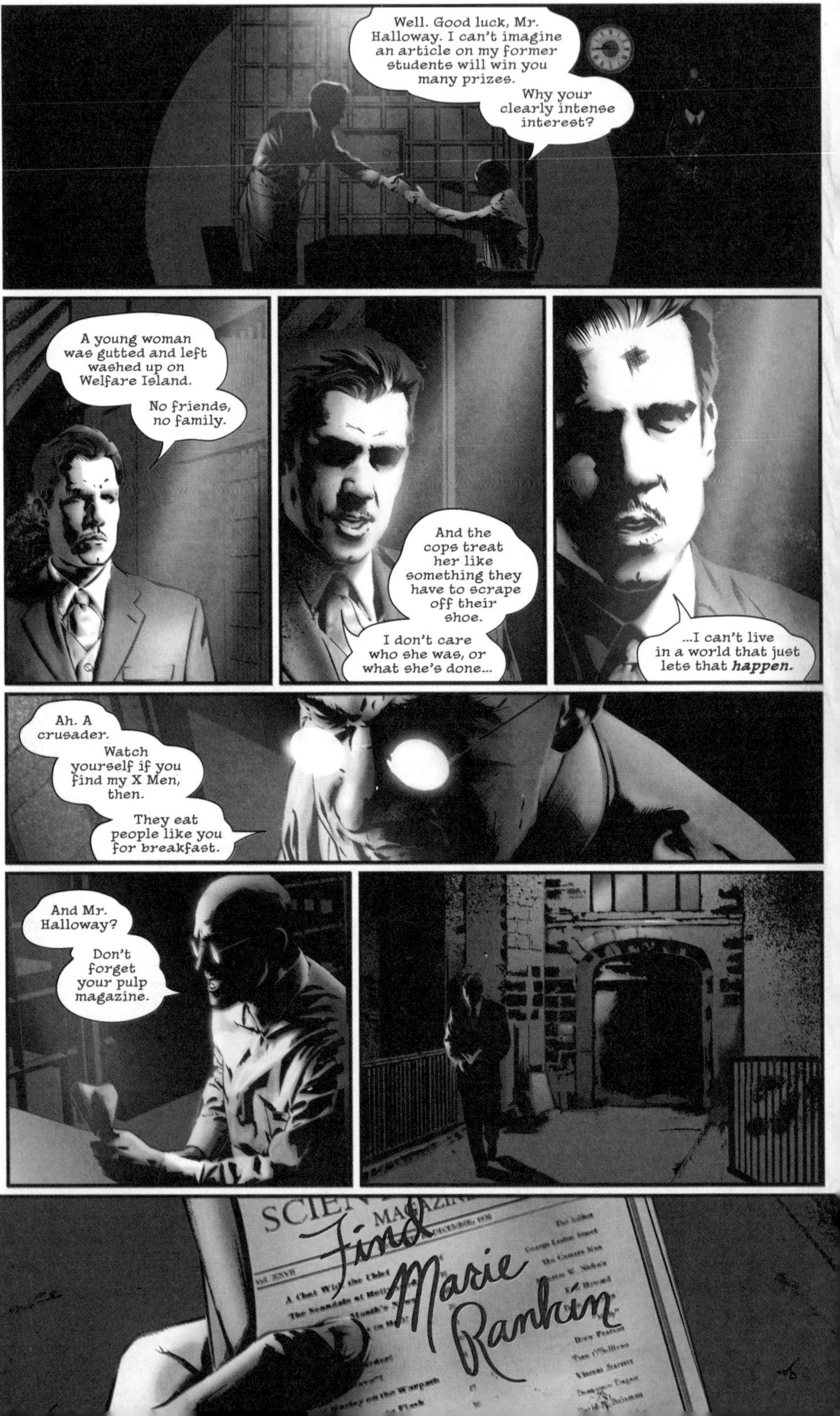
Well. Good luck, Mr. Halloway. I can't imagine an article on my former students will win you many prizes.
Why your clearly intense interest?
A young woman was gutted and left washed up on Welfare Island.
No friends, no family.
And the cops treat her like something they have to scrape off their shoe.
I don't care who she was, or what she's done...
...I can't live in a world that just lets that *happen.*
Ah. A crusader.
Watch yourself if you find my X Men, then.
They eat people like you for breakfast.
And Mr. Halloway?
Don't forget your pulp magazine.
Find Marie Rankin

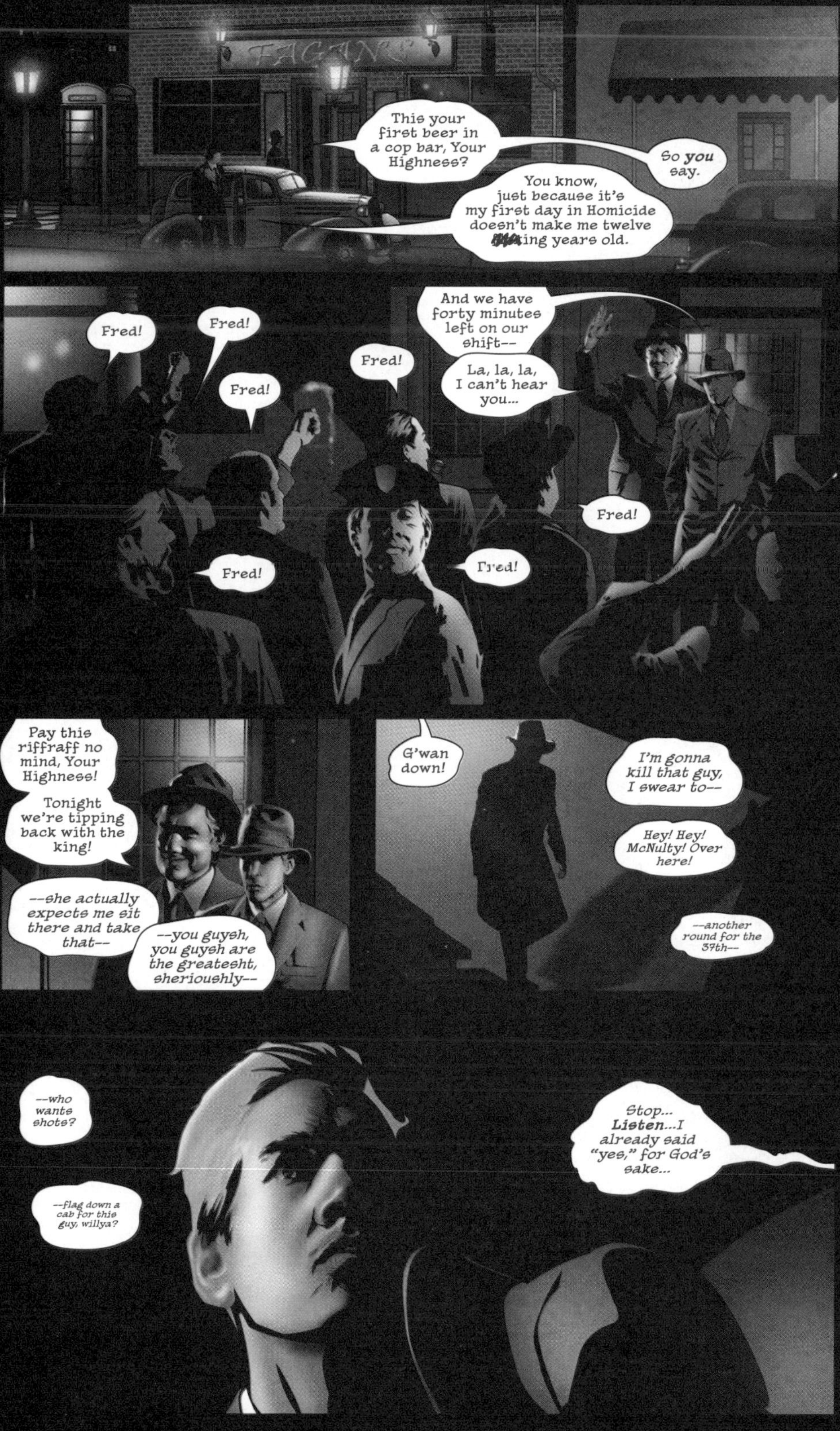
FAGAN'S
This your first beer in a cop bar, Your Highness?
You know, just because it's my first day in Homicide doesn't make me twelve [redacted]ing years old.
So **you** say.
Fred!
Fred!
Fred!
Fred!
And we have forty minutes left on our shift--
La, la, la, I can't hear you...
Fred!
Fred!
Fred!
Pay this riffraff no mind, Your Highness!
Tonight we're tipping back with the king!
--she actually expects me sit there and take that--
--you guysh, you guysh are the greatesht, sheriouslhy--
G'wan down!
I'm gonna kill that guy, I swear to--
Hey! Hey! McNulty! Over here!
--another round for the 37th--
--who wants shots?
--flag down a cab for this guy, willya?
Stop... ***Listen****...I already said "yes," for God's sake...*

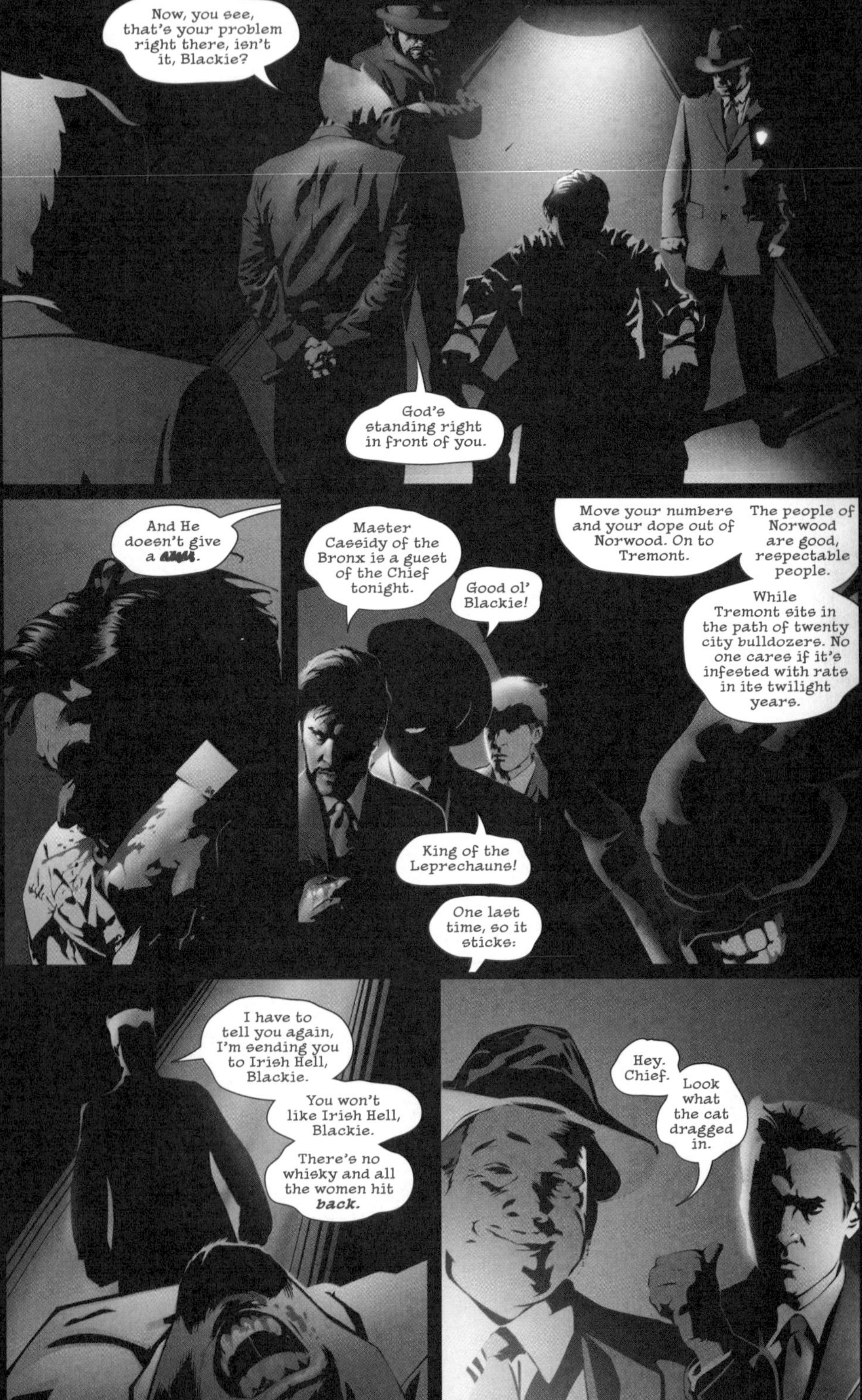
Now, you see, that's your problem right there, isn't it, Blackie?
God's standing right in front of you.
And He doesn't give a [redacted].
Master Cassidy of the Bronx is a guest of the Chief tonight.
Good ol' Blackie!
Move your numbers and your dope out of Norwood. On to Tremont.
The people of Norwood are good, respectable people.
While Tremont sits in the path of twenty city bulldozers. No one cares if it's infested with rats in its twilight years.
King of the Leprechauns!
One last time, so it sticks:
I have to tell you again, I'm sending you to Irish Hell, Blackie.
You won't like Irish Hell, Blackie.
There's no whisky and all the women hit *back.*
Hey. Chief.
Look what the cat dragged in.

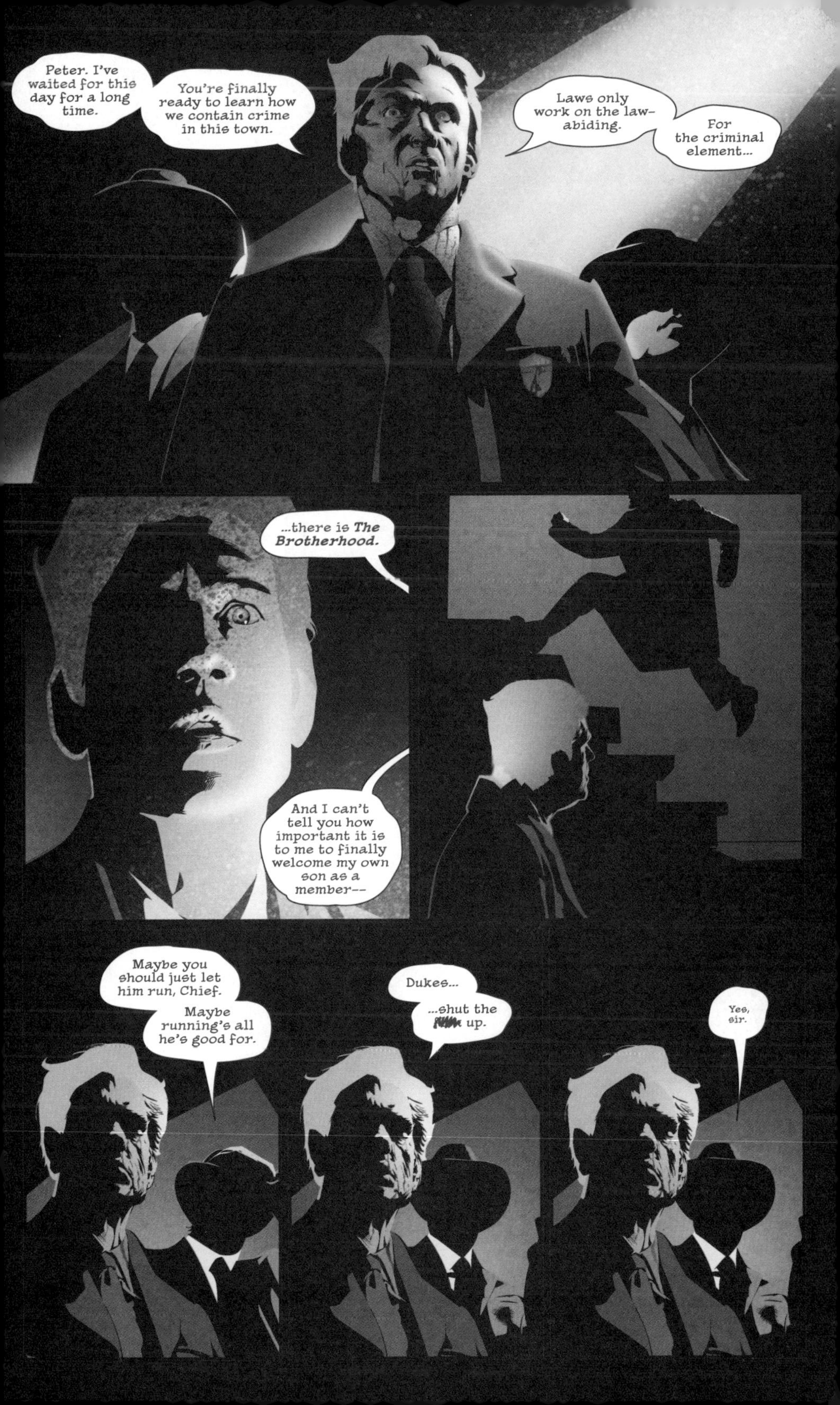

Peter. I've waited for this day for a long time.
You're finally ready to learn how we contain crime in this town.
Laws only work on the law-abiding.
For the criminal element...
...there is *The Brotherhood.*
And I can't tell you how important it is to me to finally welcome my own son as a member--
Maybe you should just let him run, Chief.
Maybe running's all he's good for.
Dukes...
...shut the up.
Yes, sir.

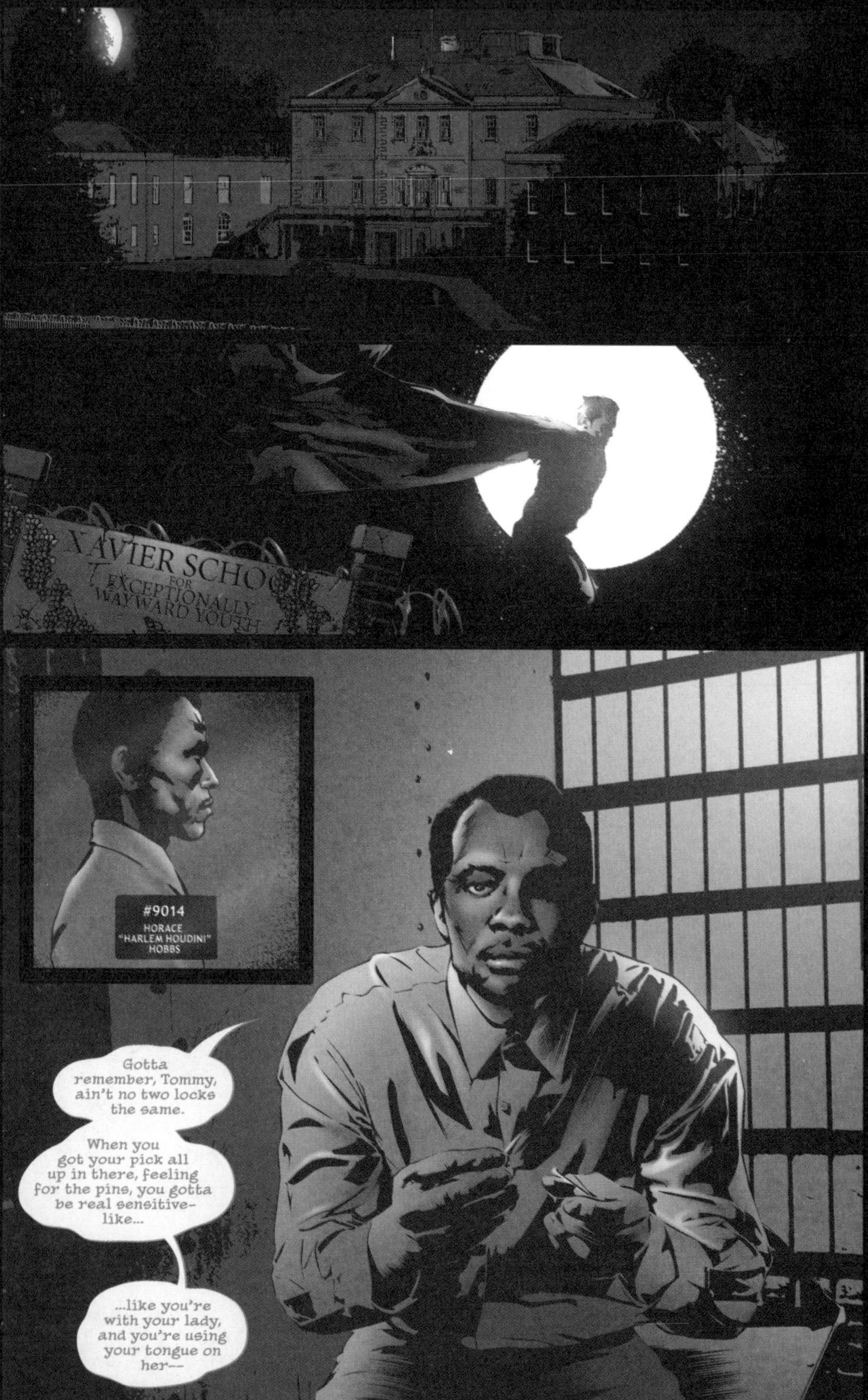
XAVIER SCHOO
FOR
EXCEPTIONALLY
WAYWARD YOUTH
#9014
HORACE
"HARLEM HOUDINI"
HOBBS
Gotta remember, Tommy, ain't no two locks the same.
When you got your pick all up in there, feeling for the pins, you gotta be real sensitive-like...
...like you're with your lady, and you're using your tongue on her--

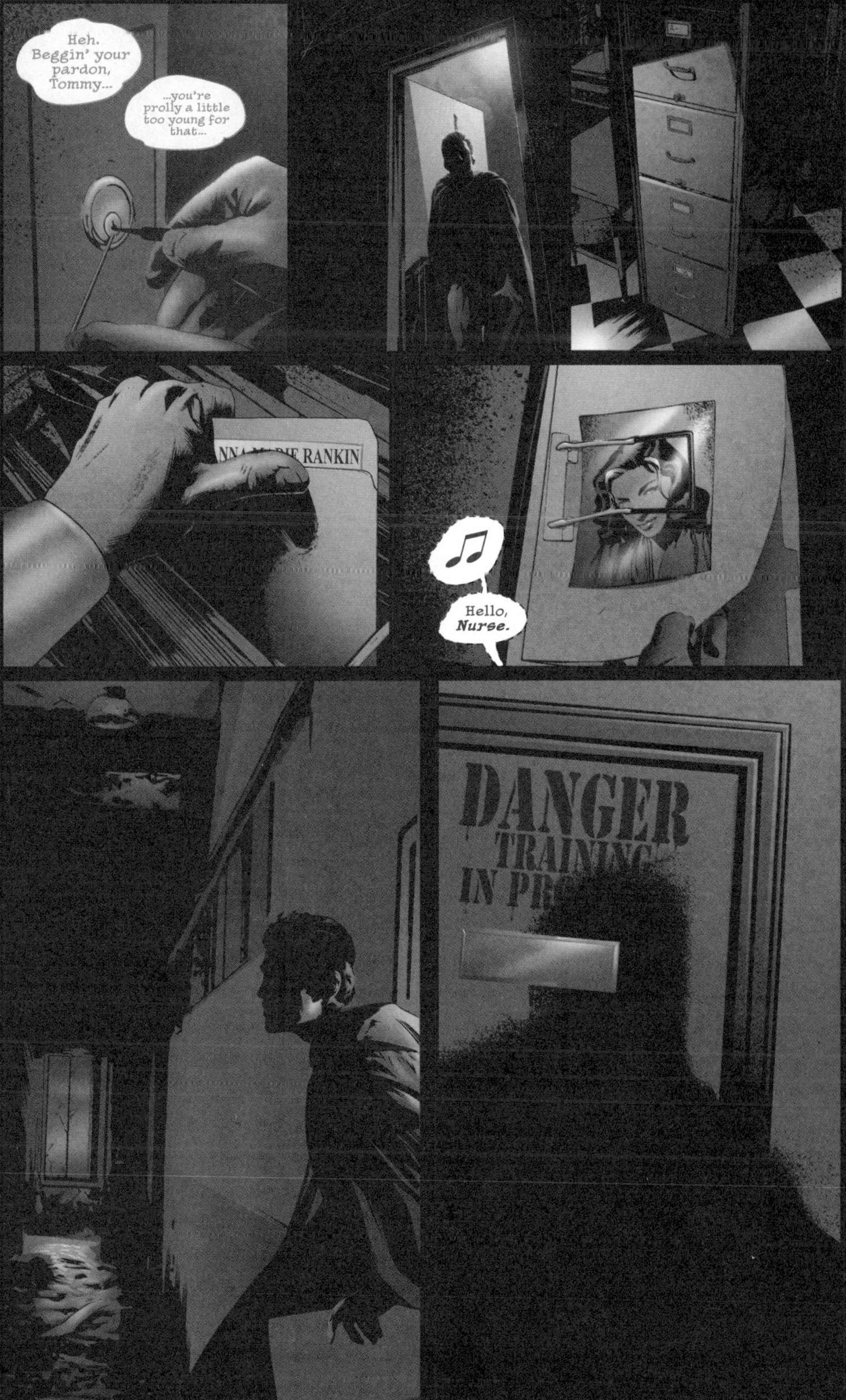
Heh. Beggin' your pardon, Tommy...
...you're prolly a little too young for that...
RANKIN
Hello, *Nurse.*
DANGER

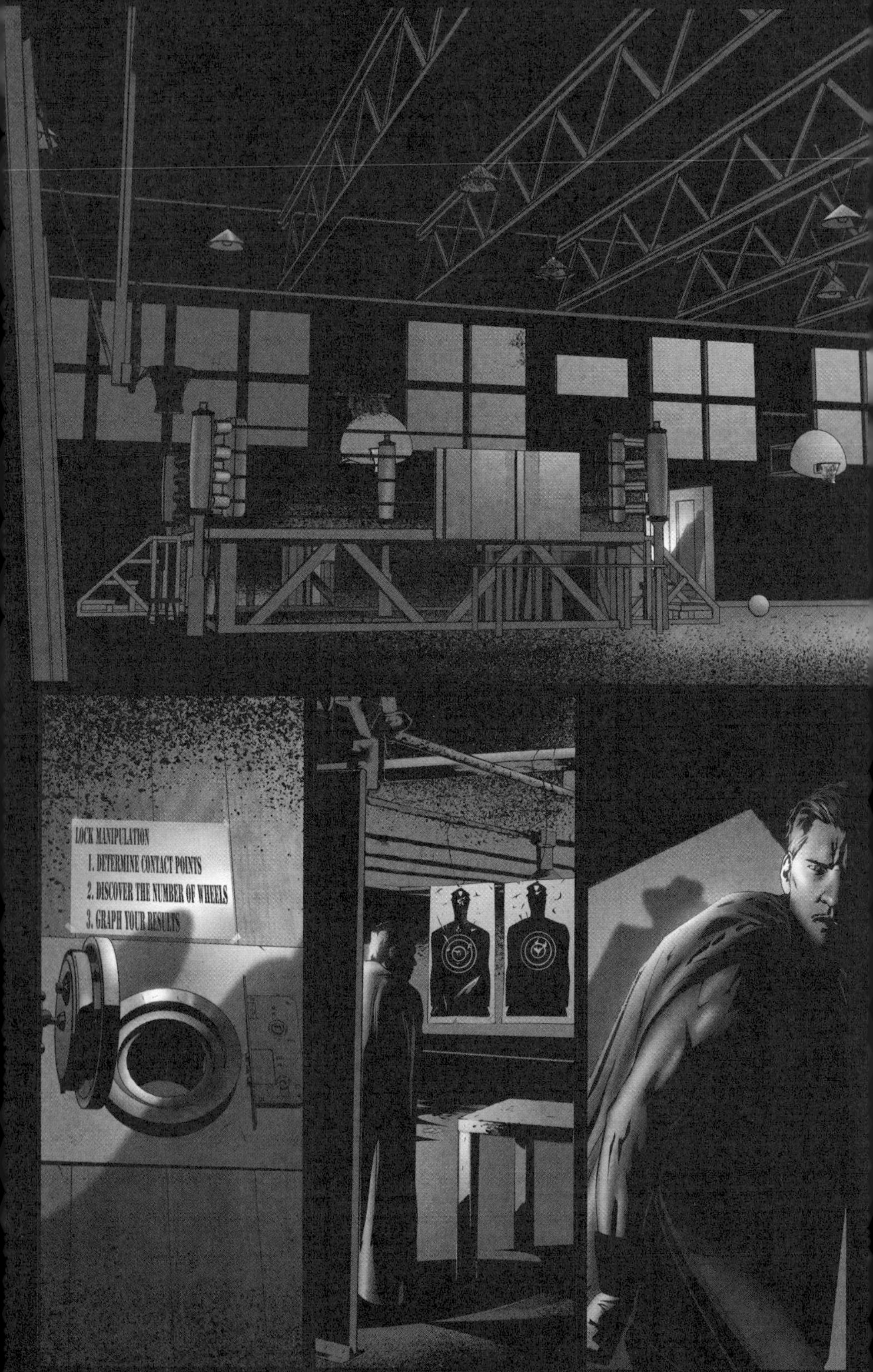
LOCK MANIPULATION
1. DETERMINE CONTACT POINTS
2. DISCOVER THE NUMBER OF WHEELS
3. GRAPH YOUR RESULTS

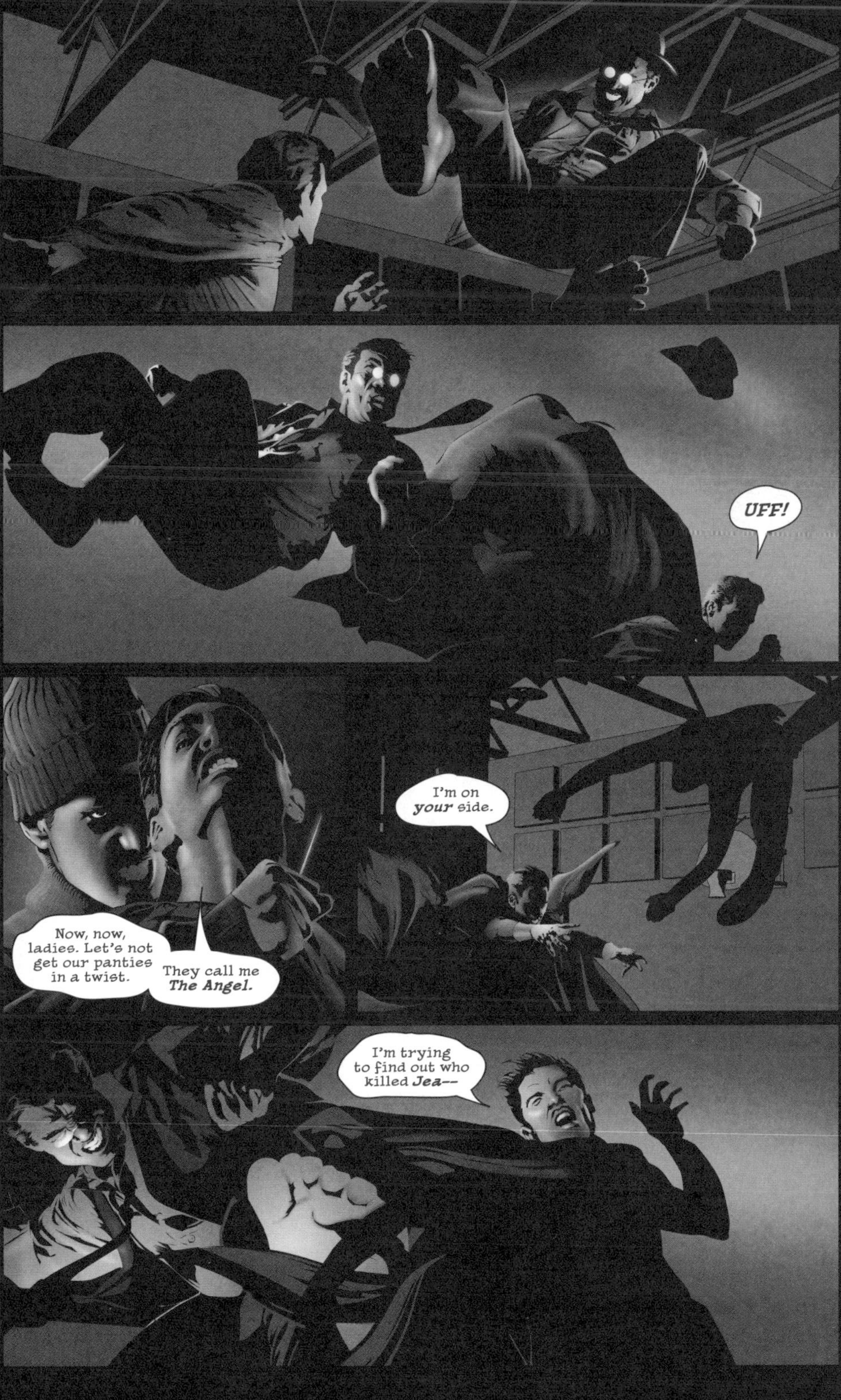
UFF!
Now, now, ladies. Let's not get our panties in a twist.
They call me *The Angel.*
I'm on *your* side.
I'm trying to find out who killed *Jea--*

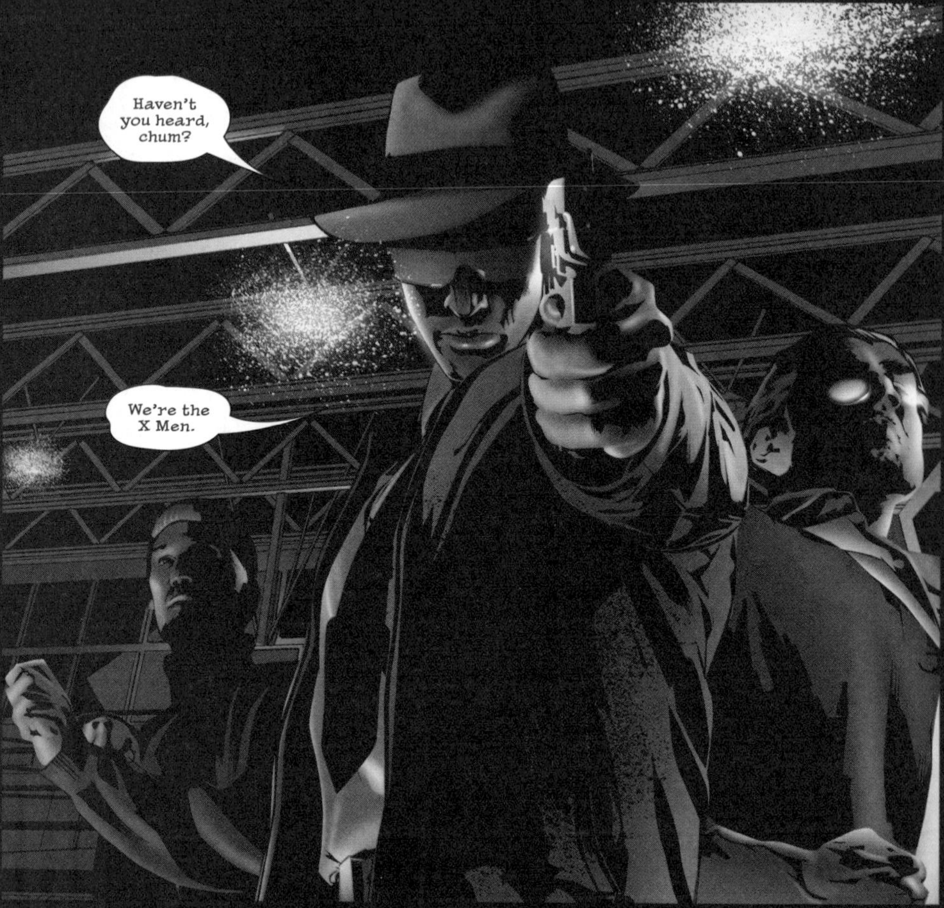
Haven't you heard, chum?
We're the X Men.
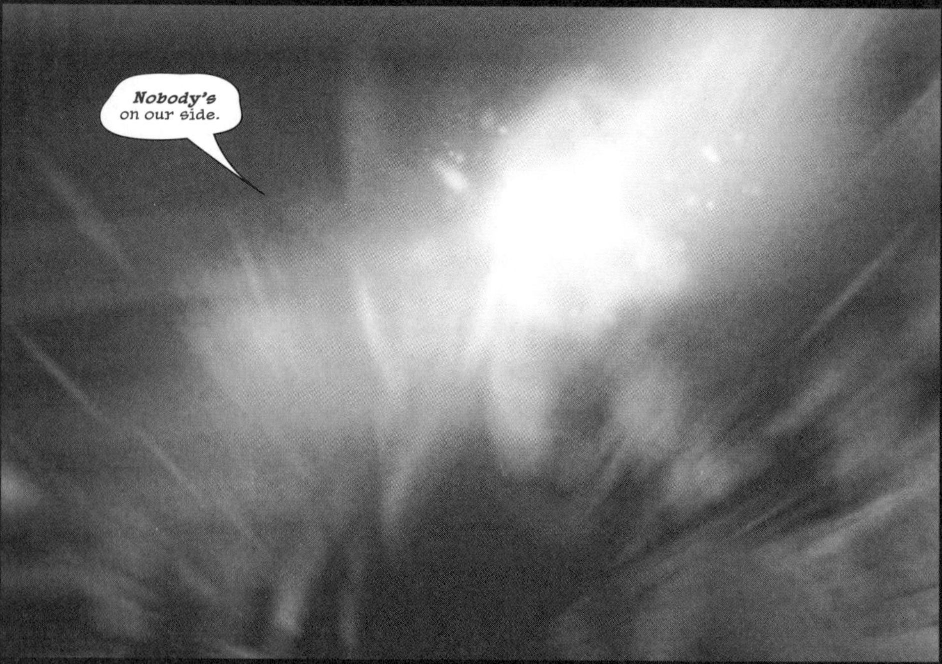
Nobody's on our side.

THE SENTINELS

By Bolivar Trask

*EDITOR'S NOTE: We are most fortunate here at **Scienti-Fiction Magazine** to have our pages graced by a luminary of Dr. Trask's incandescence. Anthropologist, sociologist, and chair of the Department of Race Betterment at the Empire State University, Dr. Trask has employed his vast expertise in this quickly expanding, cutting-edge science of **eugenics** to offer up a plausible and exciting view of the world that is to come – or, at least, we **hope** it comes!*

Chapter One: Days of Future Past

Swooping low on his propellant pack between the impossibly high, antennae-studded spires of New New New York, Sentinel 1st Class Nimrod scanned the automatic commuter tubes crisscrossing the future-city's gleaming canyons below like the great Biblical hunter for whom he was named.

His eyes, bred by the Racial Engineers of the Breeders Council from generations of Eskimo with 20/20 vision who trained themselves to hit a salmon expertly with a harpoon in tempest-tossed seas lest their igloos go hungry, picked them up almost instantly, just as the radio-stream from Commander Bastion had led him to expect. They streamed out of Robo-Womb 94 from its blown-off iris door, clutching in their soot-colored claws the screaming perfect babes of the best and the brightest of the city. In their loathsome wake, normal humans cried out helplessly and fled in terror from the sight of them.

Muties. Dirty, stinking muties. "Inadequates" was the scientific term for them, but to Nimrod and his fellow Sentinels they were a noisome stew of every chromosome the Breeders had nobly tried to purge out of each successive generation, the depraved spawn of murderers, thieves and molesters. In the march toward perfection that was the story of the human race since it first swung down from the trees, Mutants were a step back on the evolutionary scale: Reborn remnants of a primitive era of brute savagery and perpetual tribal war.

In one major sense, however, Nimrod was grateful to the Muties, even as he ambidextrously unholstered his twin neutralizers from his belt and dove down toward them, red cape flapping in the breeze like some relentless, wingless bird of prey.

After all, had there been no Muties, there would have been no need for the Breeders to create the Sentinels in the first place. And that would mean no Rachel: Beautiful, sublime Rachel, his fellow Sentinel and reason for being.

Nimrod landed before the misshapen, murderous horde and cried,

"Halt! In the name of the Council of Breeders!" Numerous times this would be all that Nimrod had to do for the superstitious Inadequates to drop to their knees and surrender. Even in some dim, wasted crevice of their twisted minds, the Muties recognized from the rippling muscles beneath his blue, skintight uniform, bred from generations of body builders and sumo wrestlers, and even his skin — an unmistakable bronze color, the shade of coffee once one, or perhaps two spoonfuls of cream have been added — that they faced not just a single man, but an Ur-man, the apotheosis of man. The singular quintessence of the Aborigine, Teuton, Zulu, Semite, Latin, Polynesian, Mongol, Slav, Brahmin, Algonquin, Norman, Mayan and more – the sum total of all the best parts of all the nations of the world stared them down with his steely, almond-shaped, robin's egg blue eyes.

When faced with such a foe, how could an Inadequate continue its futile resistance? How could one who was merely *adequate*, against the might of this pan-racial *Übermensch*?

But not this time. These Muties, who by this very crime of kidnapping seemed to be tacitly acknowledging the paucity of their own breeding pools, merely shifted the babies from one arm to the other and raised their auto-gutters high.

The auto-gutters coughed death in Nimrod's general direction, but he was no longer there. His mighty Maasai legs, coiled like steel springs for running messages from one tribal kingdom to the next across the beast-dotted veldt, let him leap to one side while he unloaded his own neutralizers into the slavering riot of evil.

Crackling arcs of bioelectric energy struck each Mutie's central nervous system with a flash and a spark. The genetic criminals cried out as their fur burned and their flesh sizzled. One blast missed, however, and the accidentally spared Mutie bounded over his fallen comrades and loped like an Ourang-Outang down the commuter tube, clutching his precious, bawling contraband. Presumably he sought one of the many open sewer entrances that led down into the warren of trenches beneath the city that served as dark sanctuary for his kind.

Nimrod cursed his carelessness. Though his reflexes had been racially honed in the Black Forest by three generations of Hessian sharpshooters, anxiousness had interfered with the brave Sentinel's aim.

For today was the day he was to have a mate chosen for him.

Unlike normal humans, whose genes were carefully culled with each new generation, Sentinels were a special case, bred to be humanity's last defense against the Muties. Rachel was his female counterpart: Her skin was as bronze as his, her eyes as blue, her hair as black and kinky. They had already pledged their love to each other outside the gaze of prying eyes; fortunately, all the Sentinels before them had been mated to one of their own, so every sign pointed to the Breeders selecting Nimrod and Rachel to be each other's life-mates. They *had* to!

Fortunately, Nimrod's anxiety did not prevent him from felling the fleeing Mutie with a perfectly aimed blast to its spinal column. He made sure the Inadequates were properly loaded into the Sterilization Wagons and the stolen children were returned to the mechanical arms of the Robo-Womb's automated wetnurses. Just as he had finished rocking the last babe to sleep he received an urgent message from Bastion to meet him at the Hall of Experimental Evolution at once.

Nimrod swallowed hard. The Hall was where the Breeders made final mating selections.

His – and Rachel's – moment of truth must have come.

The Sentinel shot up into the sky on his propellant pack, and scaled the sky up the side of the mighty ziggurat that was the Hall of Experimental Evolution. Each step depicted another advance toward mankind's ultimate perfection, beginning down by the Neanderthal and Cro-Magnon Man, continuing upward halfway to Early 20th century humanity, still locked in their racist hatreds and constant warfare, and up, now, to the enlightened era of A.D. 2013.

Nimrod alighted at the top of the step-pyramid and walked, head bowed in reverence, into the huge Breeder Council chamber. The commanding Sentinel, Bastion, stood before the legislature's high dais, looking soberly at his subordinate as Nimrod entered. He immediately saw that all the councilors shared Bastion's unease. These were not the faces of people about to tell a man he was to be married.

"Commander, what has happened?" Nimrod demanded.

"It appears the attack on Robo-Womb 94 was merely a clever distraction," Bastion said, mouth taut. "A much larger Mutie force surprise attacked your partner, Rachel, in District Twelve. She was captured … and brought down to the Muties' tunnels. Their loathsome queen, Callisto, says they will execute her unless their demands are met."

Nimrod's mind barely had time to absorb this thundering shock when Bastion turned toward the Breeders to ask for their will.

"We must deliberate on this matter for some time before we know what to do, Commander. Callisto has given us twelve hours to decide, and wisdom dictates we use every second."

"Do you understand, Nimrod?" Bastion asked, turning toward his comrade. "We know how you feel about Rachel, but the Council has spoken…"

Bastion trailed off as he looked around the Council chamber: Nimrod was nowhere to be seen!

"Great Darwin's ghost!" the Sentinels' commander cried. "He must have gone after her! The fool is going to take on the whole Mutant Nation single-handed!"

NEXT: MUTANT MASSACRE!

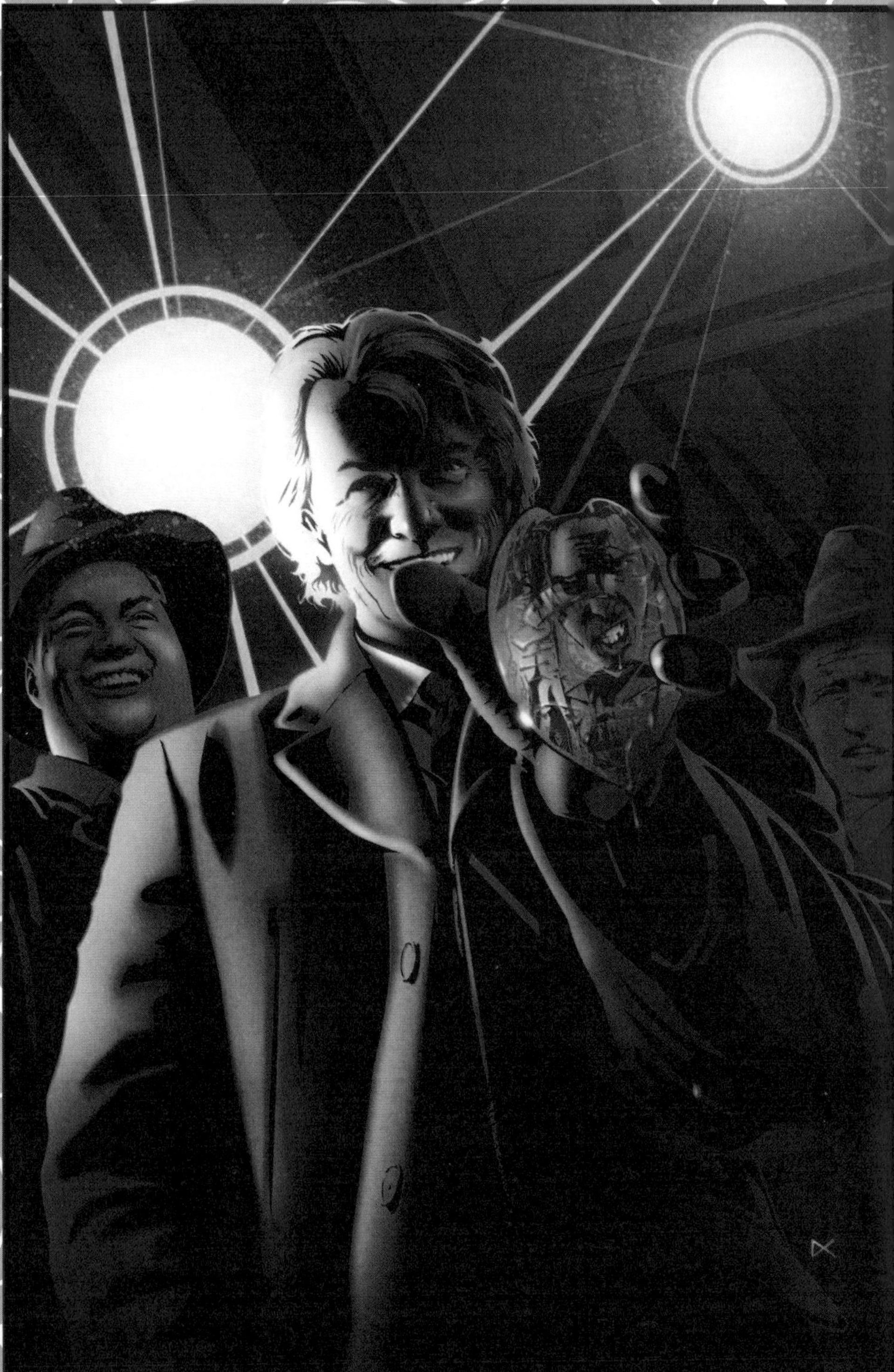

TWO

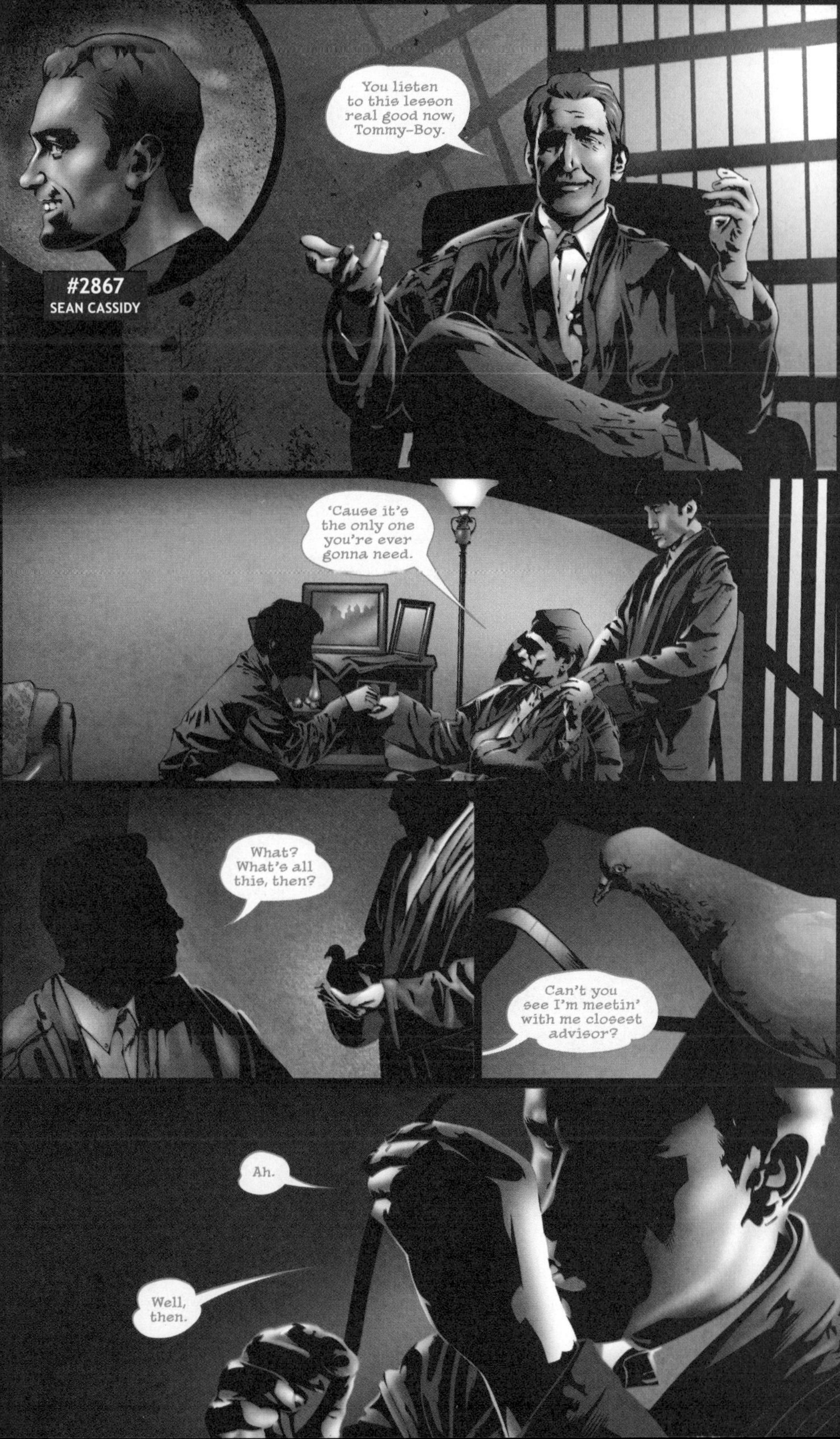
#2867
SEAN CASSIDY
You listen to this lesson real good now, Tommy-Boy.
'Cause it's the only one you're ever gonna need.
What? What's all this, then?
Can't you see I'm meetin' with me closest advisor?
Ah.
Well, then.

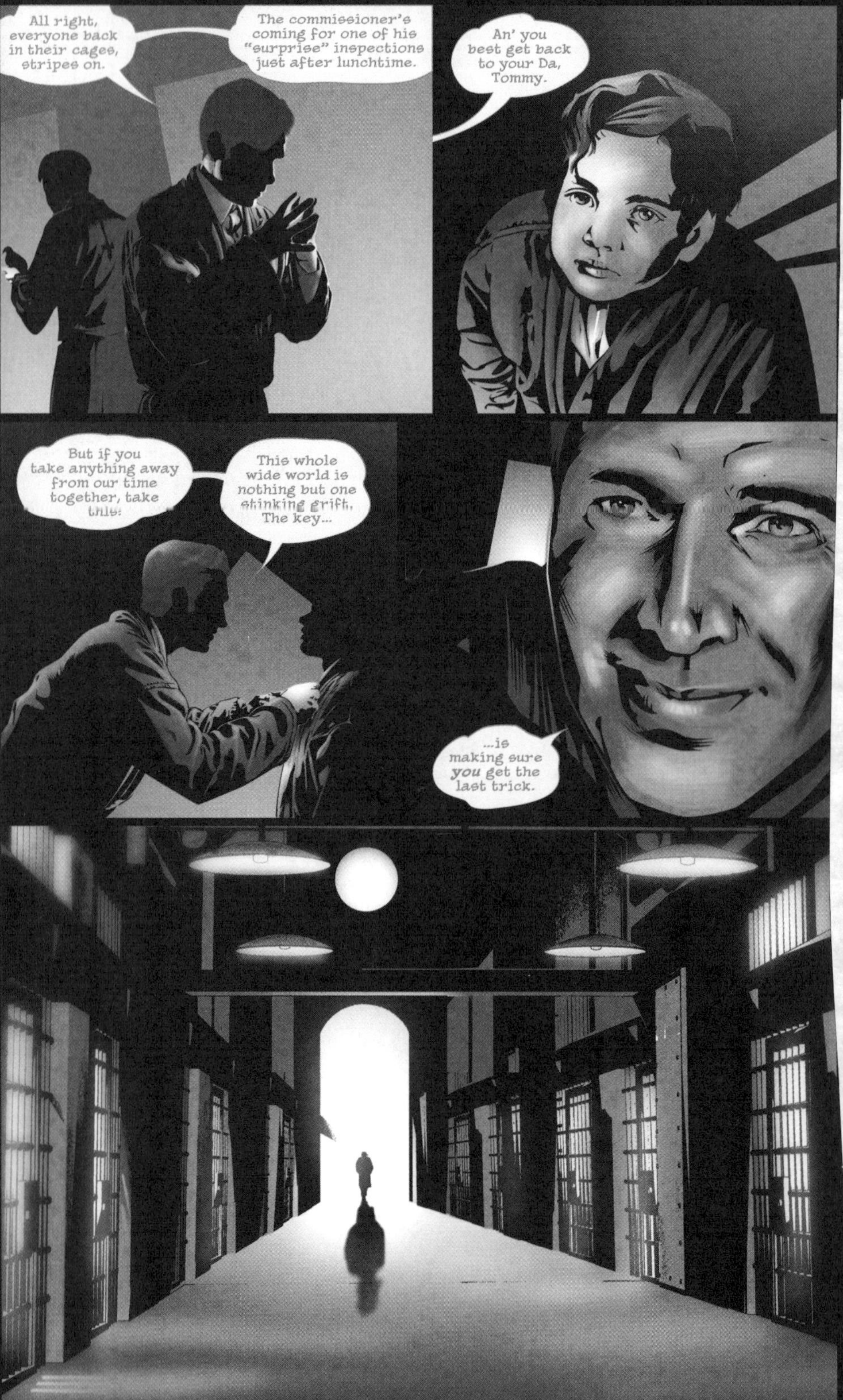
All right, everyone back in their cages, stripes on.
The commissioner's coming for one of his "surprise" inspections just after lunchtime.
An' you best get back to your Da, Tommy.
But if you take anything away from our time together, take this:
This whole wide world is nothing but one stinking grift. The key...
...is making sure *you* get the last trick.

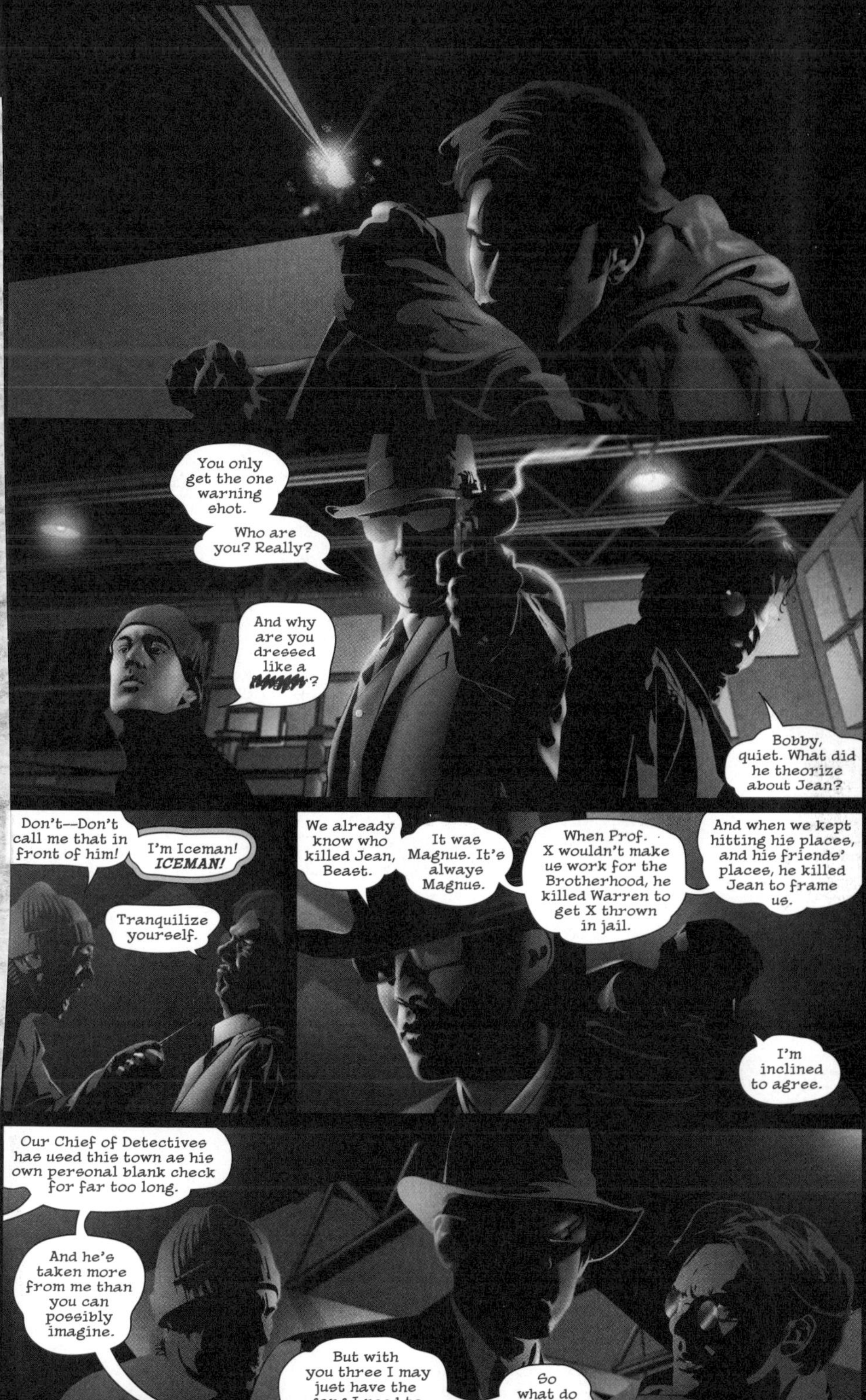
You only get the one warning shot.
Who are you? Really?
And why are you dressed like a [redacted]?
Bobby, quiet. What did he theorize about Jean?
Don't--Don't call me that in front of him!
I'm Iceman! *ICEMAN!*
Tranquilize yourself.
We already know who killed Jean, Beast.
It was Magnus. It's always Magnus.
When Prof. X wouldn't make us work for the Brotherhood, he killed Warren to get X thrown in jail.
And when we kept hitting his places, and his friends' places, he killed Jean to frame us.
I'm inclined to agree.
Our Chief of Detectives has used this town as his own personal blank check for far too long.
And he's taken more from me than you can possibly imagine.
But with you three I may just have the gang I need to take him down.
So what do you say...
...to an alliance?

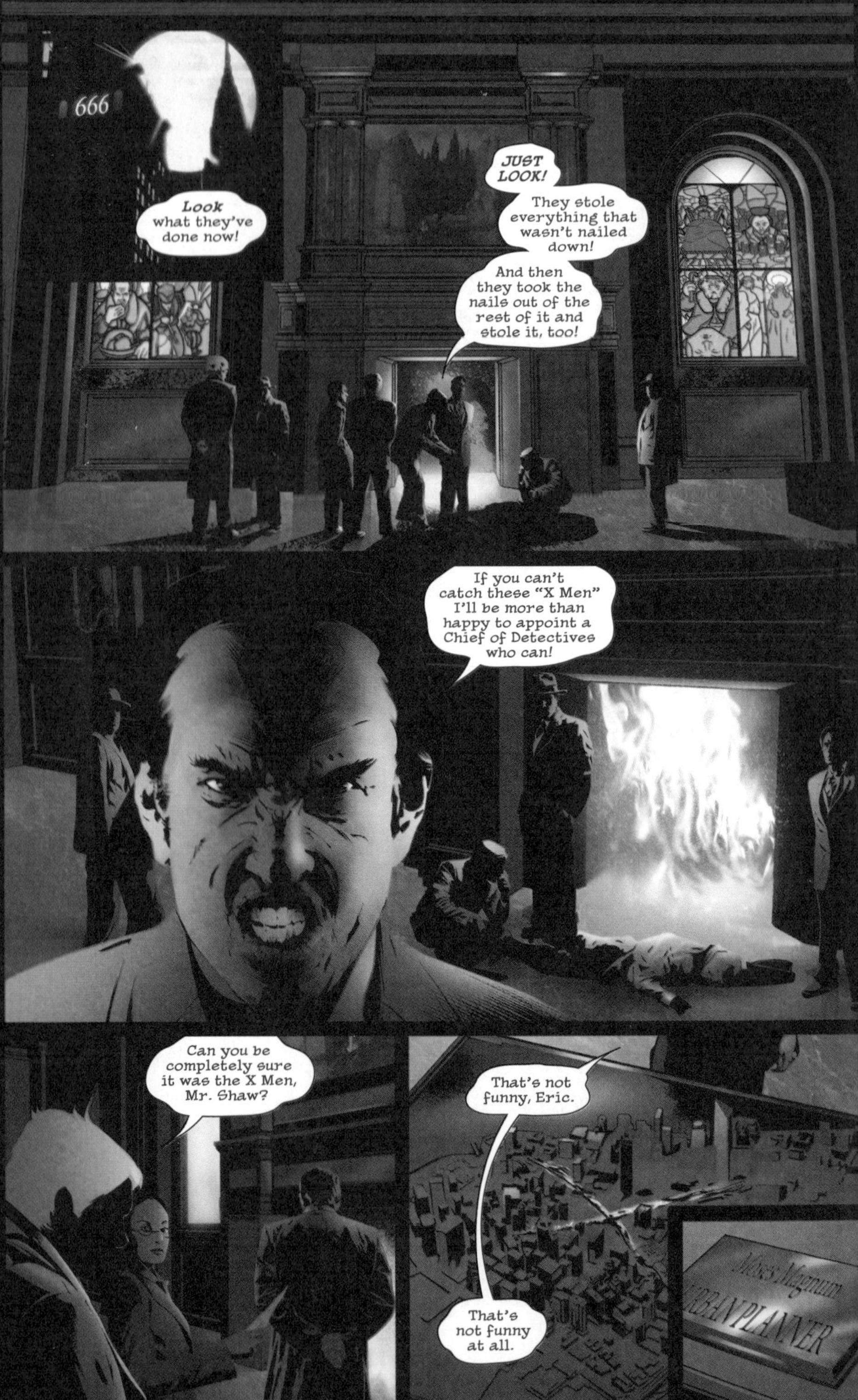
666
Look what they've done now!
JUST LOOK!
They stole everything that wasn't nailed down!
And then they took the nails out of the rest of it and stole it, too!
If you can't catch these "X Men" I'll be more than happy to appoint a Chief of Detectives who can!
Can you be completely sure it was the X Men, Mr. Shaw?
That's not funny, Eric.
That's not funny at all.
Moses Magnum
URBAN PLANNER

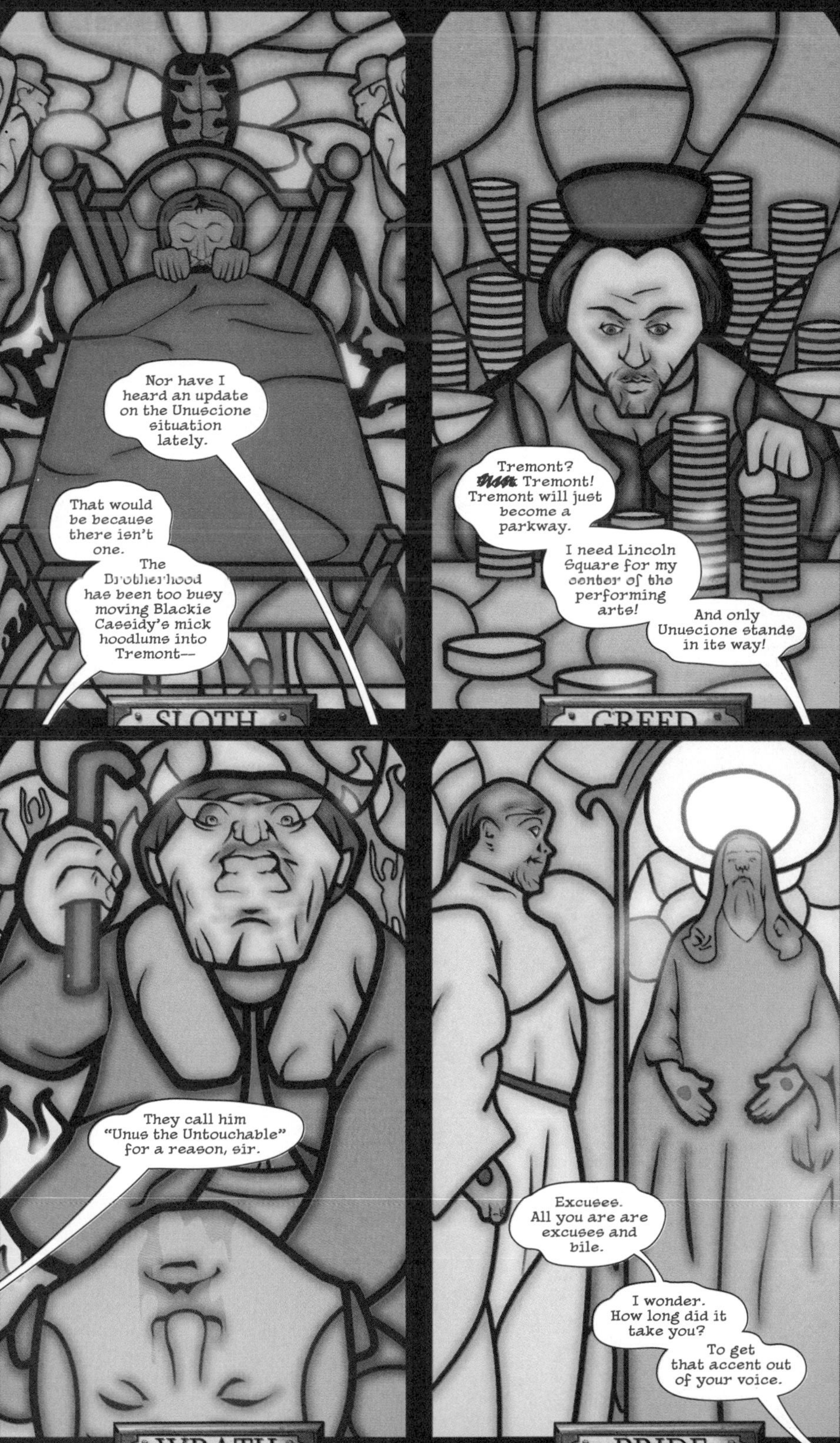

Nor have I heard an update on the Unuscione situation lately.
That would be because there isn't one.
The Brotherhood has been too busy moving Blackie Cassidy's mick hoodlums into Tremont--
SLOTH
Tremont? [redacted] Tremont! Tremont will just become a parkway.
I need Lincoln Square for my center of the performing arts!
And only Unuscione stands in its way!
GREED
They call him "Unus the Untouchable" for a reason, sir.
WRATH
Excuses. All you are are excuses and bile.
I wonder. How long did it take you?
To get that accent out of your voice.
PRIDE

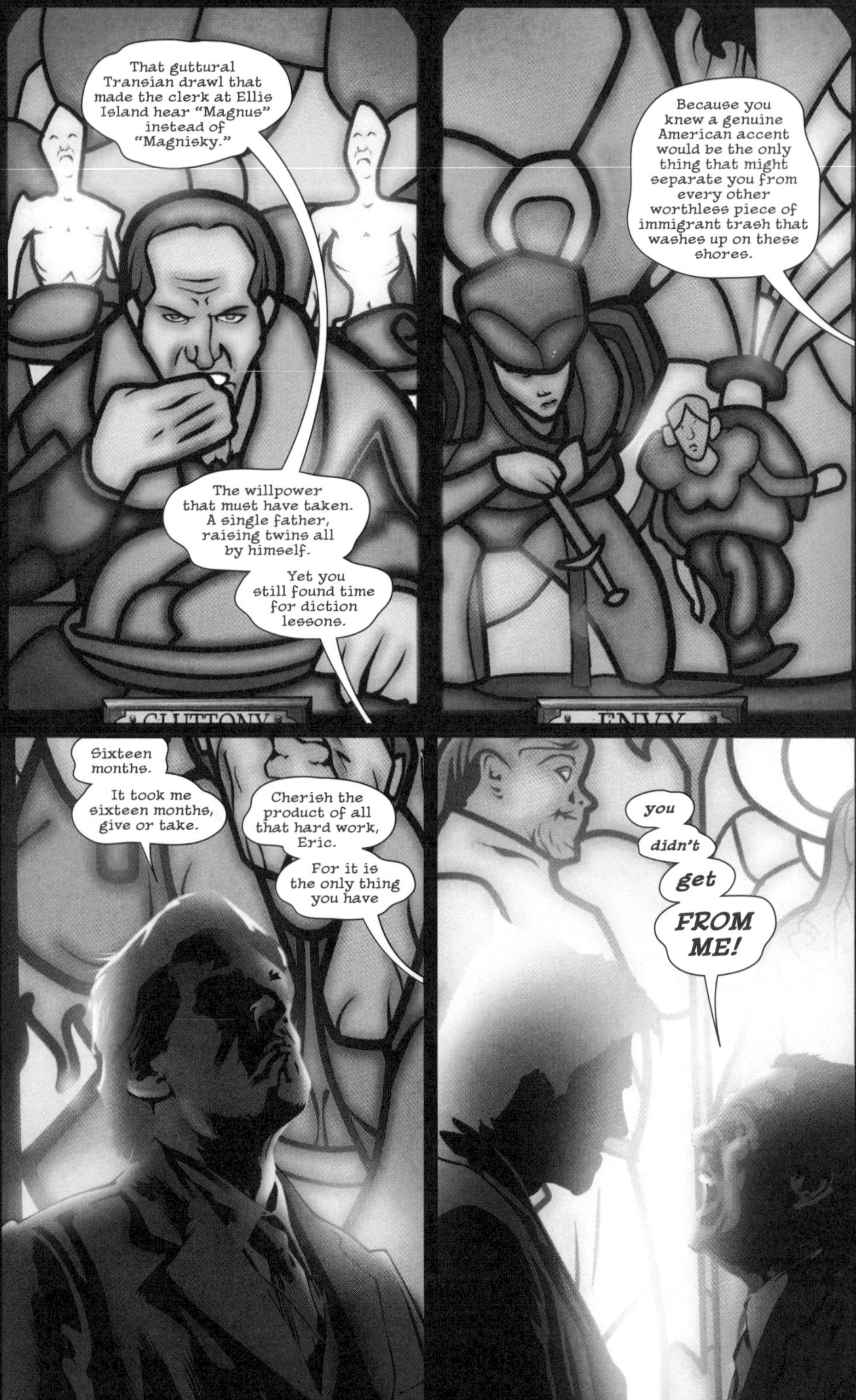
That guttural Transian drawl that made the clerk at Ellis Island hear "Magnus" instead of "Magnisky."
The willpower that must have taken. A single father, raising twins all by himself.
Yet you still found time for diction lessons.
Because you knew a genuine American accent would be the only thing that might separate you from every other worthless piece of immigrant trash that washes up on these shores.
Sixteen months.
It took me sixteen months, give or take.
Cherish the product of all that hard work, Eric.
For it is the only thing you have
you
didn't
get
FROM ME!

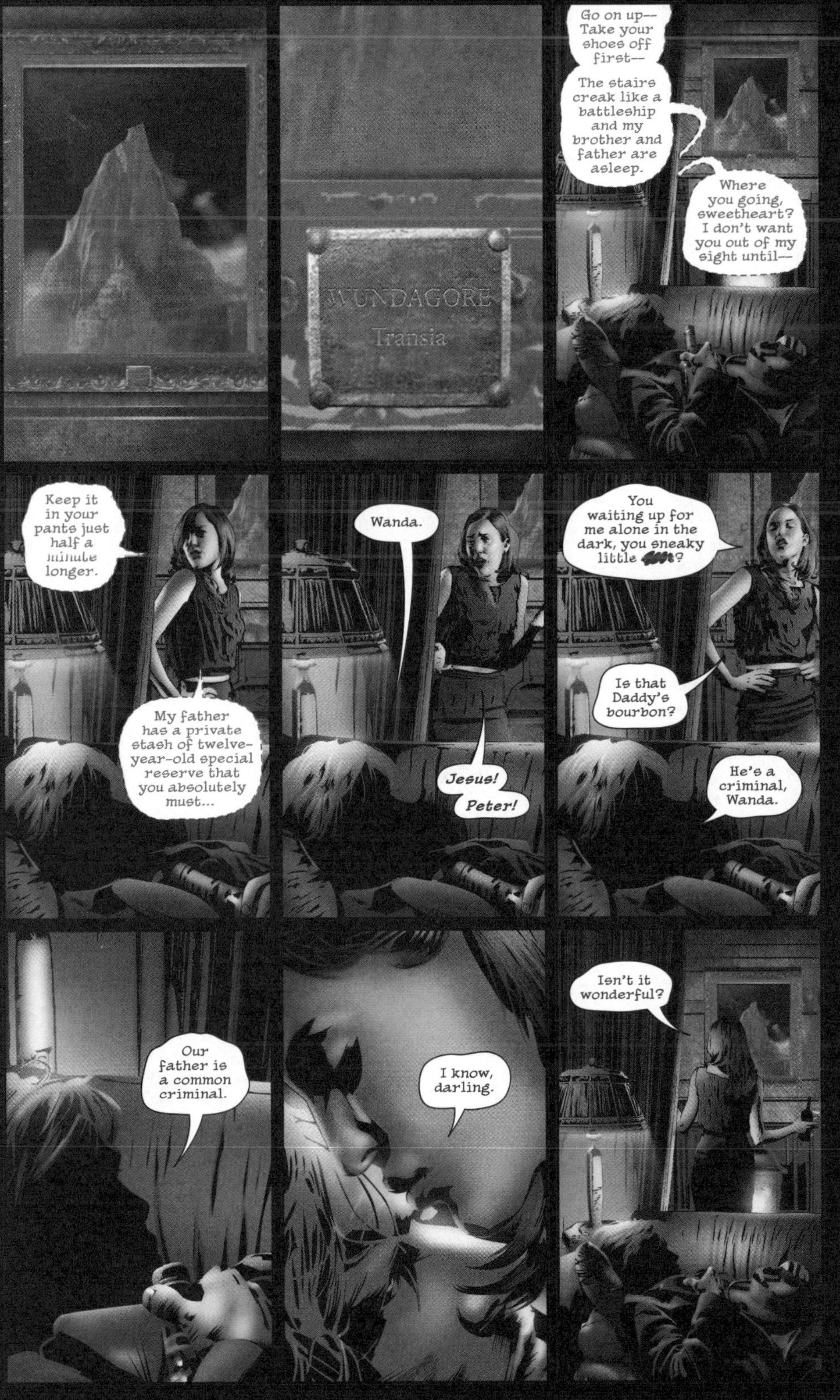
WUNDAGORE
Transia
Go on up-- Take your shoes off first--
The stairs creak like a battleship and my brother and father are asleep.
Where you going, sweetheart? I don't want you out of my sight until--
Keep it in your pants just half a minute longer.
My father has a private stash of twelve-year-old special reserve that you absolutely must...
Wanda.
Jesus!
Peter!
You waiting up for me alone in the dark, you sneaky little [redacted]?
Is that Daddy's bourbon?
He's a criminal, Wanda.
Our father is a common criminal.
I know, darling.
Isn't it wonderful?

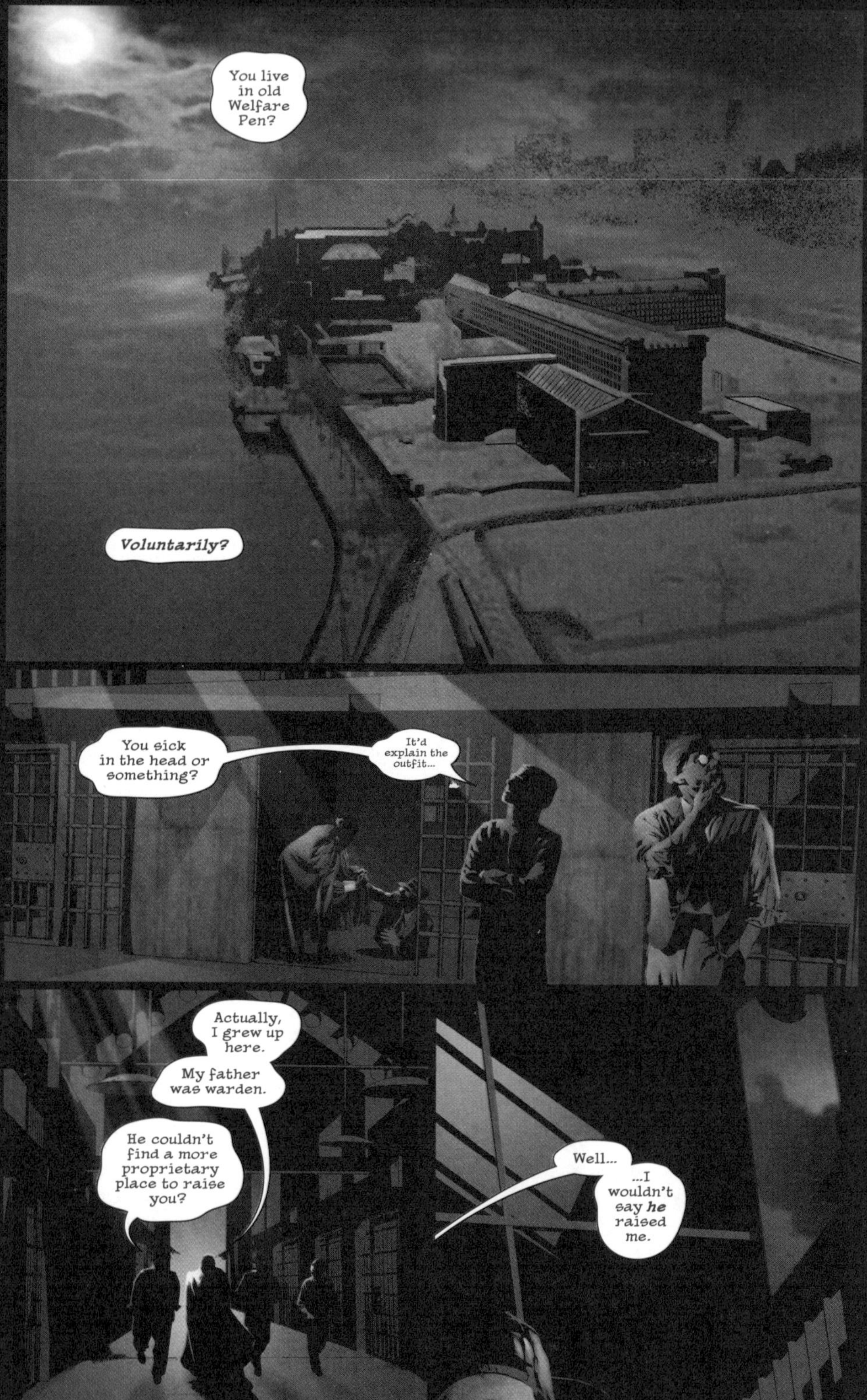
You live in old Welfare Pen?
Voluntarily?
You sick in the head or something?
It'd explain the outfit...
Actually, I grew up here.
My father was warden.
He couldn't find a more proprietary place to raise you?
Well...
...I wouldn't say *he* raised me.

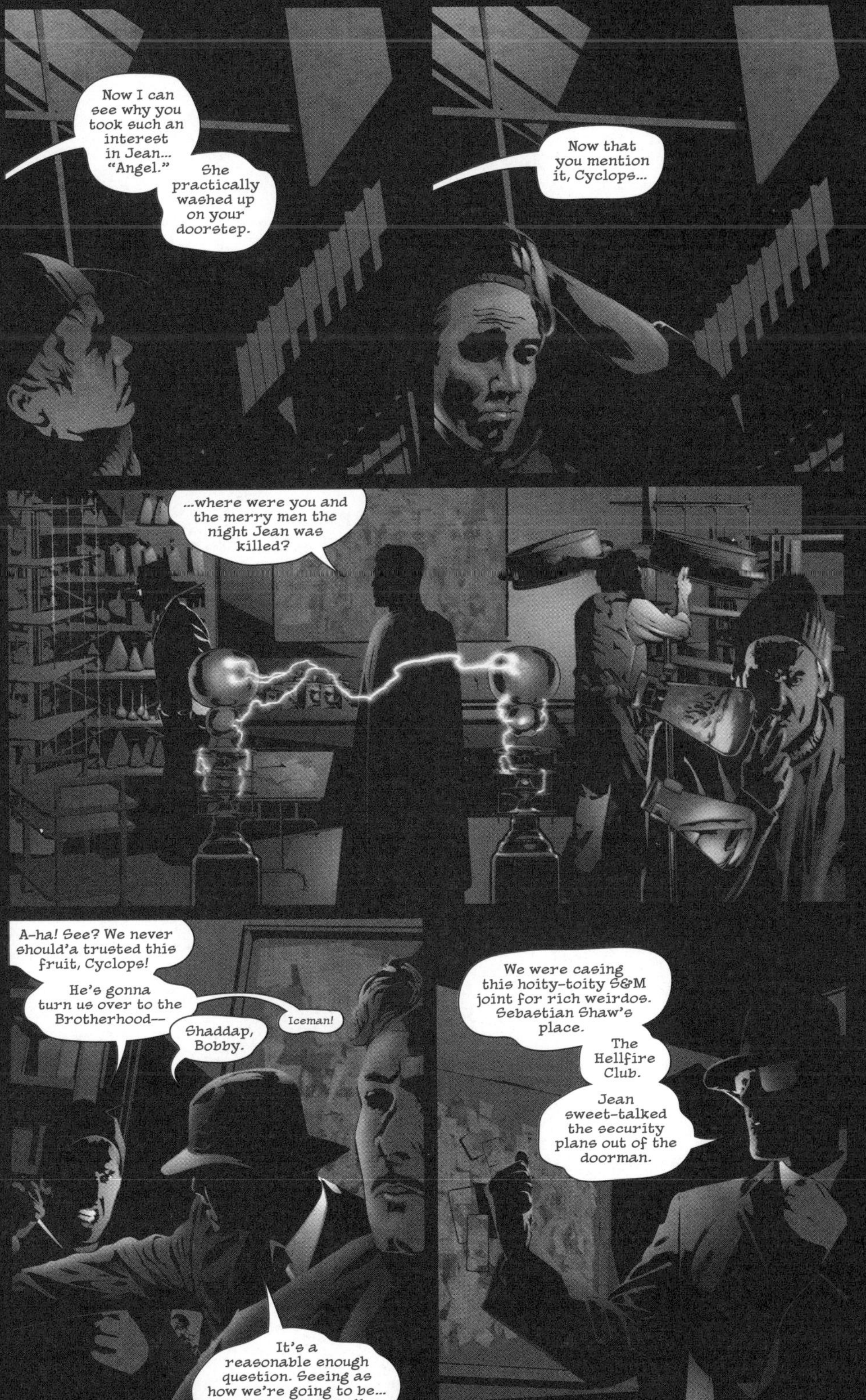
Now I can see why you took such an interest in Jean... "Angel."
She practically washed up on your doorstep.
Now that you mention it, Cyclops...
...where were you and the merry men the night Jean was killed?
A-ha! See? We never should'a trusted this fruit, Cyclops!
He's gonna turn us over to the Brotherhood--
Iceman!
Shaddap, Bobby.
It's a reasonable enough question. Seeing as how we're going to be... "partners" and all.
We were casing this hoity-toity S&M joint for rich weirdos. Sebastian Shaw's place.
The Hellfire Club.
Jean sweet-talked the security plans out of the doorman.

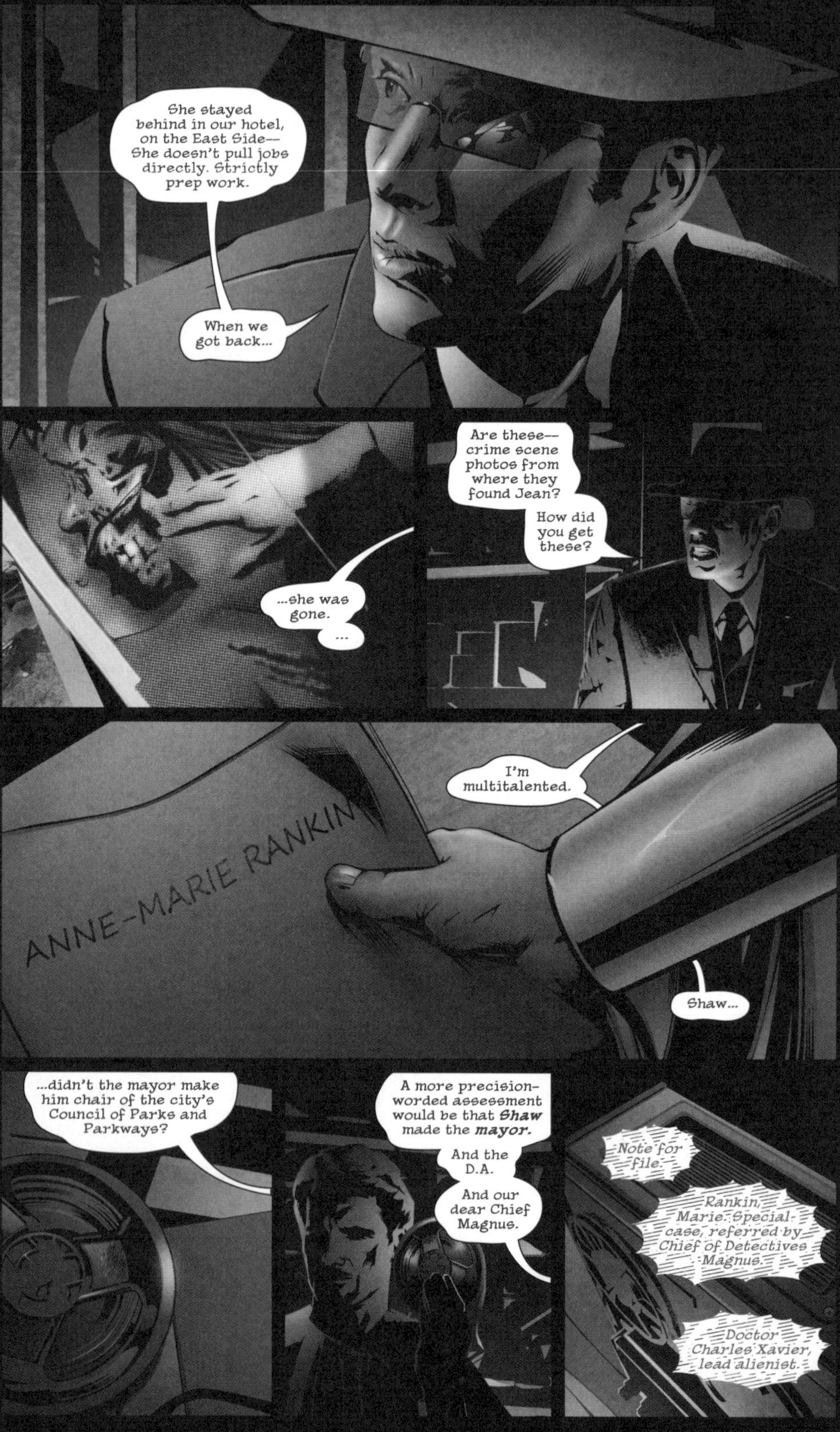
She stayed behind in our hotel, on the East Side-- She doesn't pull jobs directly. Strictly prep work.
When we got back...
...she was gone.
...
Are these-- crime scene photos from where they found Jean?
How did you get these?
ANNE-MARIE RANKIN
I'm multitalented.
Shaw...
...didn't the mayor make him chair of the city's Council of Parks and Parkways?
A more precision-worded assessment would be that Shaw made the mayor.
And the D.A.
And our dear Chief Magnus.
Note for file.
Rankin, Marie. Special case, referred by Chief of Detectives Magnus.
Doctor Charles Xavier, lead alienist.

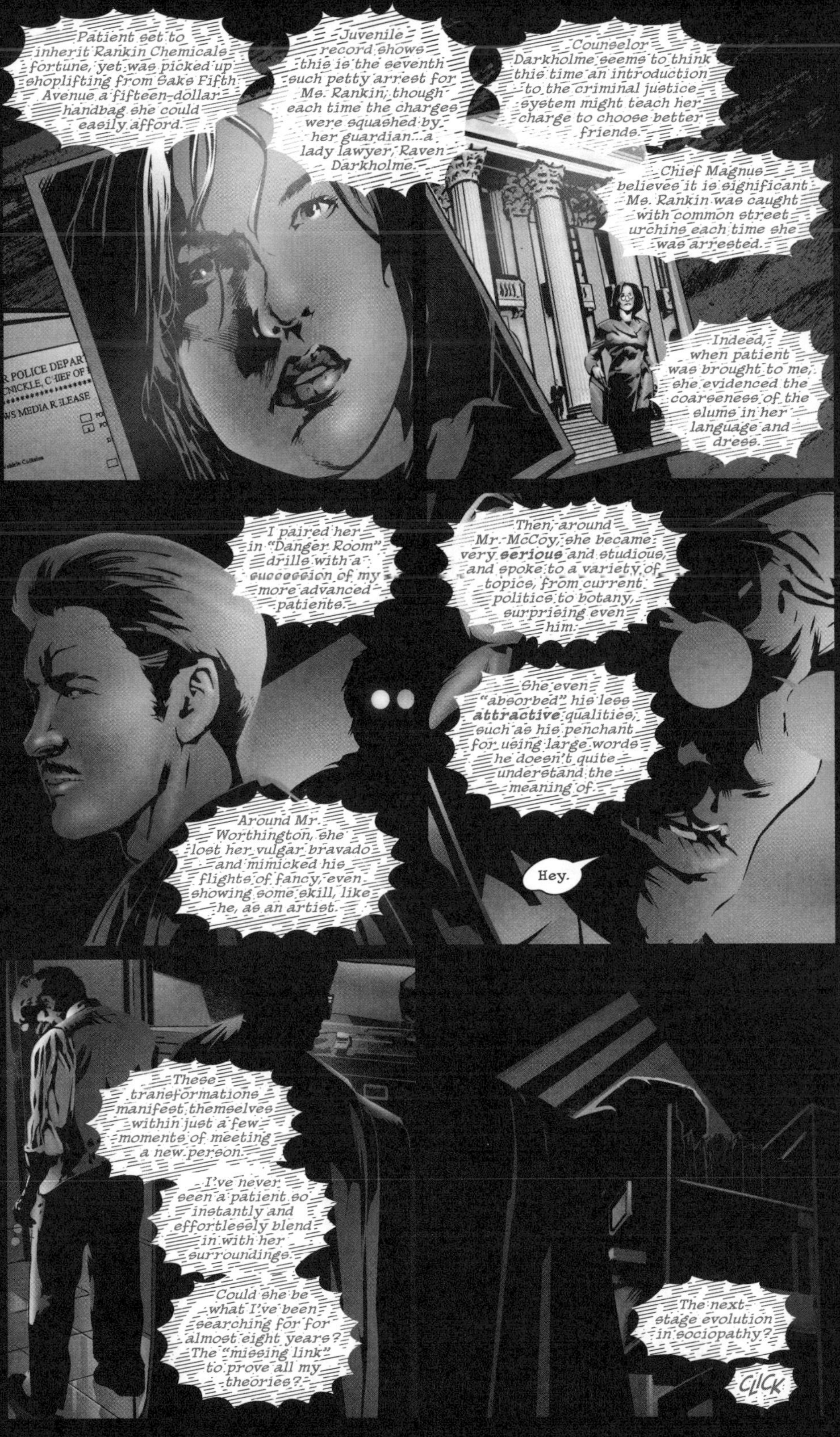

Patient set to inherit Rankin Chemicals fortune, yet was picked up shoplifting from Saks Fifth Avenue a fifteen-dollar handbag she could easily afford.
Juvenile record shows this is the seventh such petty arrest for Ms. Rankin, though each time the charges were squashed by her guardian...a lady lawyer, Raven Darkholme.
Counselor Darkholme seems to think this time an introduction to the criminal justice system might teach her charge to choose better friends.
Chief Magnus believes it is significant Ms. Rankin was caught with common street urchins each time she was arrested.
Indeed, when patient was brought to me, she evidenced the coarseness of the slums in her language and dress.
I paired her in "Danger Room" drills with a succession of my more advanced patients.
Around Mr. Worthington, she lost her vulgar bravado and mimicked his flights of fancy, even showing some skill, like he, as an artist.
Then, around Mr. McCoy, she became very **serious** and studious, and spoke to a variety of topics, from current politics to botany, surprising even him.
She even "absorbed" his less **attractive** qualities, such as his penchant for using large words he doesn't quite understand the meaning of.
Hey.
These transformations manifest themselves within just a few moments of meeting a new person.
I've never seen a patient so instantly and effortlessly blend in with her surroundings.
Could she be what I've been searching for for almost eight years? The "missing link" to prove all my theories?
The next stage evolution in sociopathy?
CLICK

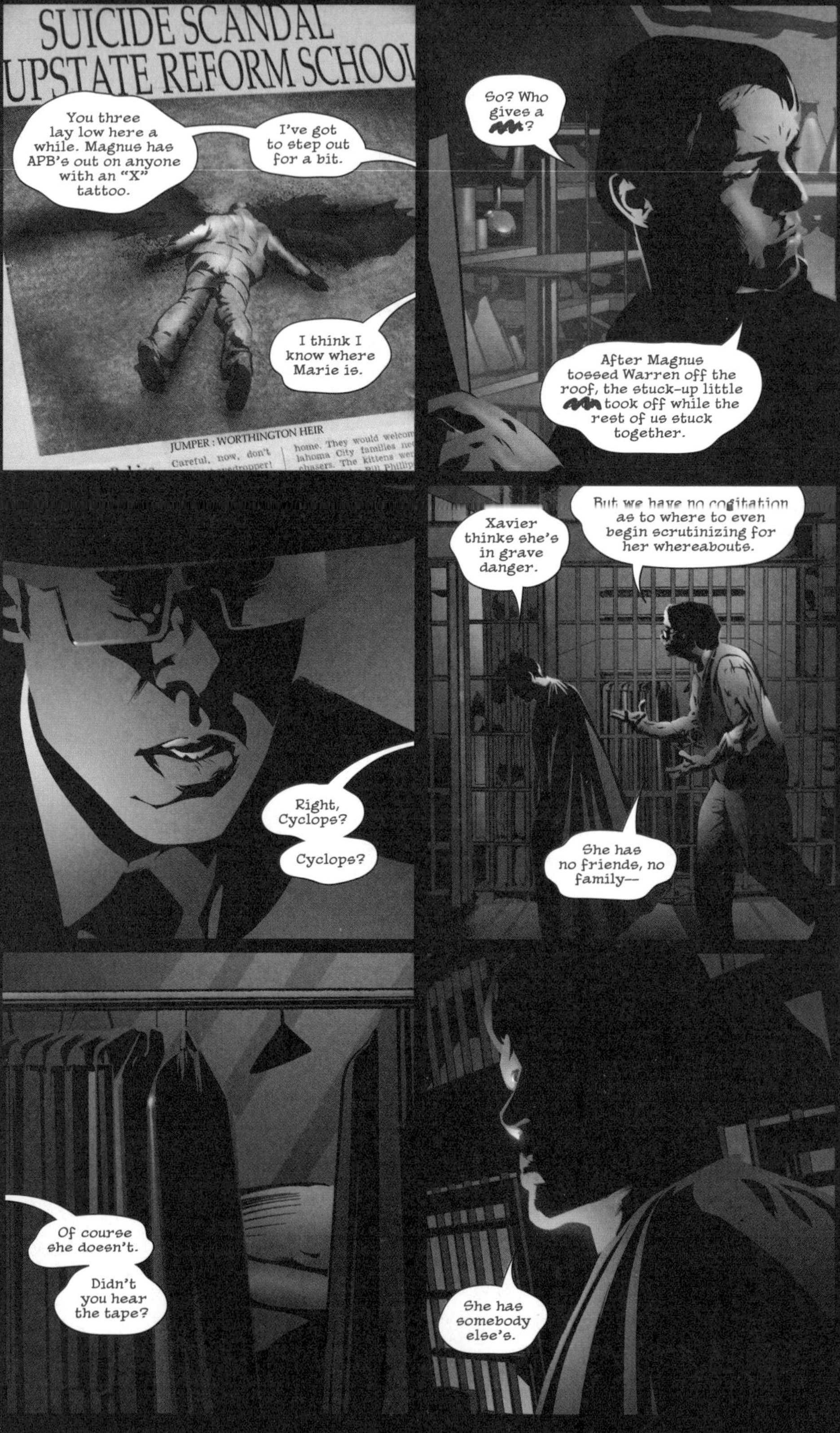

SUICIDE SCANDAL
UPSTATE REFORM SCHOO
You three lay low here a while. Magnus has APB's out on anyone with an "X" tattoo.
I've got to step out for a bit.
I think I know where Marie is.
JUMPER : WORTHINGTON HEIR
So? Who gives a [redacted]?
After Magnus tossed Warren off the roof, the stuck-up little [redacted] took off while the rest of us stuck together.
Right, Cyclops?
Cyclops?
Xavier thinks she's in grave danger.
But we have no cogitation as to where to even begin scrutinizing for her whereabouts.
She has no friends, no family--
Of course she doesn't.
Didn't you hear the tape?
She has somebody else's.

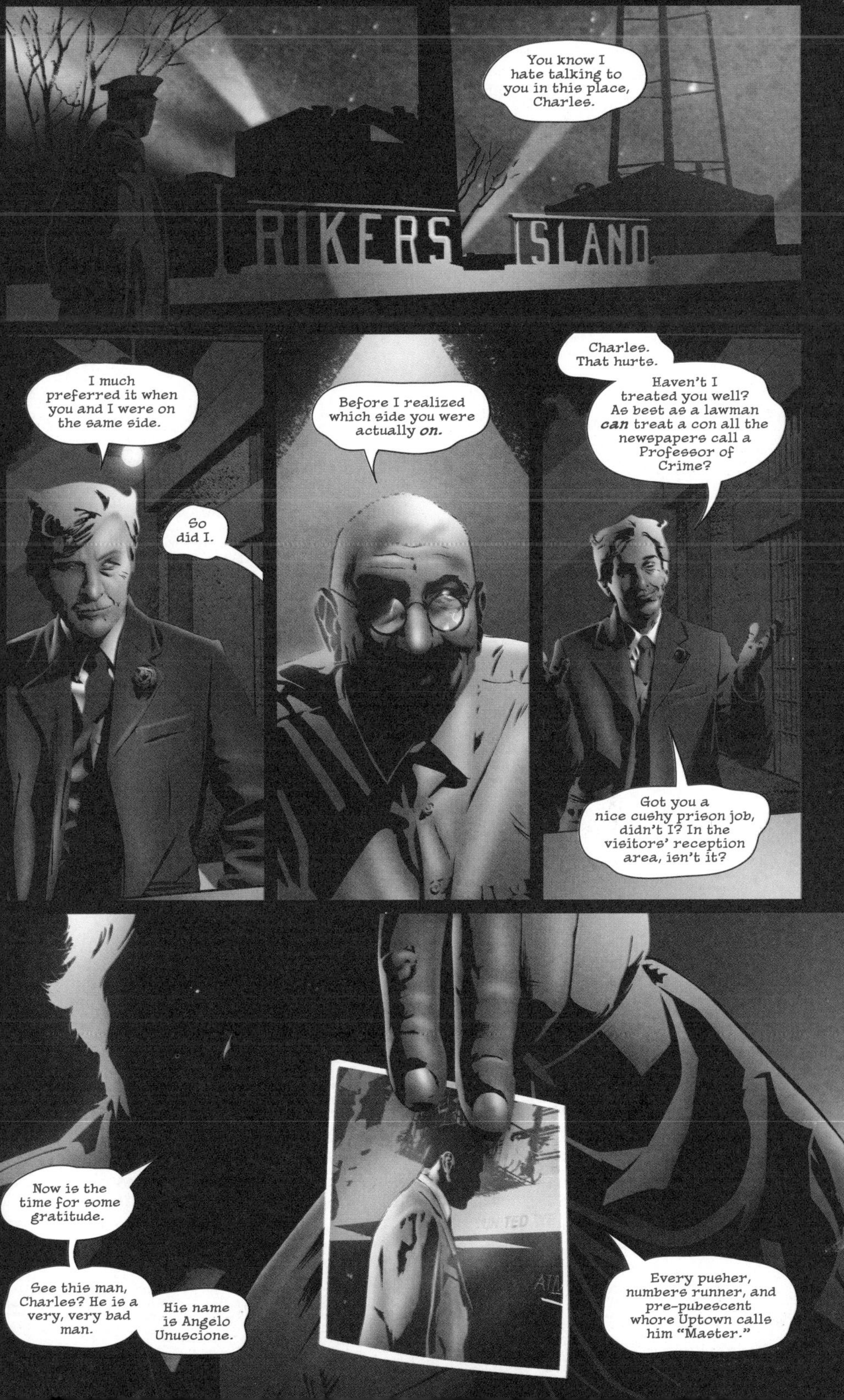
RIKERS ISLAND
You know I hate talking to you in this place, Charles.
I much preferred it when you and I were on the same side.
So did I.
Before I realized which side you were actually *on.*
Charles. That hurts.
Haven't I treated you well? As best as a lawman ***can*** treat a con all the newspapers call a Professor of Crime?
Got you a nice cushy prison job, didn't I? In the visitors' reception area, isn't it?
Now is the time for some gratitude.
See this man, Charles? He is a very, very bad man.
His name is Angelo Unuscione.
Every pusher, numbers runner, and pre-pubescent whore Uptown calls him "Master."

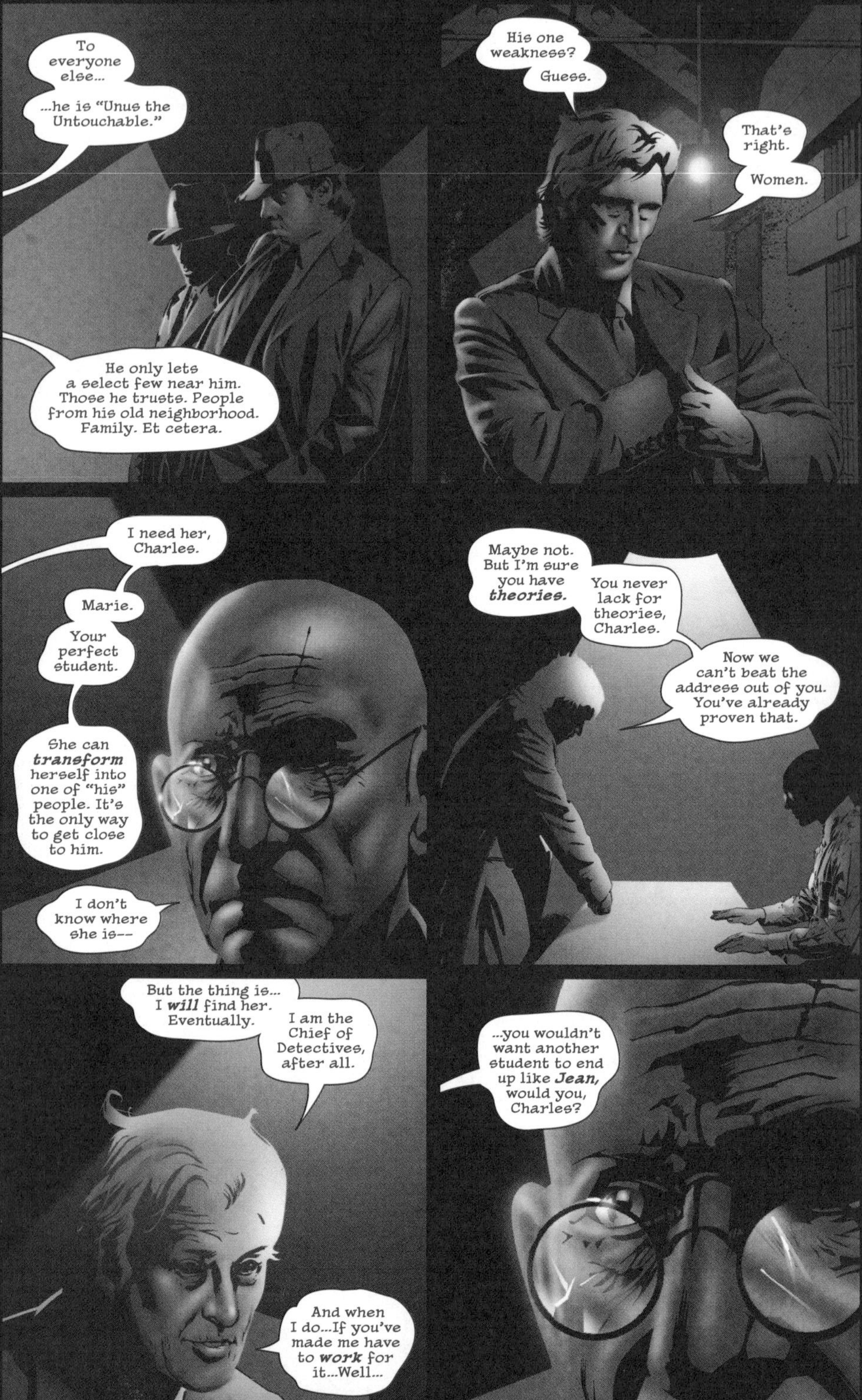
To everyone else...
...he is "Unus the Untouchable."
He only lets a select few near him. Those he trusts. People from his old neighborhood. Family. Et cetera.
His one weakness?
Guess.
That's right.
Women.
I need her, Charles.
Marie.
Your perfect student.
She can **transform** herself into one of "his" people. It's the only way to get close to him.
I don't know where she is--
Maybe not. But I'm sure you have **theories.**
You never lack for theories, Charles.
Now we can't beat the address out of you. You've already proven that.
But the thing is... I **will** find her. Eventually.
I am the Chief of Detectives, after all.
And when I do...If you've made me have to **work** for it...Well...
...you wouldn't want another student to end up like **Jean,** would you, Charles?

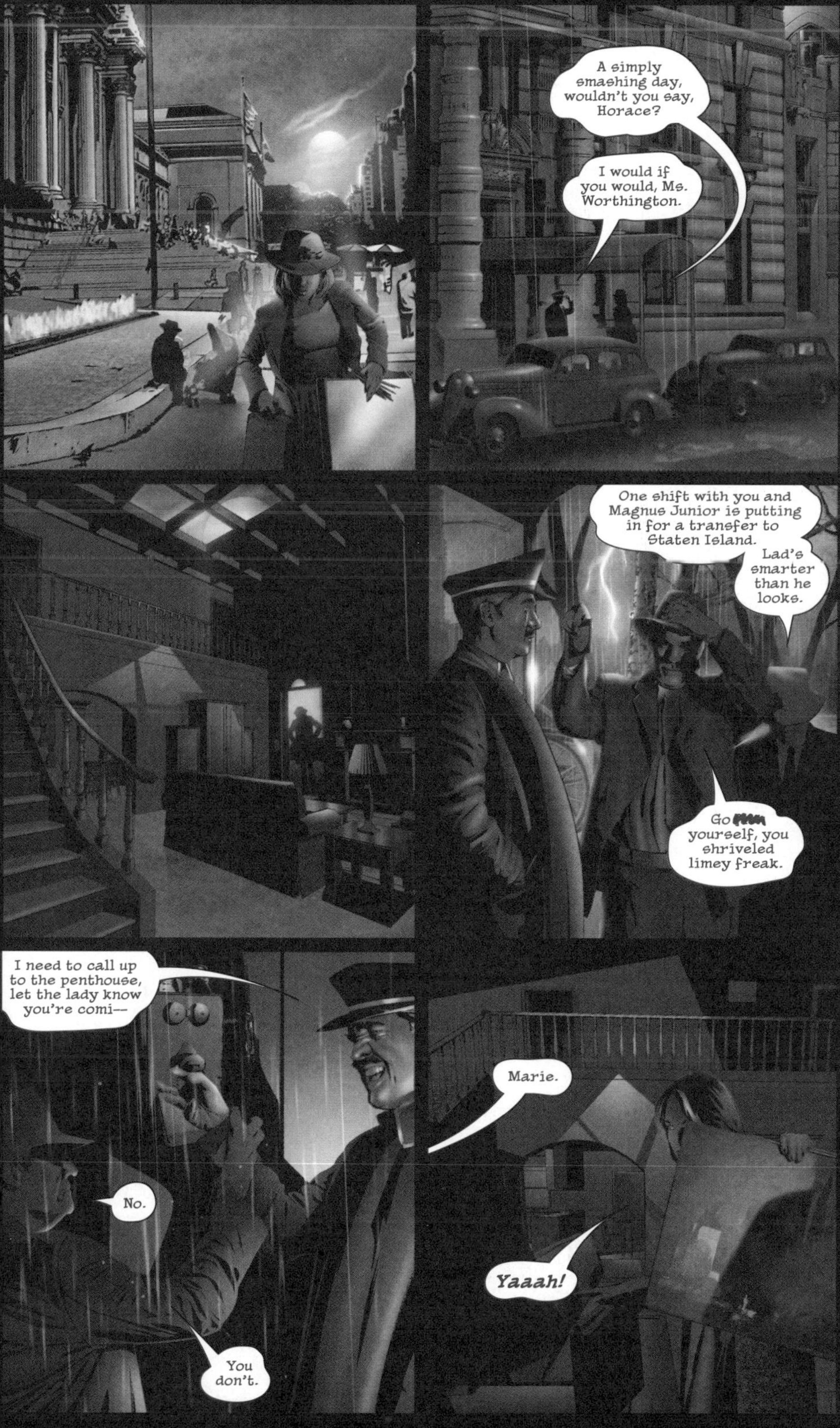

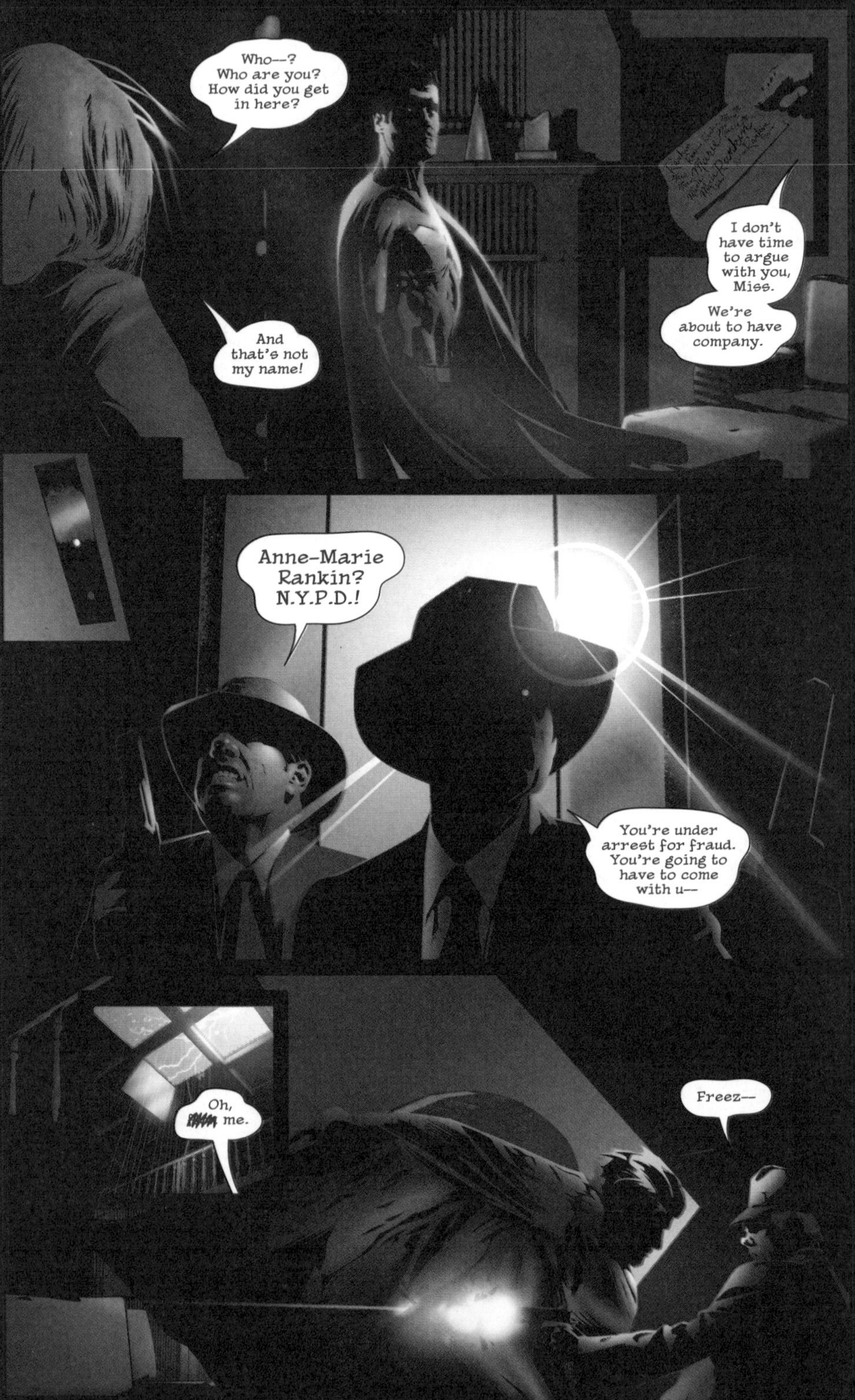

Who--? Who are you? How did you get in here?
And that's not my name!
I don't have time to argue with you, Miss.
We're about to have company.
Anne-Marie Rankin? N.Y.P.D.!
You're under arrest for fraud. You're going to have to come with u--
Oh, [redacted] me.
Freez--

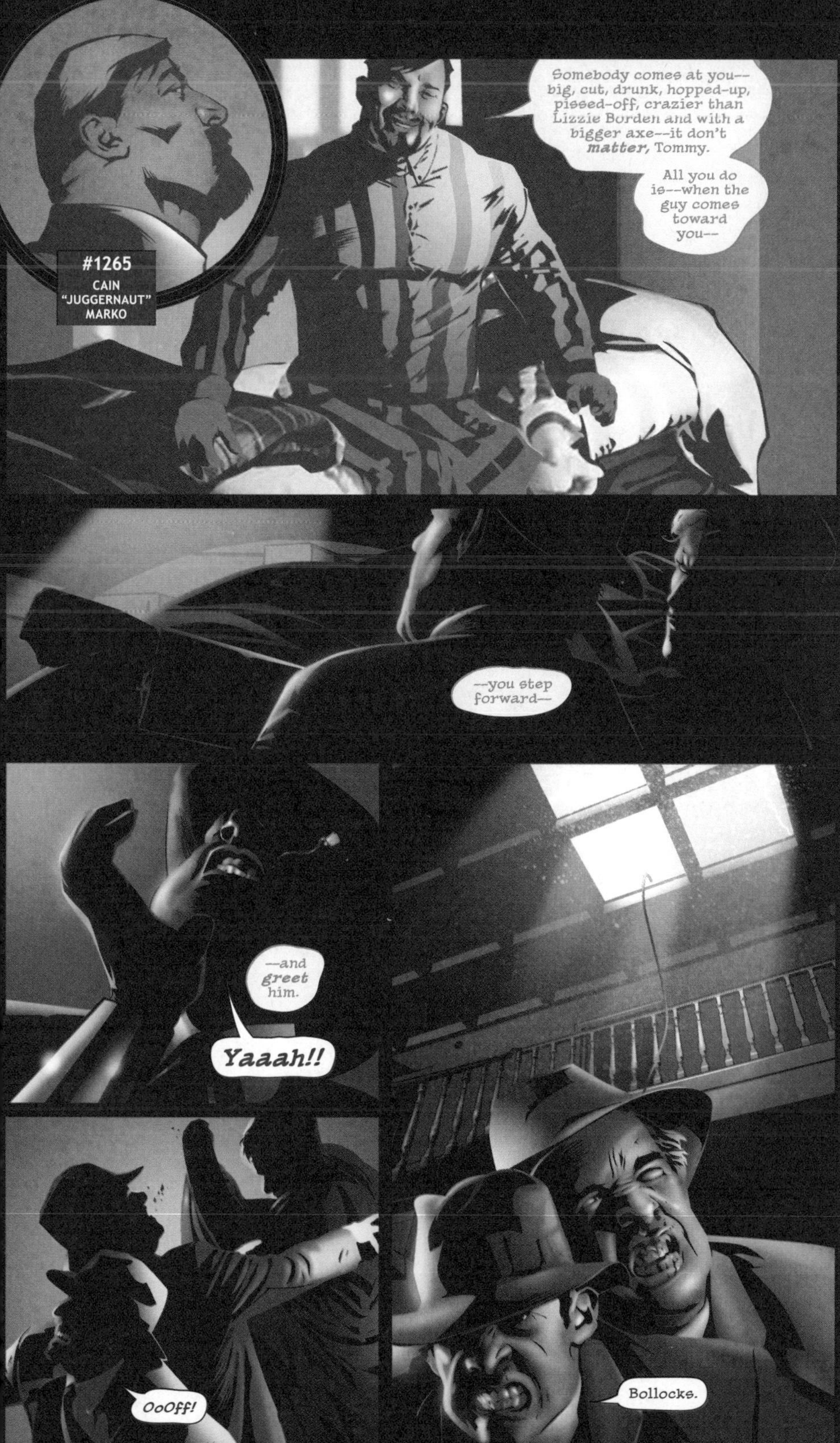
#1265
CAIN
"JUGGERNAUT"
MARKO
Somebody comes at you--big, cut, drunk, hopped-up, pissed-off, crazier than Lizzie Borden and with a bigger axe--it don't *matter,* Tommy.
All you do is--when the guy comes toward you--
--you step forward--
--and *greet* him.
Yaaah!!
OoOff!
Bollocks.

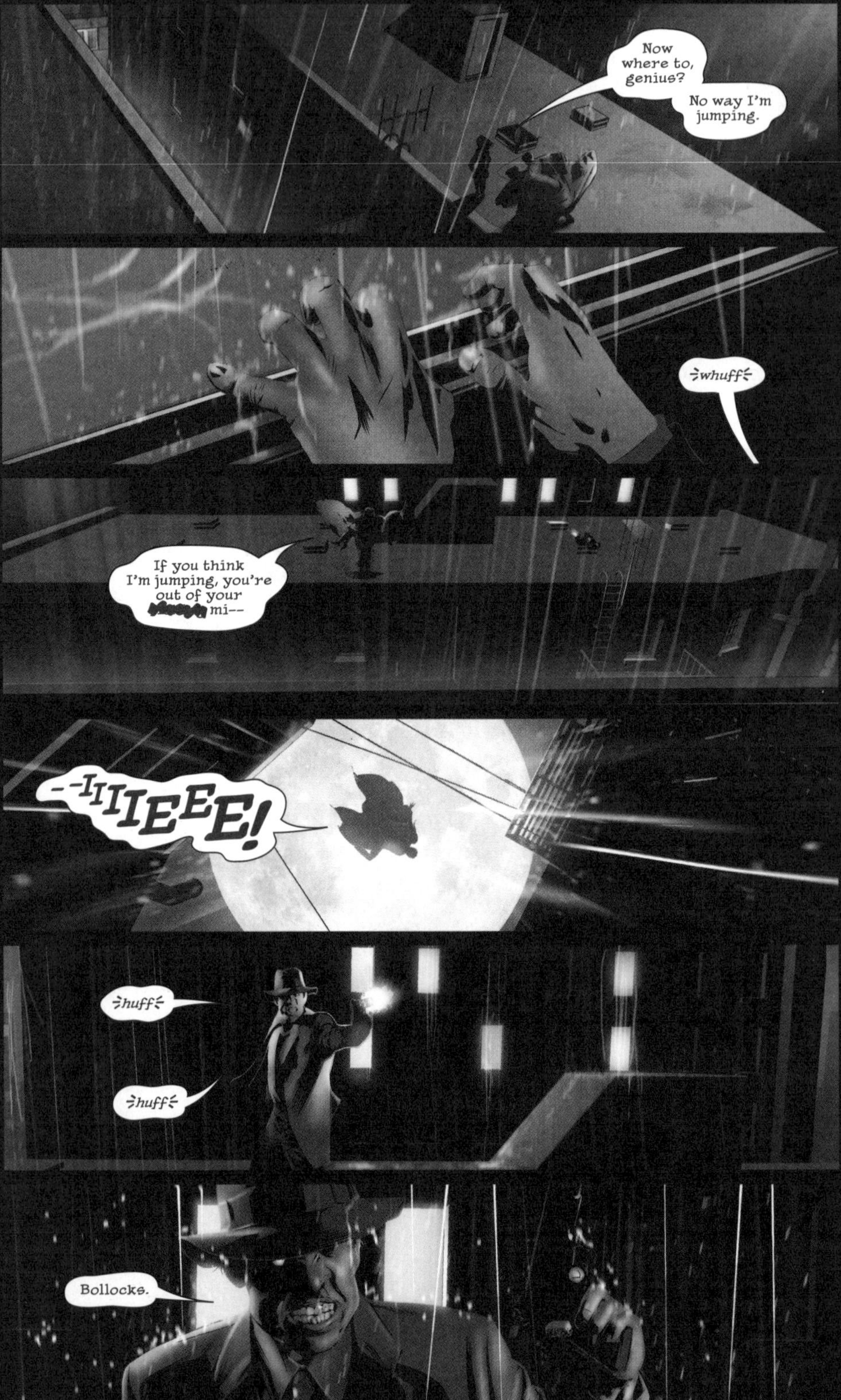
Now where to, genius?
No way I'm jumping.
whuff
If you think I'm jumping, you're out of your [redacted] mi--
--IIIIEEEE!
huff
huff
Bollocks.

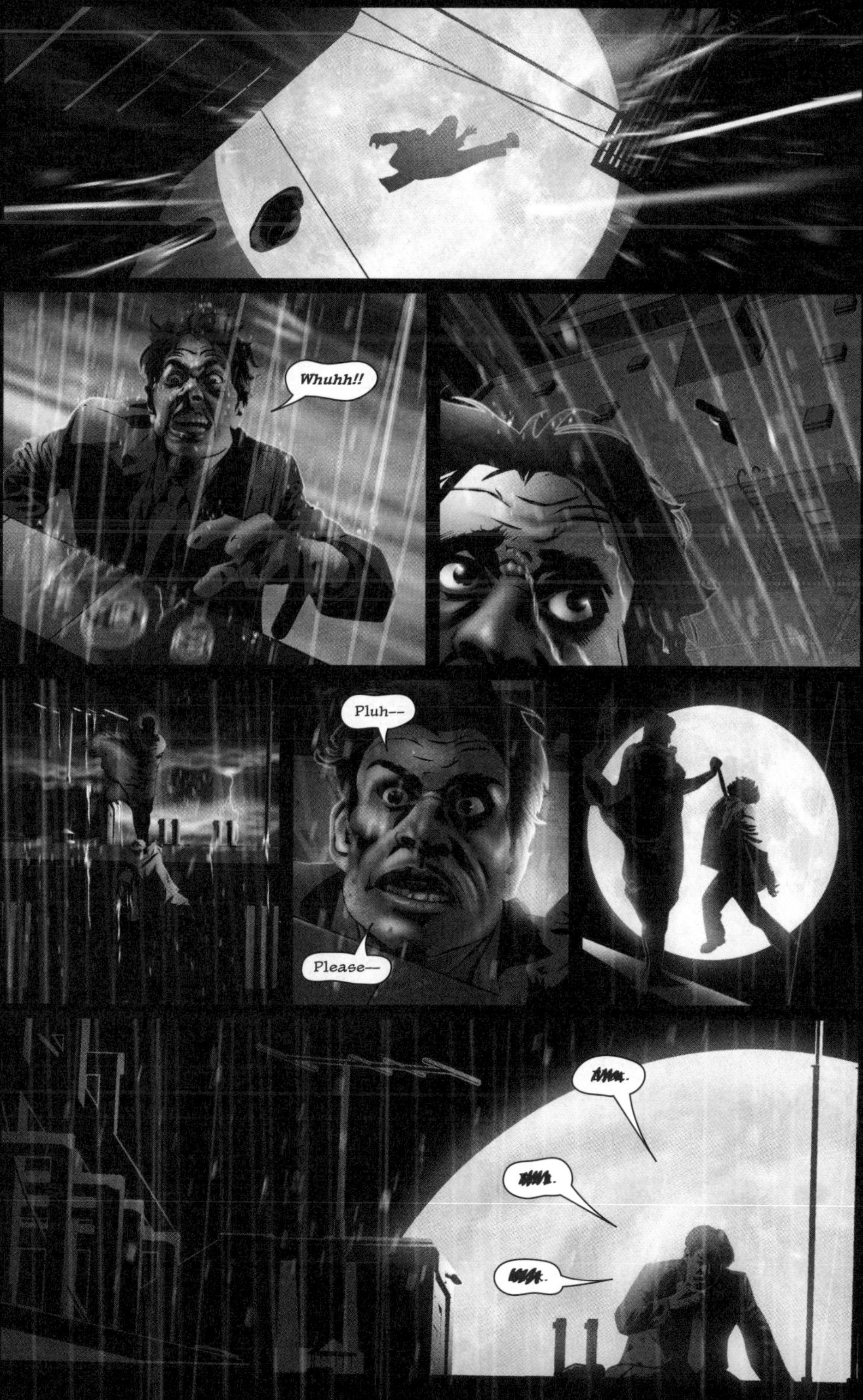
Whuhh!!
Pluh--
Please--

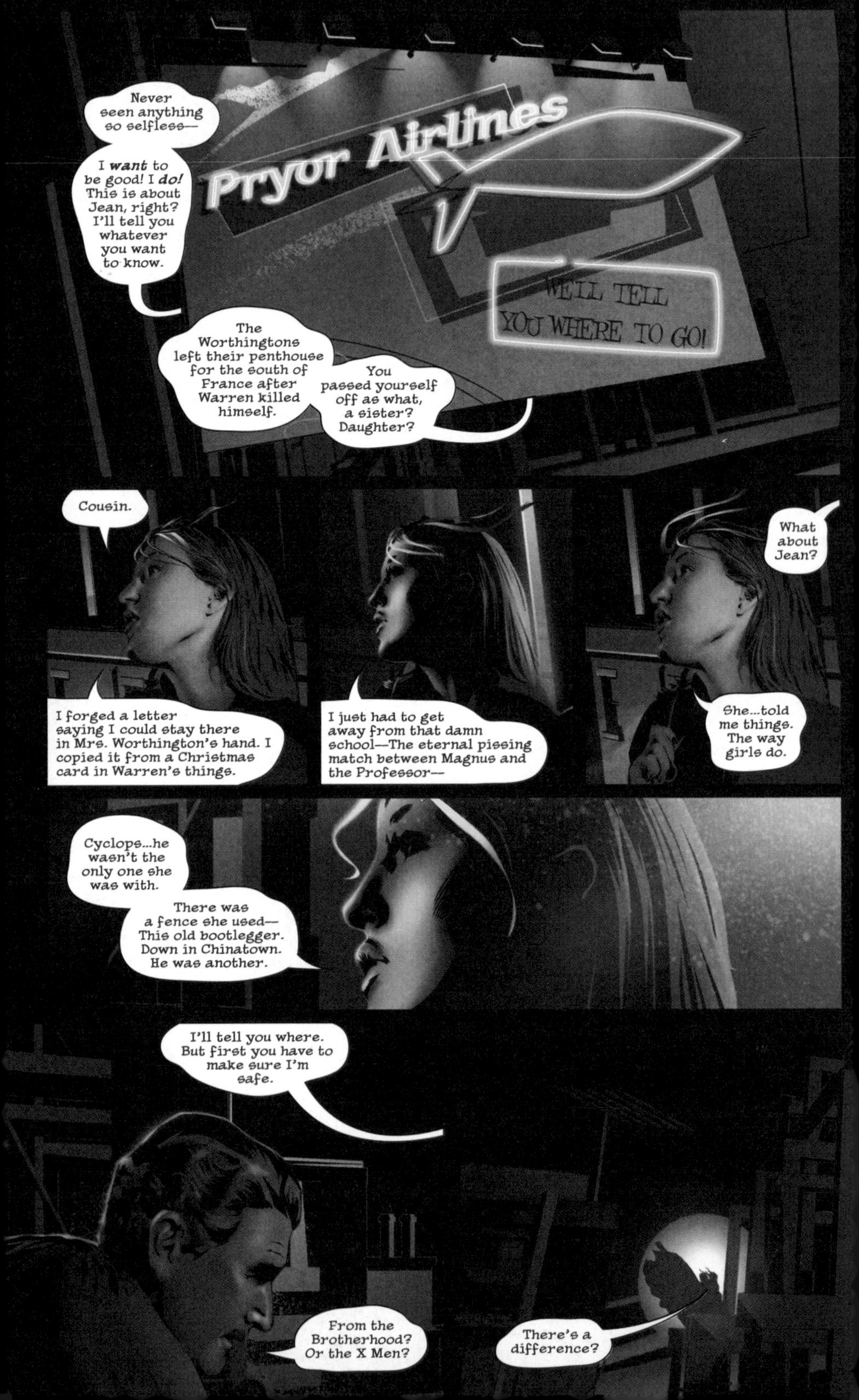
Never seen anything so selfless--
I *want* to be good! I *do!* This is about Jean, right? I'll tell you whatever you want to know.
Pryor Airlines
WE'LL TELL YOU WHERE TO GO!
The Worthingtons left their penthouse for the south of France after Warren killed himself.
You passed yourself off as what, a sister? Daughter?
Cousin.
I forged a letter saying I could stay there in Mrs. Worthington's hand. I copied it from a Christmas card in Warren's things.
I just had to get away from that damn school--The eternal pissing match between Magnus and the Professor--
What about Jean?
She...told me things. The way girls do.
Cyclops...he wasn't the only one she was with.
There was a fence she used-- This old bootlegger. Down in Chinatown. He was another.
I'll tell you where. But first you have to make sure I'm safe.
From the Brotherhood? Or the X Men?
There's a difference?

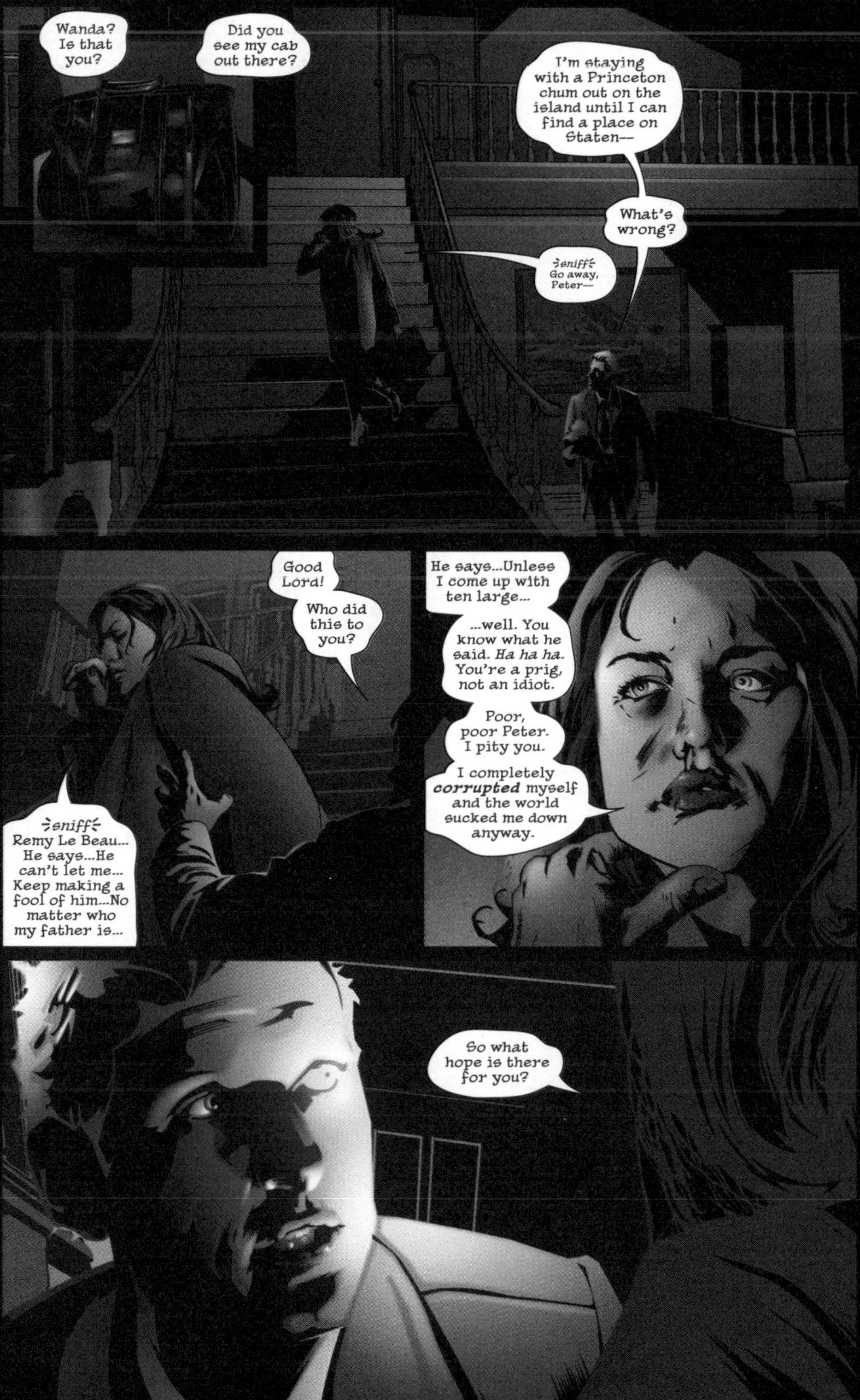

Wanda? Is that you?
Did you see my cab out there?
I'm staying with a Princeton chum out on the island until I can find a place on Staten--
What's wrong?
sniff Go away, Peter--
Good Lord!
Who did this to you?
sniff Remy Le Beau... He says...He can't let me... Keep making a fool of him...No matter who my father is...
He says...Unless I come up with ten large...
...well. You know what he said. *Ha ha ha.* You're a prig, not an idiot.
Poor, poor Peter. I pity you.
I completely ***corrupted*** myself and the world sucked me down anyway.
So what hope is there for you?

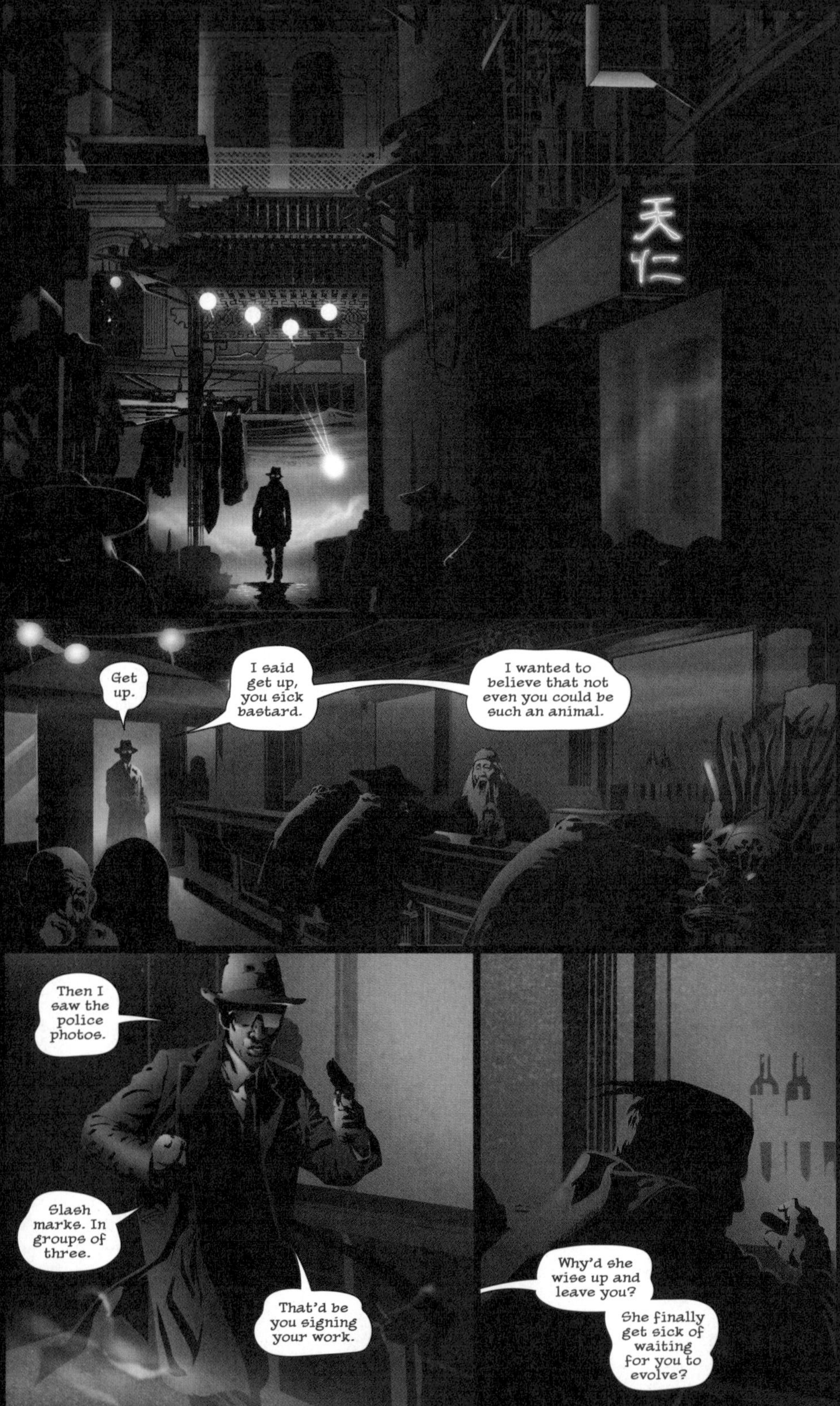
天仁
Get up.
I said get up, you sick bastard.
I wanted to believe that not even you could be such an animal.
Then I saw the police photos.
Slash marks. In groups of three.
That'd be you signing your work.
Why'd she wise up and leave you?
She finally get sick of waiting for you to evolve?

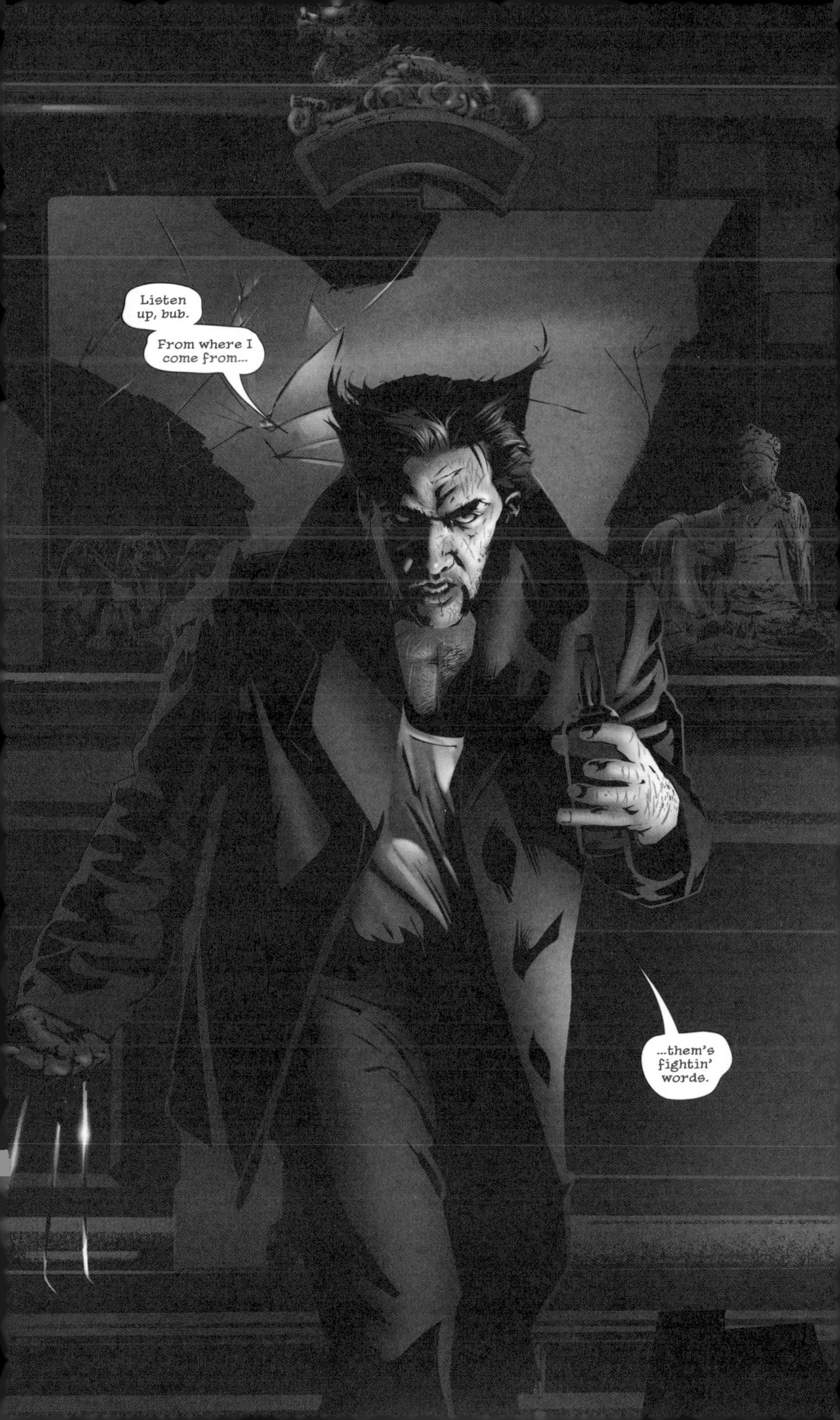
Listen up, bub.
From where I come from...
...them's fightin' words.

THE SENTINELS

By Bolivar Trask

*EDITOR'S NOTE: Loyal **Scienti-Fiction** readers will recall that in Dr. Trask's previous installment, our hero, the genetically perfect man, NIMROD, descended into the tunnels below New New New York to rescue his beloved fellow Sentinel RACHEL from the queen of the evolutionary backwards Muties, CALLISTO.*

Chapter Two: Mutant Massacre!

His mouth set in a grim line, Nimrod flew on his propellant pack through the arches of the Golden Aquifer, past the radiating rings of the city's central Macrowave Emitter.

He had read about the university archeological dig in the morning's news-fiche, and spotted it from the air miles before he actually reached it: graduate students in their purple college overalls busied themselves with magnetic artifact elevators and vibro-picks in a bathtub-shaped pit carved out of the city's firmament, exposing to the air a strata of rubble of New New York, the old ruin today's gleaming metropolis was built upon.

Muscles rippling beneath his skin-tight blue jumpsuit, red cape flapping, the Sentinel dropped to his feet in the middle of the excavation site, startling the professors recounting the day's findings into their Dicta-Bots and causing the fresh-faced co-eds shaking dirt from pottery shards at the auto-sifters to drop swooning into their male classmates' arms.

Nimrod strode boldly up to the most grizzled, whitest-haired scholar in the group, whom he assumed correctly was the lead archeologist. "Is it true that in your excavations you've discovered a shaft that penetrates all the way down to the original New York?" Nimrod had no time to lose. He prayed the authority in his voice, resonating as it did from throat muscles constructed from the genes of history's most accomplished Neapolitan baritones, would cow the professor into unquestioned obedience. If the old maestro demanded to know on what authority Nimrod made such queries, or asked to contact his superior officer, Bastion, the fact that this was an unauthorized operation lacking the sanction of the Breeders Council would soon be revealed.

Fortunately for Nimrod, however, the looming presence of his physical perfection robbed the wizened scholar of any protest. He pointed to a large hole in the ground surrounded by probing equipment. "Y-yes. Our expedition discovered the remains of another dig, one that must have been started by the archeologists of New New York right before Apocalypse hit—"

Without hesitation, and to a chorus of shocked gasps from the on-looking graduate students, Nimrod bounded over to the gaping maw and dove in headfirst!

The Sentinel dropped like a stone for several minutes through seemingly endless night until, with a flick of the dial on his left gauntlet, he activated his propellant pack to slow his descent. Shortly, his hunter-bred eyes became attuned to the gloom, and he began to see around him layers upon layers of toppled spires that once rose proudly for thousands of stories.

This was all that remained of the towers of New New York, brought down by the Phoenix Bomb-filled aero-gyros of the mad Egyptian despot, En Sabah Nur. This Apocalypse, as it was called, was what finally forced the League of Nations to instill the breeding program long recommended by the greatest of all eugenicists, Dr. Stephen Lang. With the continued advances in the science of weaponry, combined with the never-dying prejudice and hatred of one tribe of humanity for another, only Lang's plan to breed the evil out of human nature through selectively mating the best of the species with each other seemed to offer any hope for peace on Earth. Though the usual reactionary forces of tradition and conservatism were raised in protest, when New New New York was built upon the ruins of the old, the Hall of Experimental Evolution rose with it. The Breeders Council began the selective mating process, through which Bastion, Nimrod, Rachel and the other Sentinels were created.

Then the unthinkable was inflicted upon them. Dr. Stephen Lang was slain in his bed by a pack of ravenous Muties, and his secrets were lost forever. Only by mating Sentinels with other Sentinels could the line be continued – surely the Muties knew this, and kidnapped Nimrod's beloved Rachel to prevent their genetically blessed union.

As Nimrod descended, down, down into the Stygian pit of history, a crimson light began shining up toward him, as if he descended into the Inferno of legend. But such ancient superstitions had fallen along with the spires of New New York. Nimrod knew from his university history-fiches that the blood-red luminescence was chemical, not sinful, in nature. Phosphorescent fungi clung to the remnants of the original city of New York, the trenches that were built from the Old Battery to Ancient Harlem to protect against the vaporous death rained down from the war-dirigibles of the Crimson Bands of Cyttorak, the descendants of that nation succumbing to the worst urges of their conquering forbearers and bringing their chemical weapons of mass destruction across the seas.

In the aftermath of that war, the tunnel-ridden city was rendered all but uninhabitable by three years of continual mustard gas bombardment, and had to be sealed off and the towers of New New York built atop it. Its atmosphere – and the poisonous spores that thrived off the gas's residue – was lethal to regular humans. However, the cilia lining Nimrod's trachea had been bred from the chromosomes of the hardiest Atomic Doughboys that survived the fierce fighting, and so the mighty Sentinel breathed its fetid air as easily as if it were a summer's breeze.

The mongrel Muties, with their coarse lungs and barbarous throats, thrived in the oppressive climate as well – as Nimrod soon learned when he was greeted by a snarling pack of them. They surged forward out of the shadows as soon as his feet alighted on the concrete slab-floor of the trench. Not wanting to alert the rest of their monstrous fellows by the sharp discharge of his neutralizers, Nimrod realized he would have to dispatch this rabble with his bare hands.

Fortunately, those hands were the product of ten carefully selected bloodlines of Malay street-fighters, and more than up to the task.

One grotesque freak, completely hairless and white as bleached bones, eyes bulging yellowishly from their sockets, attempted to swing his fists at the Sentinel with the monstrous strength of Shakespeare's brutish Caliban. But Nimrod, swinging his elbow-like blade of a mighty battle-axe, smashed into the albino's windpipe, crushing it instantly. The monster fell to the ground, clutching his throat and choking out a death rattle.

Another hideous genetic throwback, a long-armed beast who swung from the overhead pipes like some degenerate ape, attempted to plant its loathsome feet, with its impossibly long, almost finger-like toes, into Nimrod's chest, but the mighty Sentinel pivoted on his hips and sent a sternum-shattering kick into the Mutie's ribcage, breaking at least one or two bones and piercing its lungs with them. Down the throwback fell, drowning with a gurgle in his own foaming blood.

A plague-ridden freak wrapped in rags and a filthy knit cap pulled low over stringy hair attempted to grapple Nimrod to the ground, but the Sentinel grabbed the Mutie's head in both hands and forced his thumbs into the creature's eyes, blinding him! This creature of pestilence attempted to cry out in pain, or for mercy, but Nimrod offered neither, giving his foe's grotesque head a sharp twist, breaking the spine instantly.

Now the only attacker to remain was a diminutive green Mutie with a distended head like that of a fetus, the crown covered in bloated bumps and boils. Obviously the latest in a long line of despicable cowards, the dwarf succumbed to his genetic pre-dispositions and attempted to flee, but swift Nimrod grabbed him by the collar and dragged him close. He covered the Mutie's mouth with his other hand, and nearly shivered with repulsion – the creature had the same slick, rubbery skin as a blood-sucking leech.

Employing the same tone of voice he had used with the timorous archeologist above, Nimrod said, "Take me to Rachel – the other Sentinel, the one who looks like me – or I end your life here and now."

The Mutie Leech's fear-filled eyes flashed with dull comprehension and nodded quickly.

Nimrod wagged a finger at him. "And if you make one more sound, or call out for the rest of your mongrel horde, I will not hesitate to dispatch you just as surely."

Leech led the Sentinel through the twisting, crimson-glowing trenches like the scurrying vermin that he was. Even though his sense of direction had been carefully selected from the chromosomes of the hardiest Bedouin nomads, Nimrod had no doubt that if he had been left to navigate the labyrinth of tunnels of Old New York by himself he would have been lost to human sight forever. In fact, the main reason he and his fellow Sentinels had been unable to utterly exterminate the Muties was that only the freaks themselves knew the correct routes from the upper city above to their infernal trenches—hence Nimrod's need to make use of the accidental excavation of the university dig.

At last, the leech-child opened a rickety wooden door and admitted Nimrod into a dank chamber. Water-stained cardboard crates served as furniture, yellowing news-fiches as carpeting. Immediately, however, Nimrod's spirits lifted. A bronze beauty lay upon a crude mattress that was little more than a tarpaulin thrown on clumps of luminescent moss. Even if she were not still wearing the skin-tight blue jumpsuit and red cape of her office, Nimrod would have recognized his betrothed Rachel anywhere.

To her bedside he flew and gently shook her shoulder until her perfect eyelashes, the amalgamation of twenty-eight Swedish models', fluttered open.

"Beloved, 'tis I," Nimrod smiled.

"Nimrod!" Rachel sat up sharply and looked around the room. "What are you doing here?"

"Why … to rescue you and return you to the surface world at once, of course."

Nimrod's heart shriveled to a husk as Rachel emitted a high shriek. "To the surface world? No … never! I love it here with the Muties, and I don't want to go back!"

"My dearest Rachel … what are you saying?!"

"That I have shown your beauteous Sentinel the lies and falsehoods your world is built on!" a voice behind Nimrod cried, and he whirled to see the gaunt, scarred form of Callisto, Queen of the Muties, burst into the room with her hulking, sword-wielding guard! Beside her was Leech, who must have run to summon her when Nimrod's attention was drawn wholly to the sight of his beloved.

"Guards — seize him!"

NEXT: AGE OF APOCALPYSE!

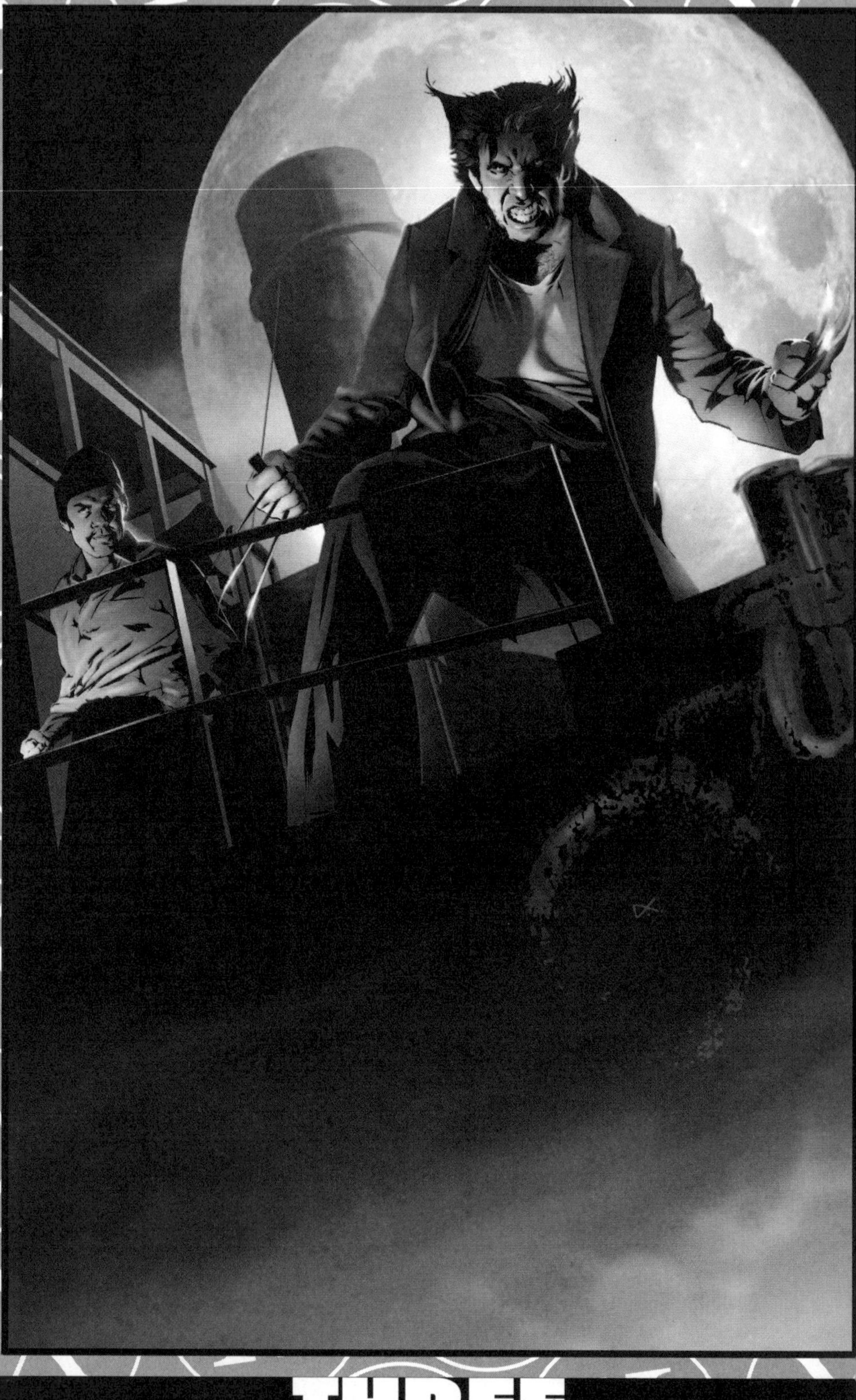

THREE

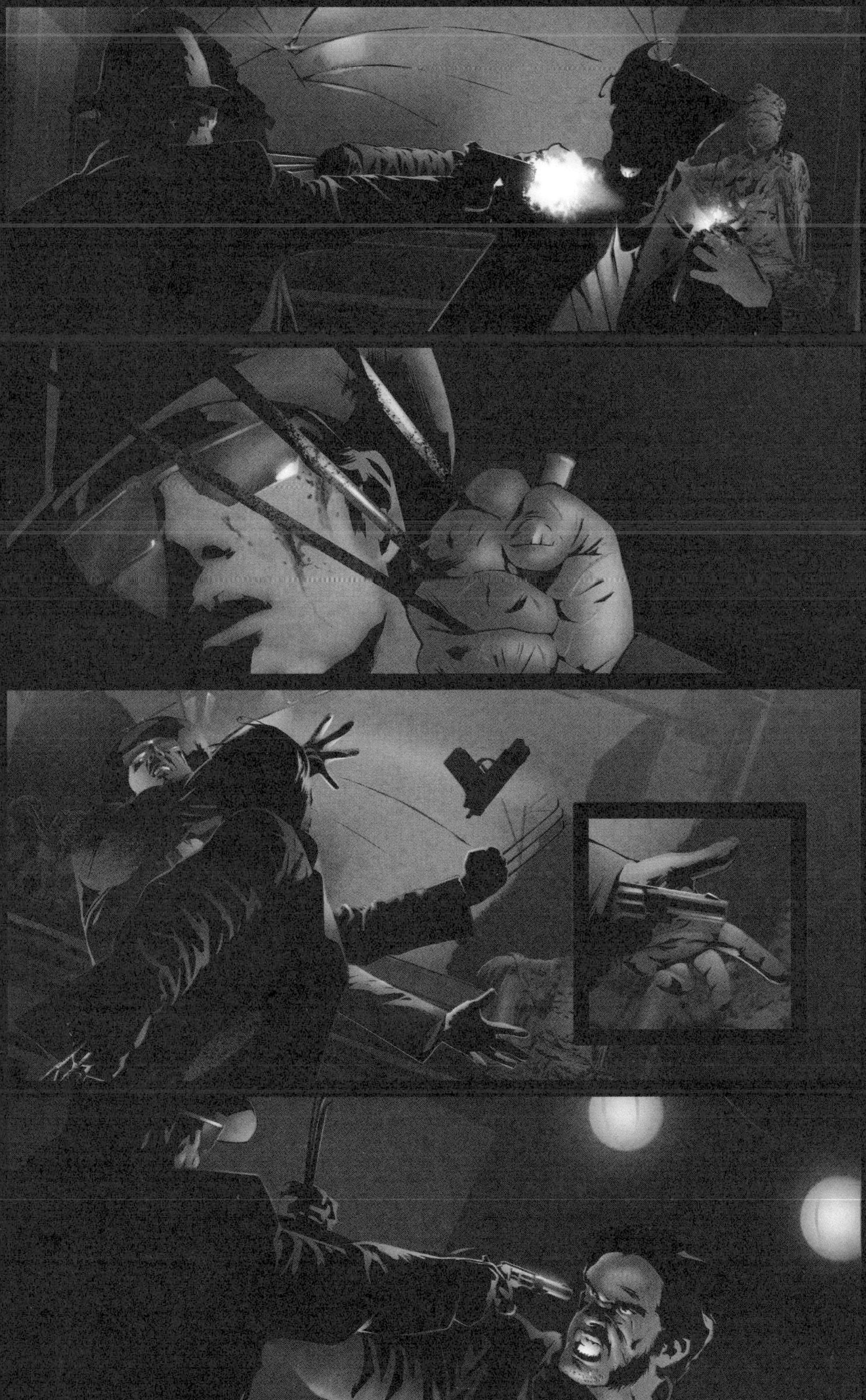

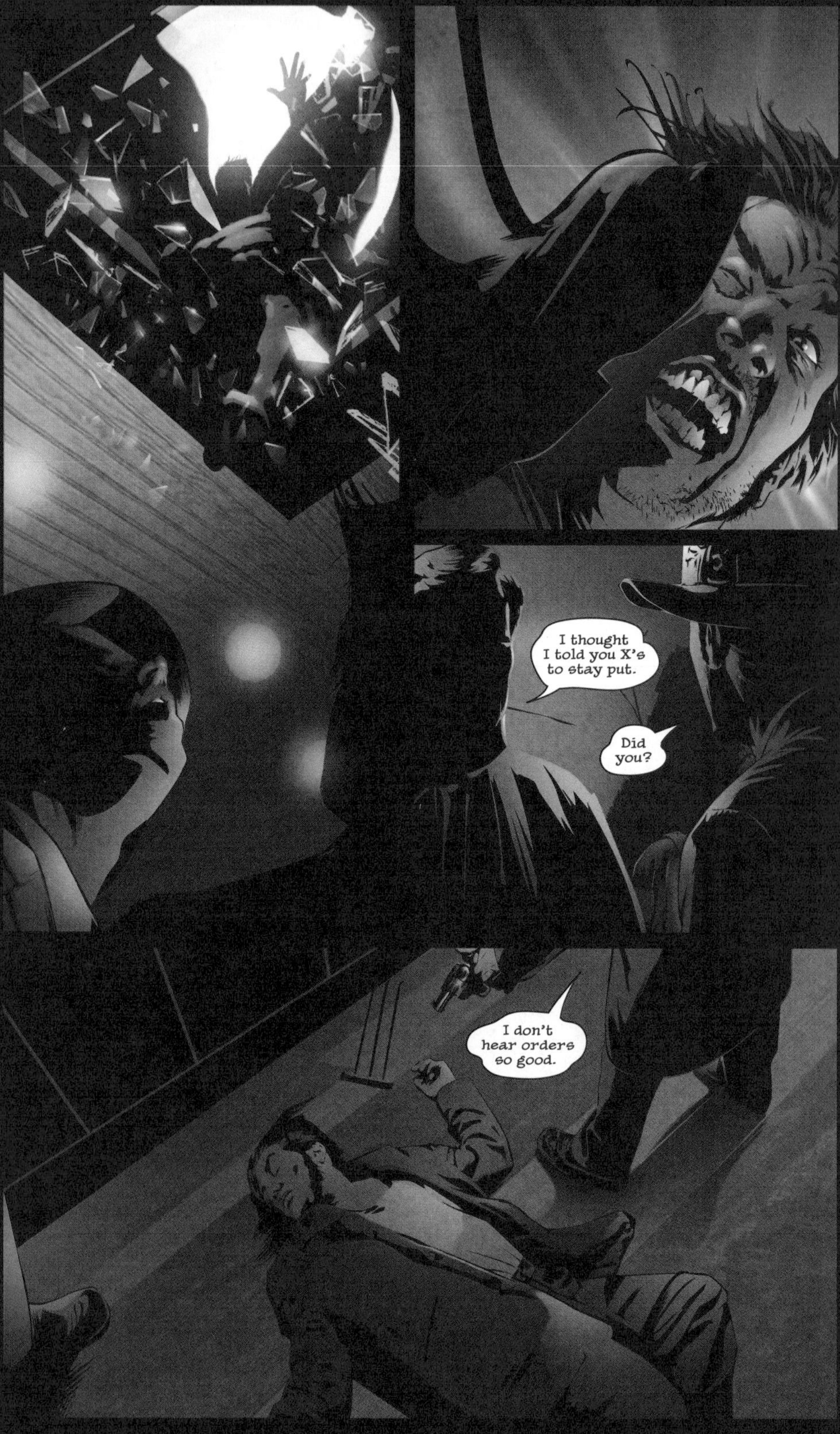
I thought I told you X's to stay put.
Did you?
I don't hear orders so good.

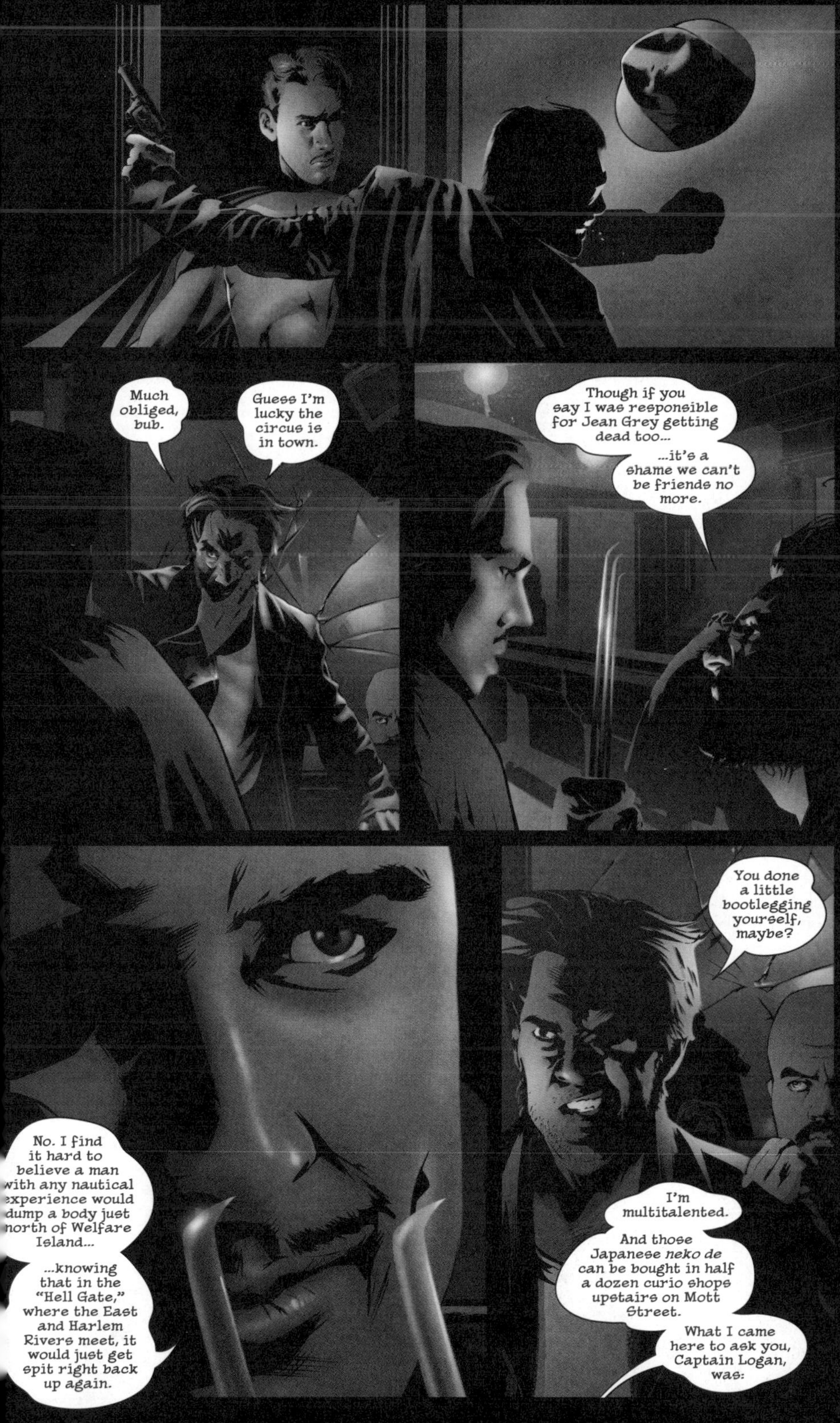
Much obliged, bub.
Guess I'm lucky the circus is in town.
Though if you say I was responsible for Jean Grey getting dead too...
...it's a shame we can't be friends no more.
You done a little bootlegging yourself, maybe?
No. I find it hard to believe a man with any nautical xperience would dump a body just orth of Welfare Island...
...knowing that in the "Hell Gate," where the East and Harlem Rivers meet, it would just get spit right back up again.
I'm multitalented.
And those Japanese *neko de* can be bought in half a dozen curio shops upstairs on Mott Street.
What I came here to ask you, Captain Logan, was:

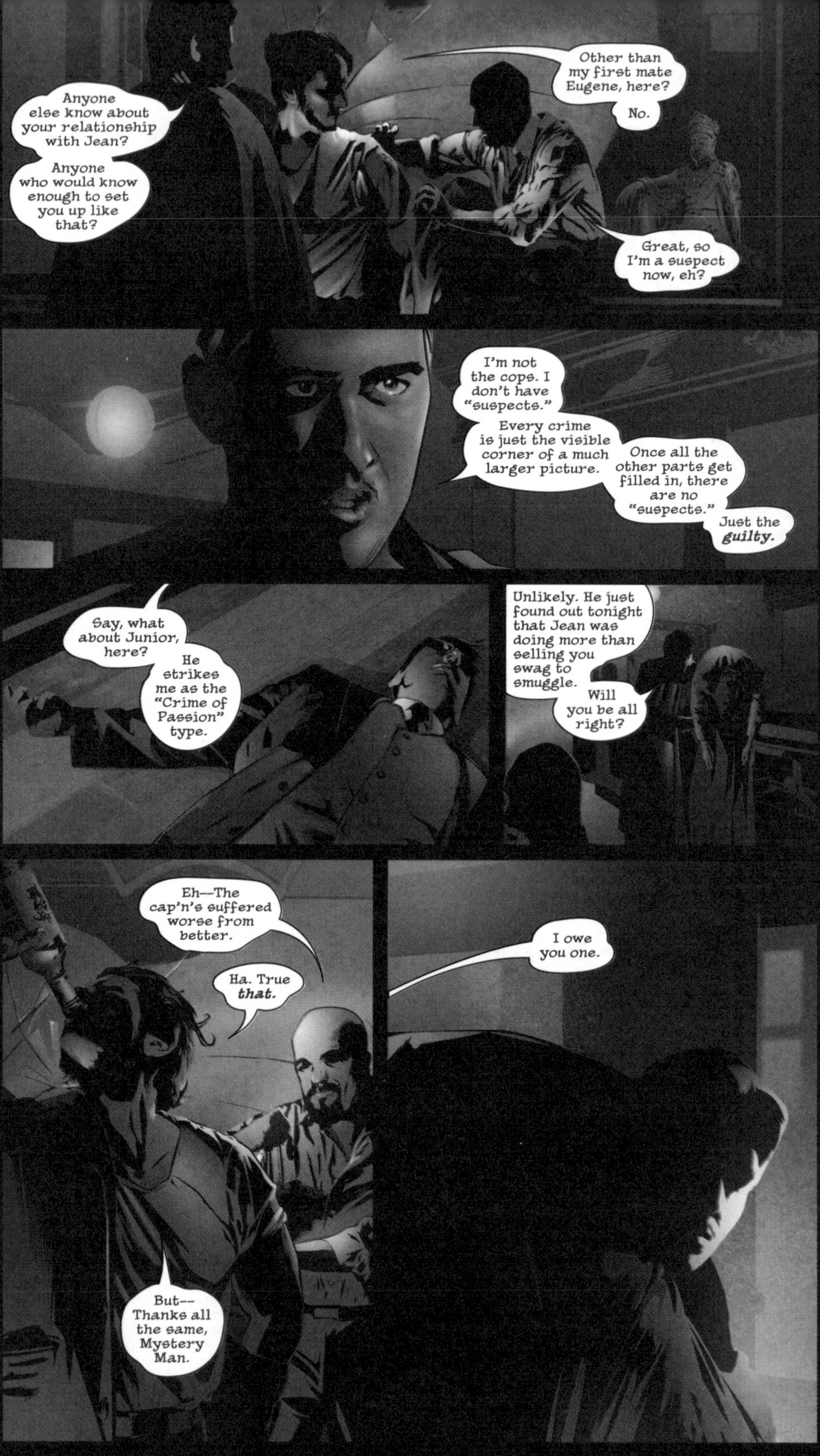
Anyone else know about your relationship with Jean?
Anyone who would know enough to set you up like that?
Other than my first mate Eugene, here?
No.
Great, so I'm a suspect now, eh?
I'm not the cops. I don't have "suspects."
Every crime is just the visible corner of a much larger picture.
Once all the other parts get filled in, there are no "suspects."
Just the *guilty.*
Say, what about Junior, here?
He strikes me as the "Crime of Passion" type.
Unlikely. He just found out tonight that Jean was doing more than selling you swag to smuggle.
Will you be all right?
Eh--The cap'n's suffered worse from better.
Ha. True *that.*
But--Thanks all the same, Mystery Man.
I owe you one.

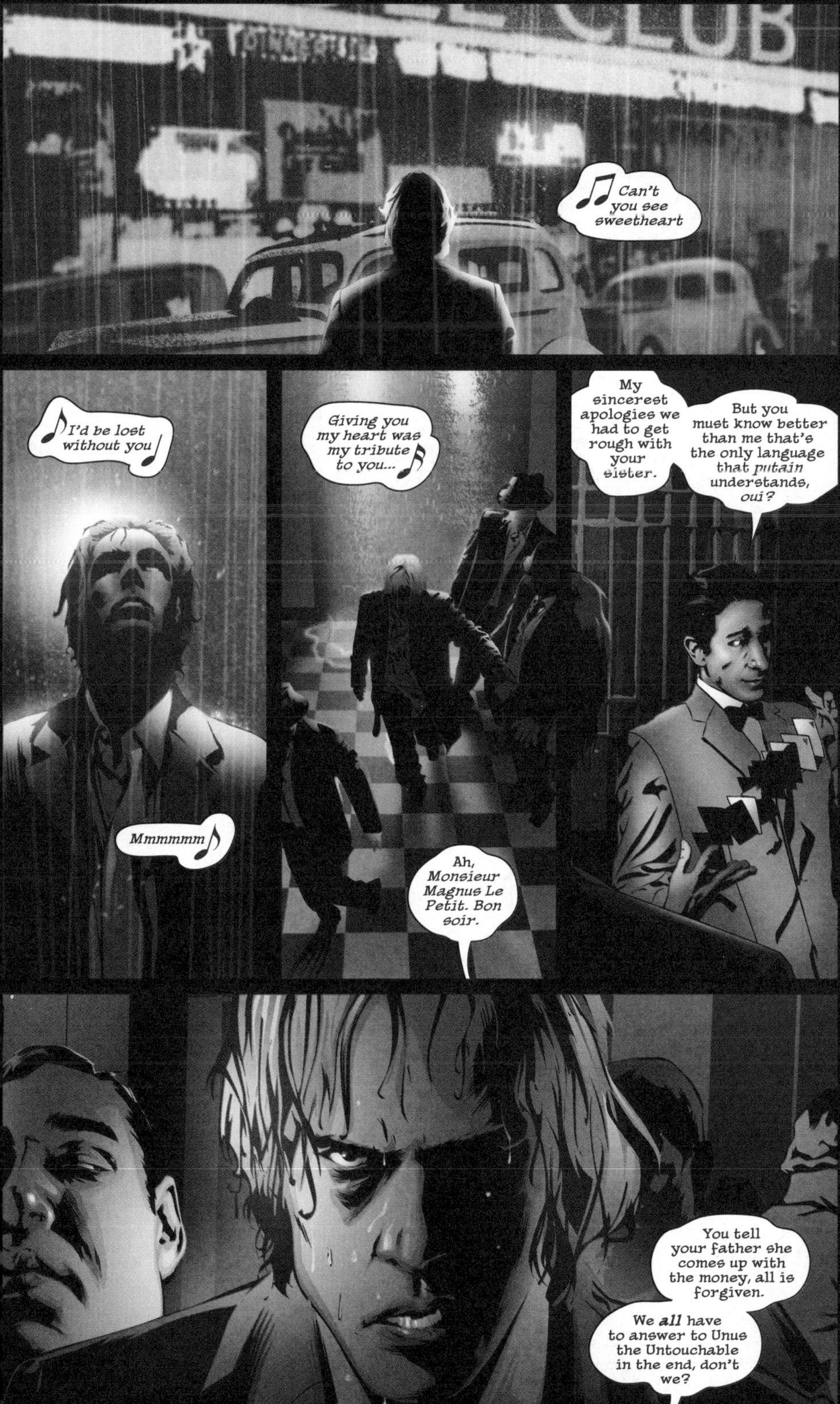
CLUB
♫ Can't you see sweetheart
♪ I'd be lost without you ♪
Mmmmmm ♪
Giving you my heart was my tribute to you... ♬
Ah, Monsieur Magnus Le Petit. Bon soir.
My sincerest apologies we had to get rough with your sister.
But you must know better than me that's the only language that *putain* understands, *oui?*
You tell your father she comes up with the money, all is forgiven.
We ***all*** have to answer to Unus the Untouchable in the end, don't we?

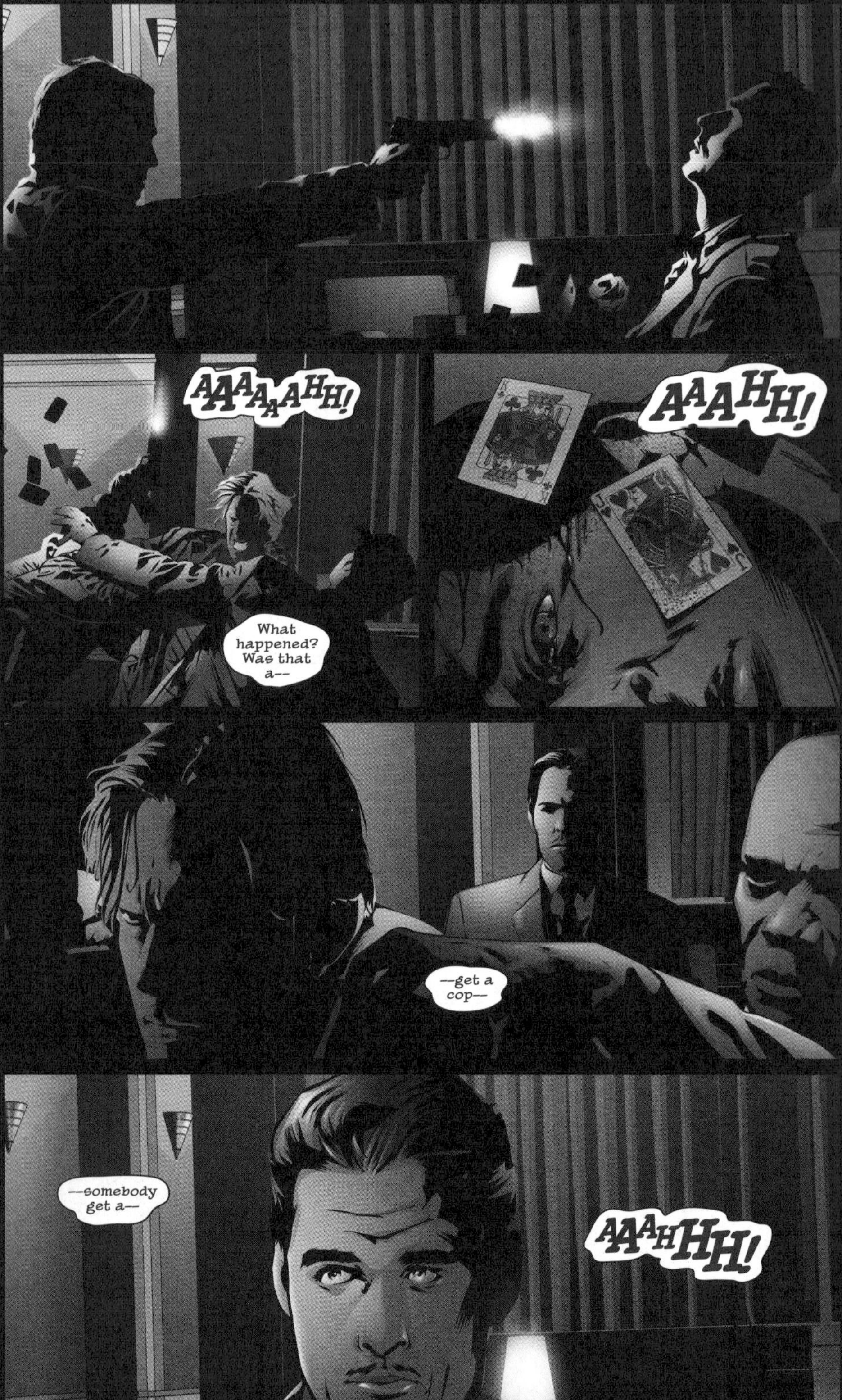
AAAAAAHH!
AAAHH!
What happened? Was that a--
--get a cop--
--somebody get a--
AAAHHH!

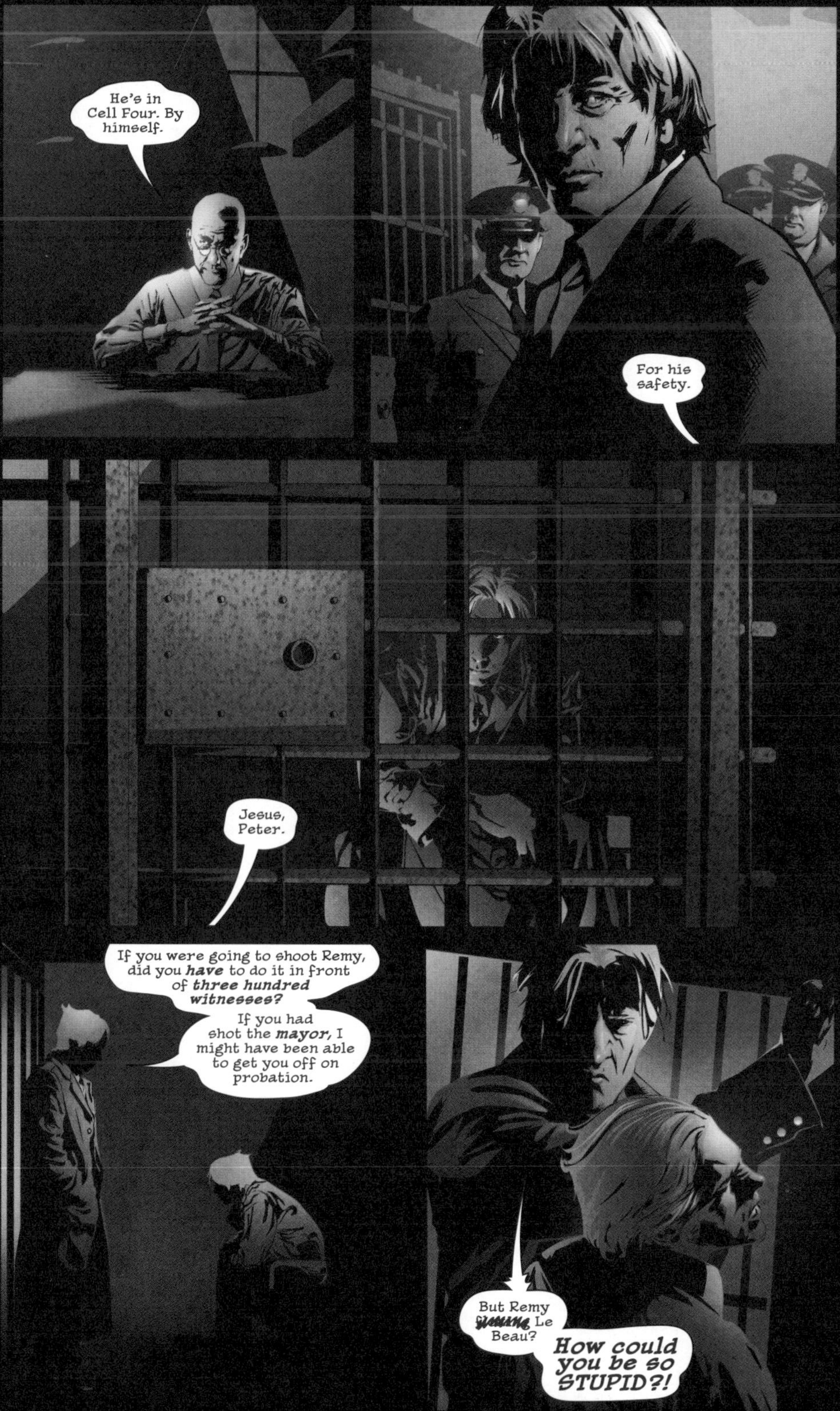
He's in Cell Four. By himself.
For his safety.
Jesus, Peter.
If you were going to shoot Remy, did you *have* to do it in front of *three hundred witnesses?*
If you had shot the *mayor,* I might have been able to get you off on probation.
But Remy Le Beau?
How could you be so STUPID?!

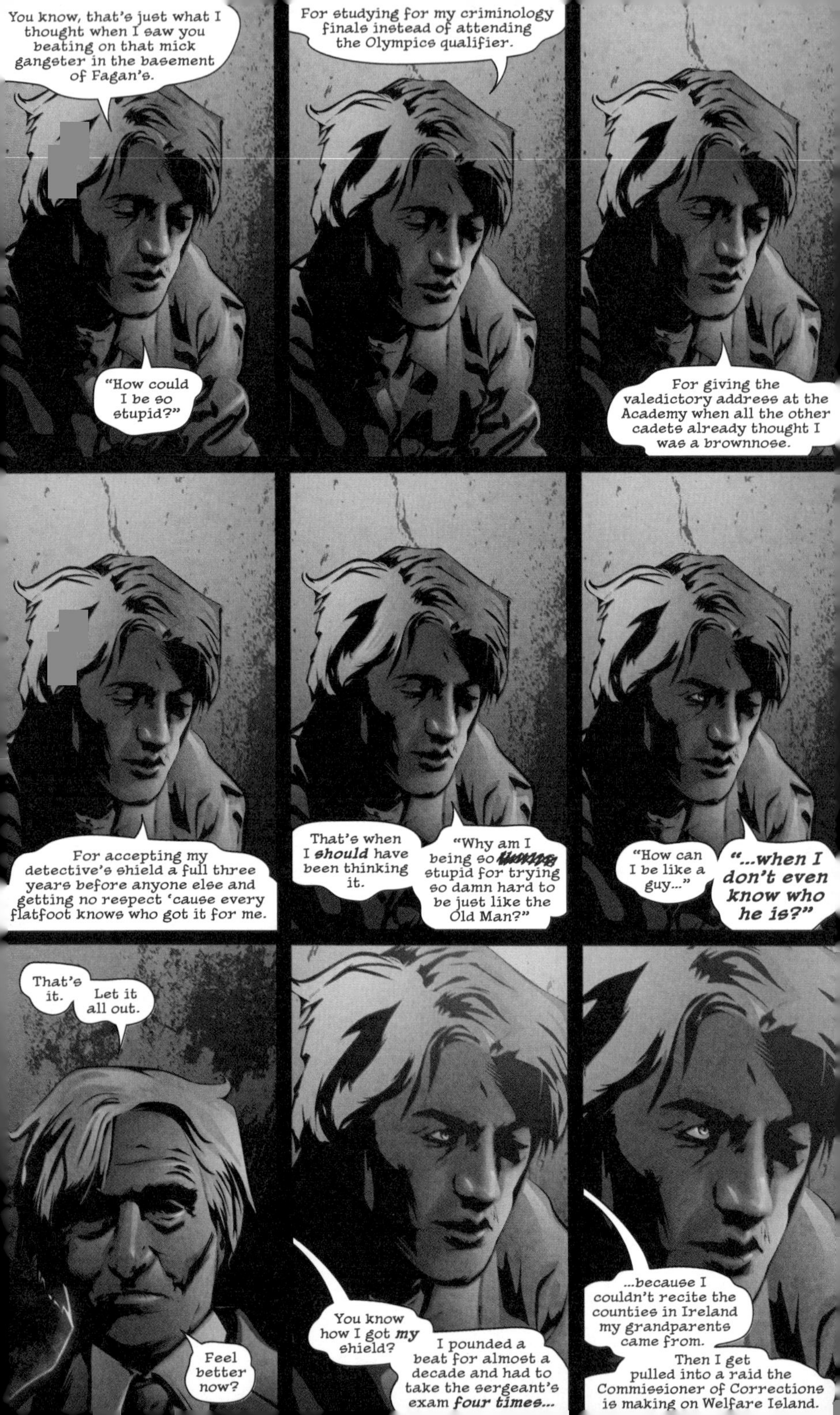

You know, that's just what I thought when I saw you beating on that mick gangster in the basement of Fagan's.
"How could I be so stupid?"
For studying for my criminology finals instead of attending the Olympics qualifier.
For giving the valedictory address at the Academy when all the other cadets already thought I was a brownnose.
For accepting my detective's shield a full three years before anyone else and getting no respect 'cause every flatfoot knows who got it for me.
That's when I *should* have been thinking it.
"Why am I being so stupid for trying so damn hard to be just like the Old Man?"
"How can I be like a guy..."
"...when I don't even know who he is?"
That's it.
Let it all out.
Feel better now?
You know how I got *my* shield?
I pounded a beat for almost a decade and had to take the sergeant's exam ***four times...***
...because I couldn't recite the counties in Ireland my grandparents came from.
Then I get pulled into a raid the Commissioner of Corrections is making on Welfare Island.

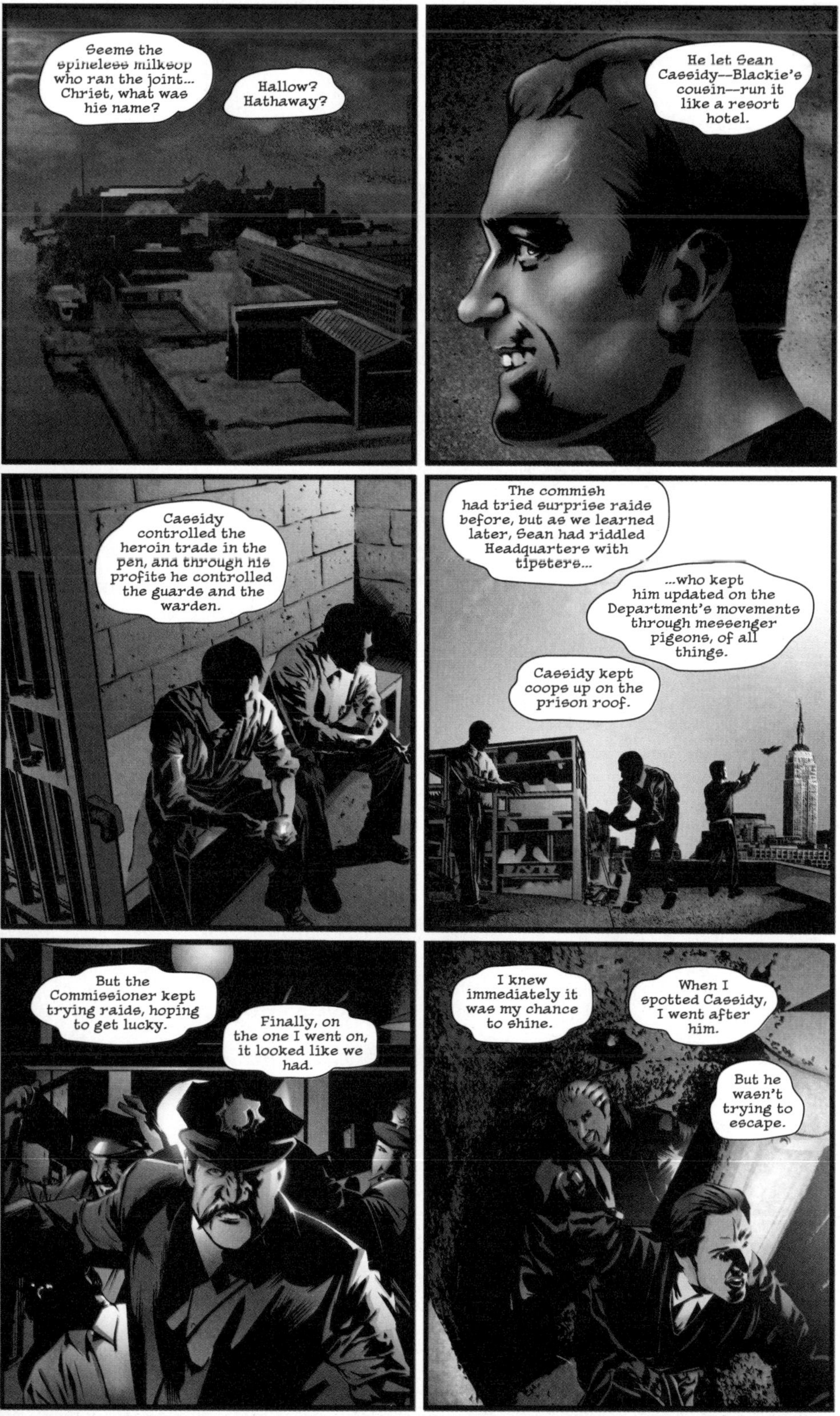
Seems the spineless milksop who ran the joint... Christ, what was his name?
Hallow? Hathaway?
He let Sean Cassidy--Blackie's cousin--run it like a resort hotel.
Cassidy controlled the heroin trade in the pen, and through his profits he controlled the guards and the warden.
The commish had tried surprise raids before, but as we learned later, Sean had riddled Headquarters with tipsters...
...who kept him updated on the Department's movements through messenger pigeons, of all things.
Cassidy kept coops up on the prison roof.
But the Commissioner kept trying raids, hoping to get lucky.
Finally, on the one I went on, it looked like we had.
I knew immediately it was my chance to shine.
When I spotted Cassidy, I went after him.
But he wasn't trying to escape.

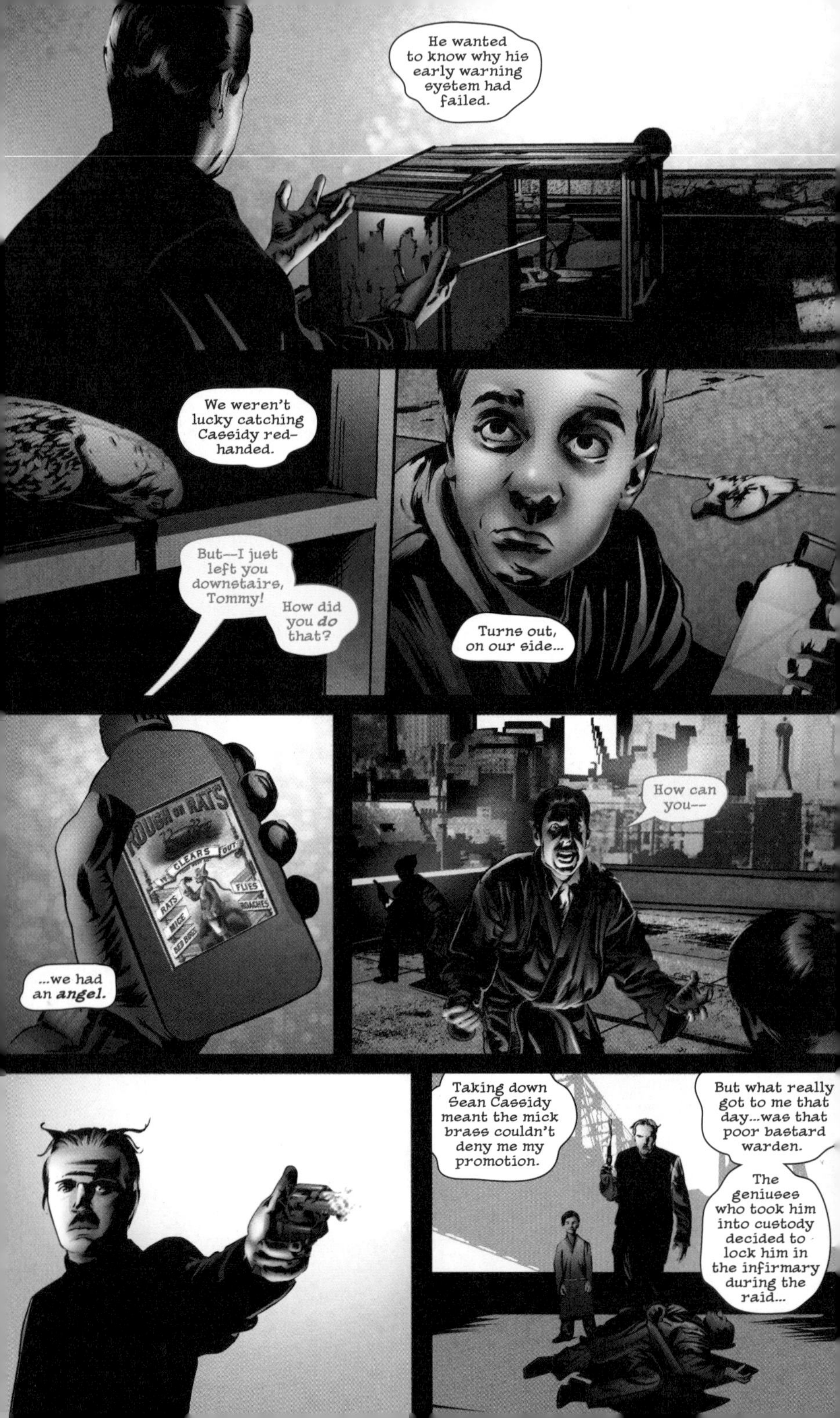
He wanted to know why his early warning system had failed.
We weren't lucky catching Cassidy red-handed.
But--I just left you downstairs, Tommy!
How did you *do* that?
Turns out, on our side...
ROUGH ON RATS
CLEARS OUT
RATS
MICE
FLIES
ROACHES
BED BUGS
...we had an ***angel.***
How can you--
Taking down Sean Cassidy meant the mick brass couldn't deny me my promotion.
But what really got to me that day...was that poor bastard warden.
The geniuses who took him into custody decided to lock him in the infirmary during the raid...

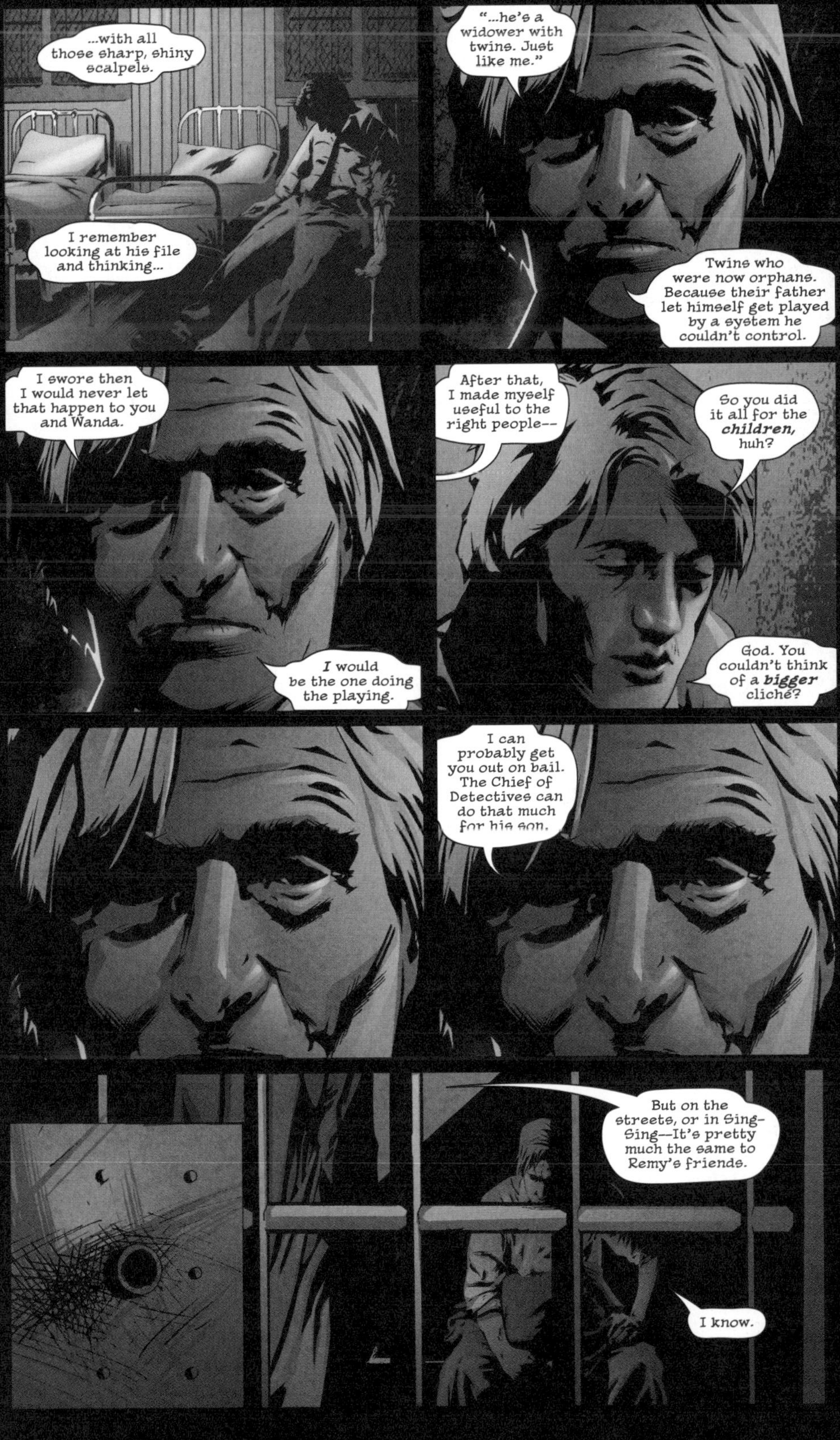
...with all those sharp, shiny scalpels.
I remember looking at his file and thinking...
"...he's a widower with twins. Just like me."
Twins who were now orphans. Because their father let himself get played by a system he couldn't control.
I swore then I would never let that happen to you and Wanda.
I would be the one doing the playing.
After that, I made myself useful to the right people--
So you did it all for the children, huh?
God. You couldn't think of a bigger cliché?
I can probably get you out on bail. The Chief of Detectives can do that much for his son.
But on the streets, or in Sing-Sing--It's pretty much the same to Remy's friends.
I know.

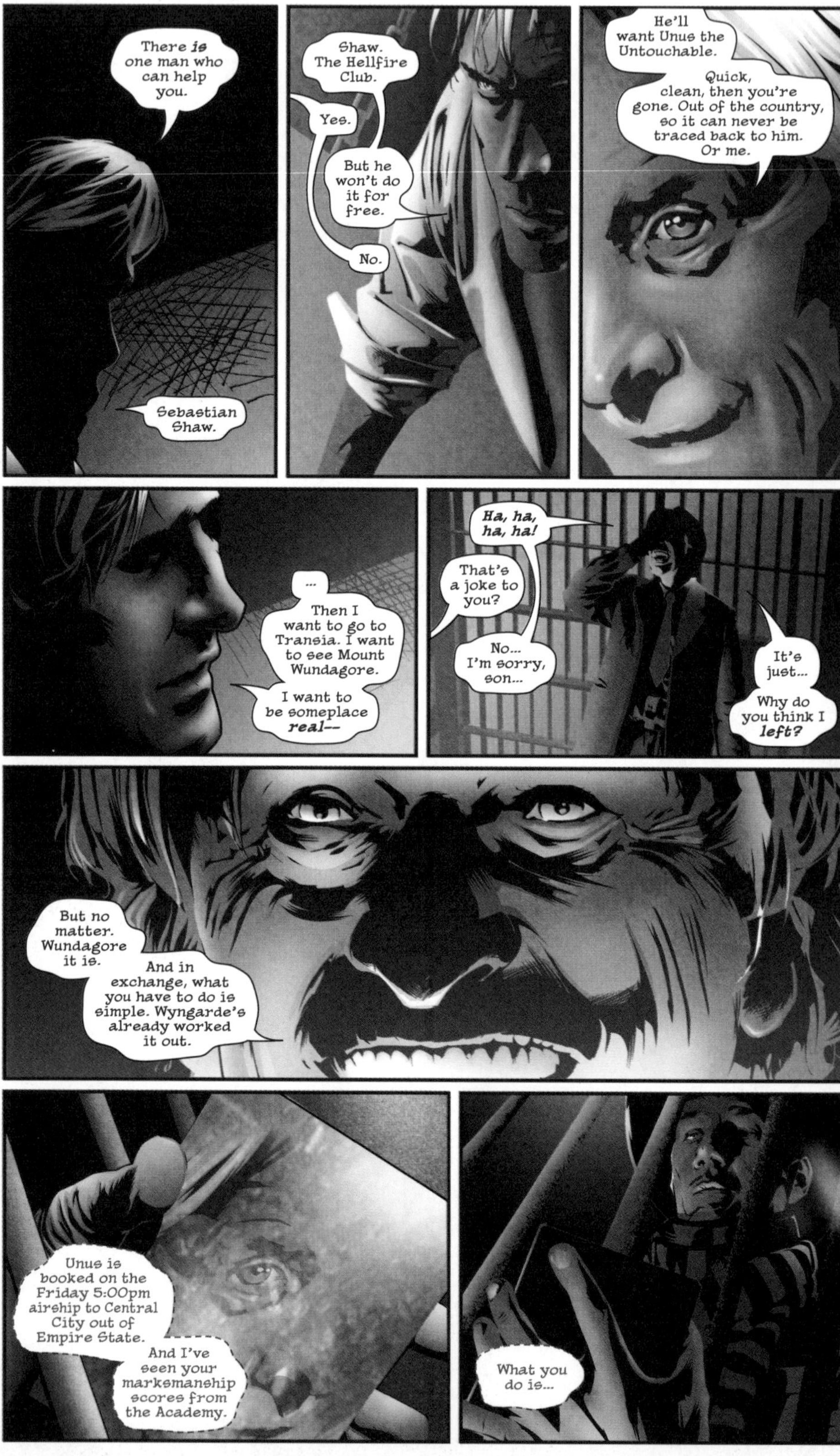

There *is* one man who can help you.
Sebastian Shaw.
Shaw. The Hellfire Club.
Yes.
But he won't do it for free.
No.
He'll want Unus the Untouchable.
Quick, clean, then you're gone. Out of the country, so it can never be traced back to him. Or me.
...
Then I want to go to Transia. I want to see Mount Wundagore.
I want to be someplace *real*--
Ha, ha, ha, ha!
That's a joke to you?
No... I'm sorry, son...
It's just...
Why do you think I *left?*
But no matter. Wundagore it is.
And in exchange, what you have to do is simple. Wyngarde's already worked it out.
Unus is booked on the Friday 5:00pm airship to Central City out of Empire State.
And I've seen your marksmanship scores from the Academy.
What you do is...

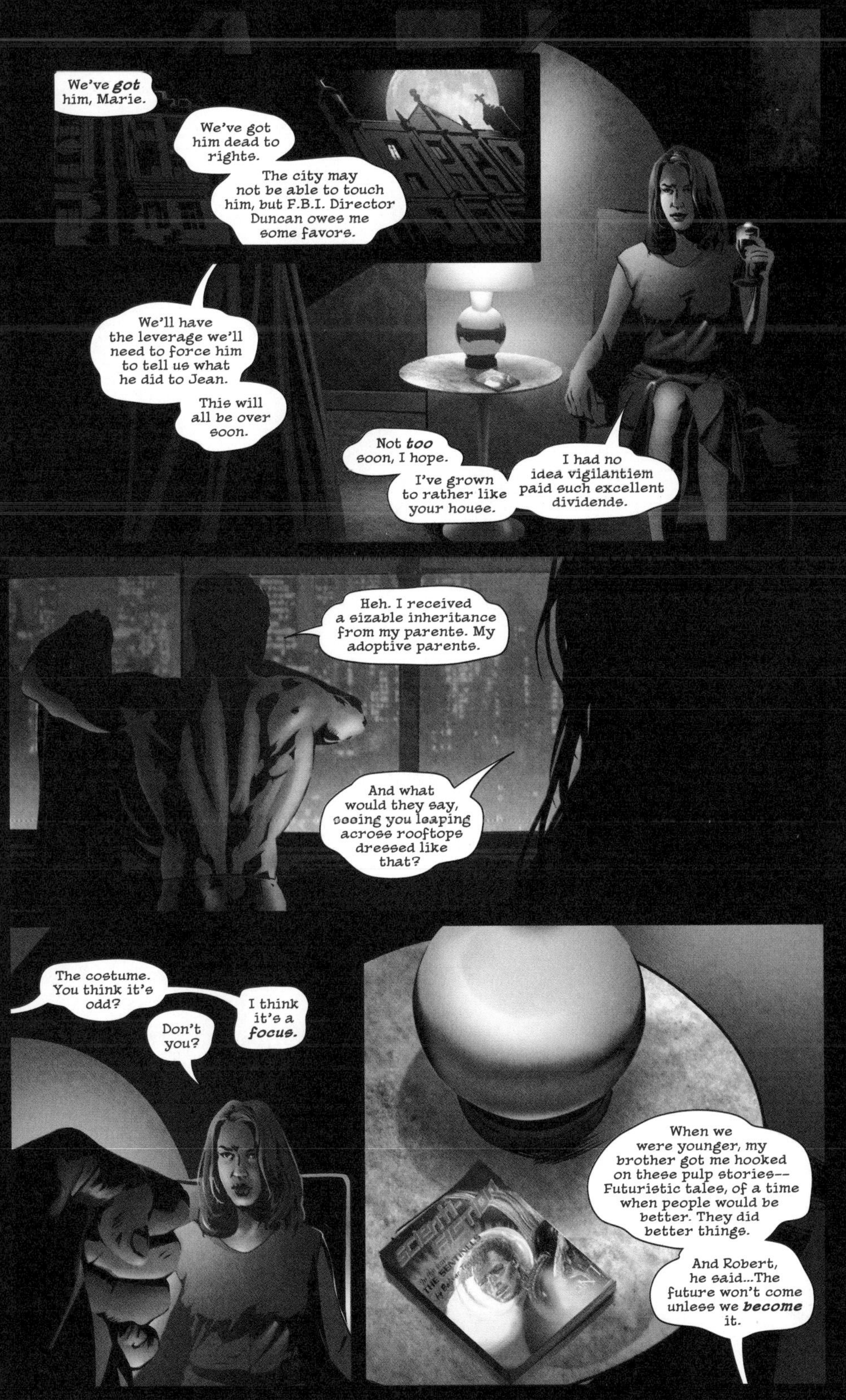

We've *got* him, Marie.
We've got him dead to rights.
The city may not be able to touch him, but F.B.I. Director Duncan owes me some favors.
We'll have the leverage we'll need to force him to tell us what he did to Jean.
This will all be over soon.
Not *too* soon, I hope.
I've grown to rather like your house.
I had no idea vigilantism paid such excellent dividends.
Heh. I received a sizable inheritance from my parents. My adoptive parents.
And what would they say, seeing you leaping across rooftops dressed like that?
The costume. You think it's odd?
I think it's a *focus.*
Don't you?
When we were younger, my brother got me hooked on these pulp stories-- Futuristic tales, of a time when people would be better. They did better things.
And Robert, he said...The future won't come unless we *become* it.

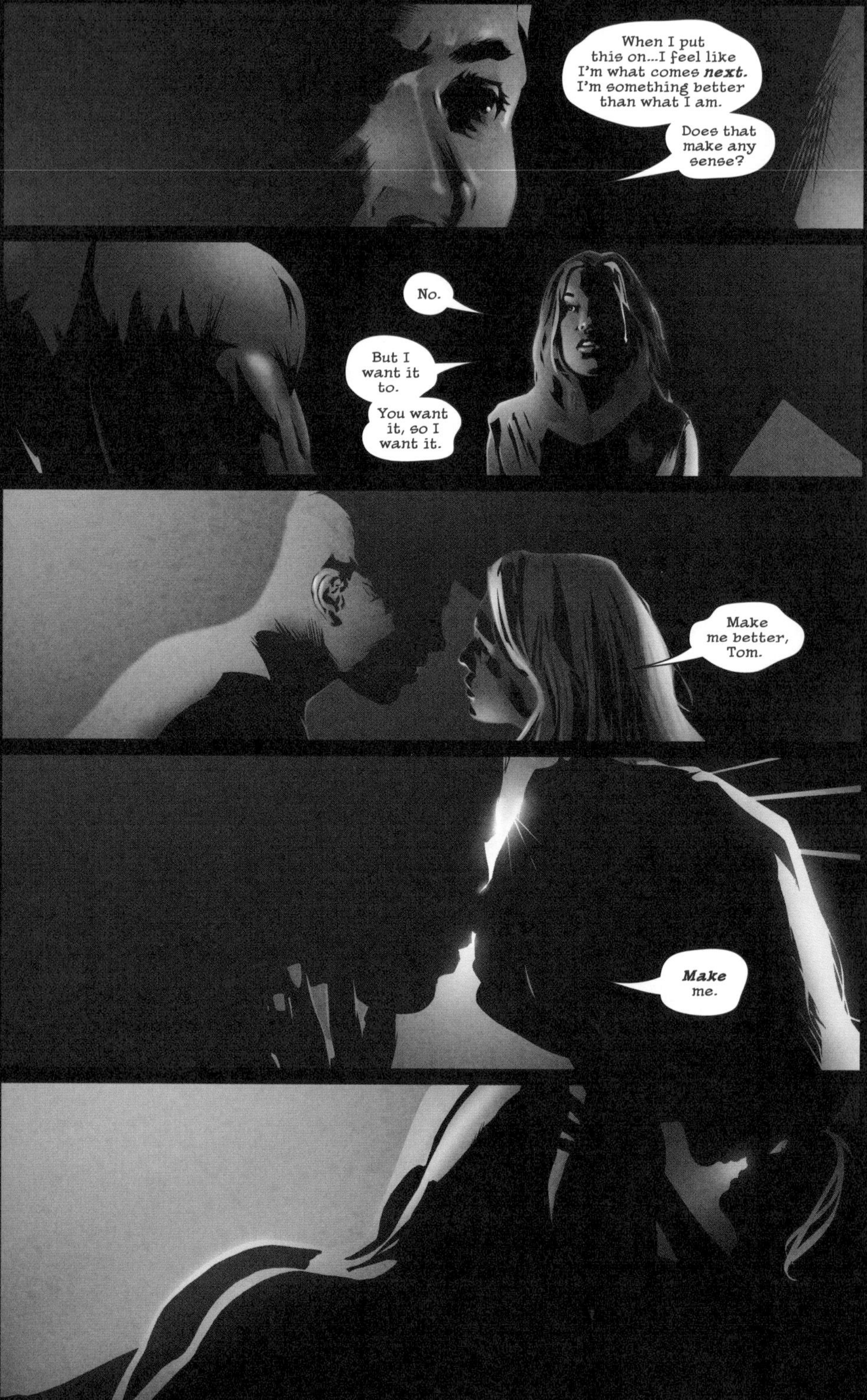

When I put this on...I feel like I'm what comes ***next.*** I'm something better than what I am.
Does that make any sense?
No.
But I want it to.
You want it, so I want it.
Make me better, Tom.
Make me.

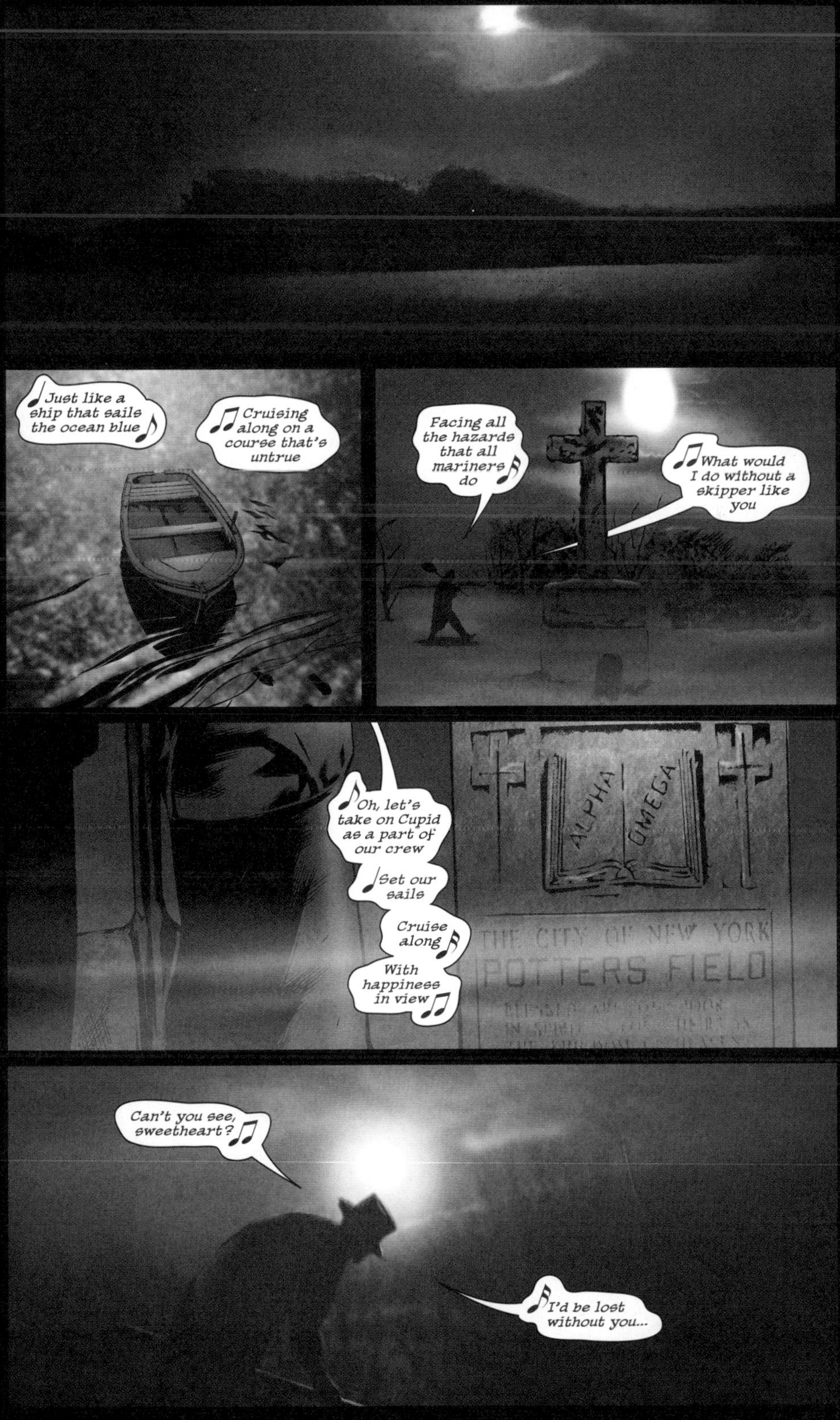
Just like a ship that sails the ocean blue
Cruising along on a course that's untrue
Facing all the hazards that all mariners do
What would I do without a skipper like you
Oh, let's take on Cupid as a part of our crew
ALPHA
OMEGA
Set our sails
Cruise along
With happiness in view
THE CITY OF NEW YORK
POTTERS FIELD
Can't you see, sweetheart?
I'd be lost without you...

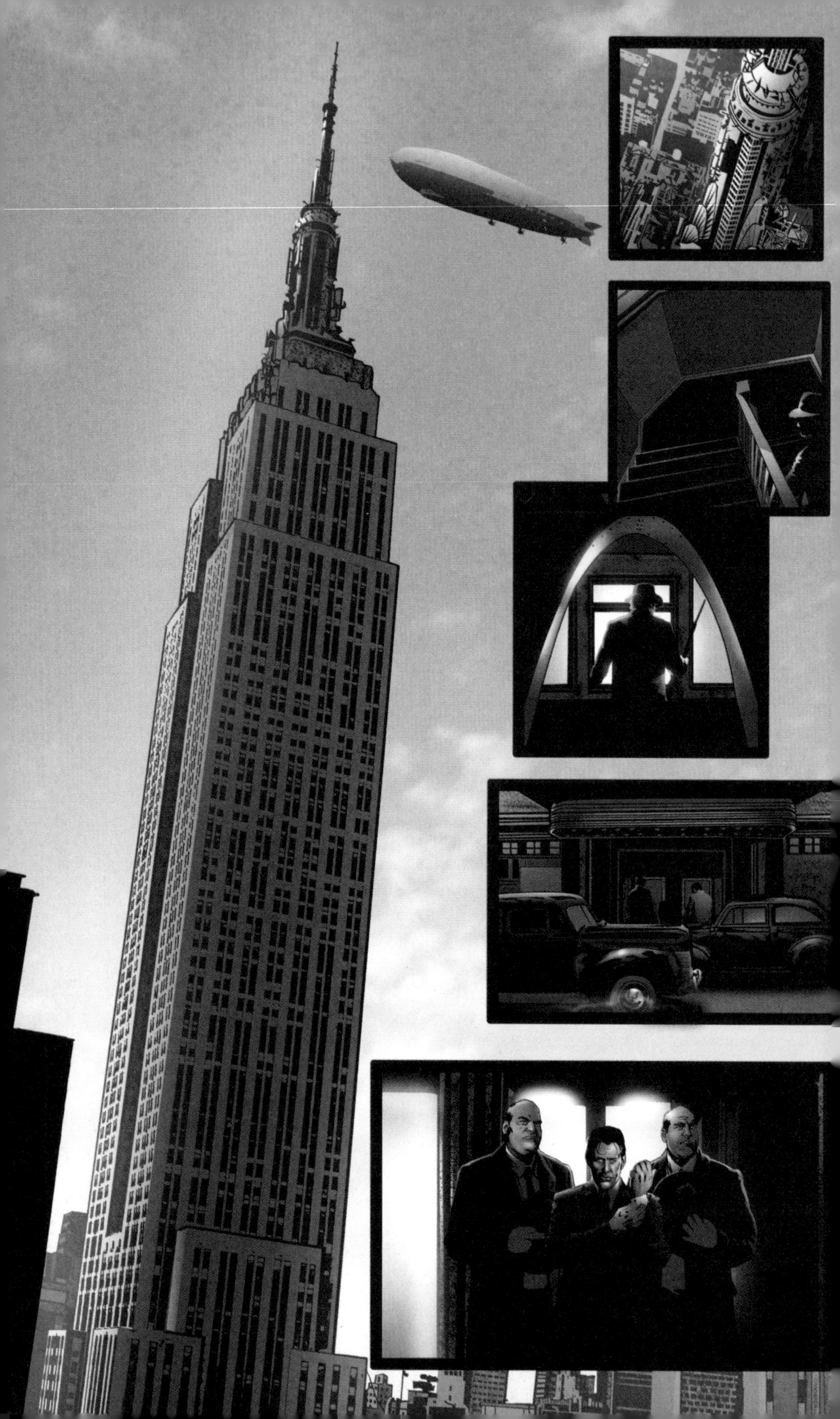

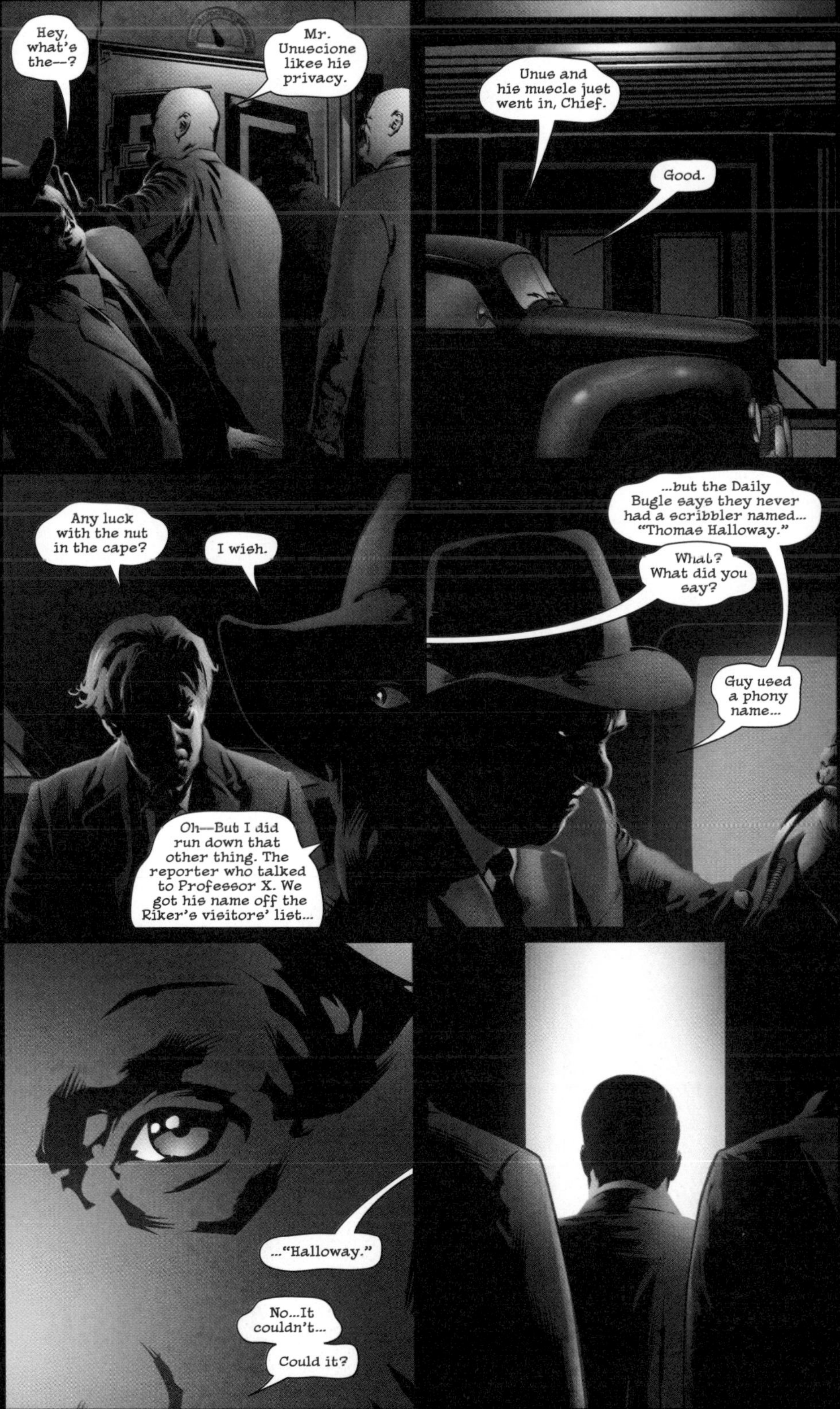

Hey, what's the--?
Mr. Unuscione likes his privacy.
Unus and his muscle just went in, Chief.
Good.
Any luck with the nut in the cape?
I wish.
Oh—But I did run down that other thing. The reporter who talked to Professor X. We got his name off the Riker's visitors' list...
...but the Daily Bugle says they never had a scribbler named... "Thomas Halloway."
What? What did you say?
Guy used a phony name...
..."Halloway."
No...It couldn't...
Could it?

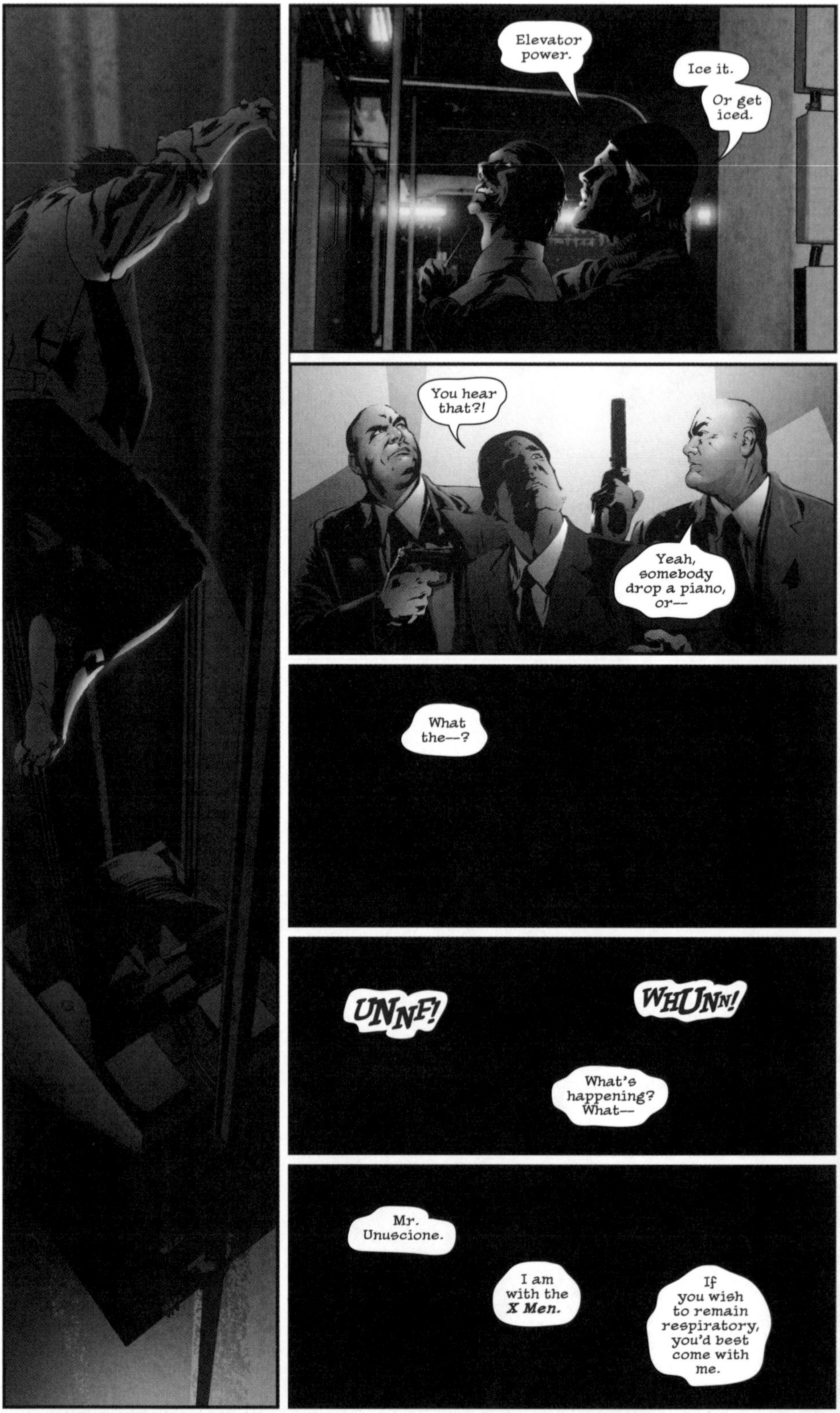
Elevator power.
Ice it.
Or get iced.
You hear that?!
Yeah, somebody drop a piano, or--
What the--?
UNNF!
WHUNN!
What's happening? What--
Mr. Unuscione.
I am with the *X Men.*
If you wish to remain respiratory, you'd best come with me.

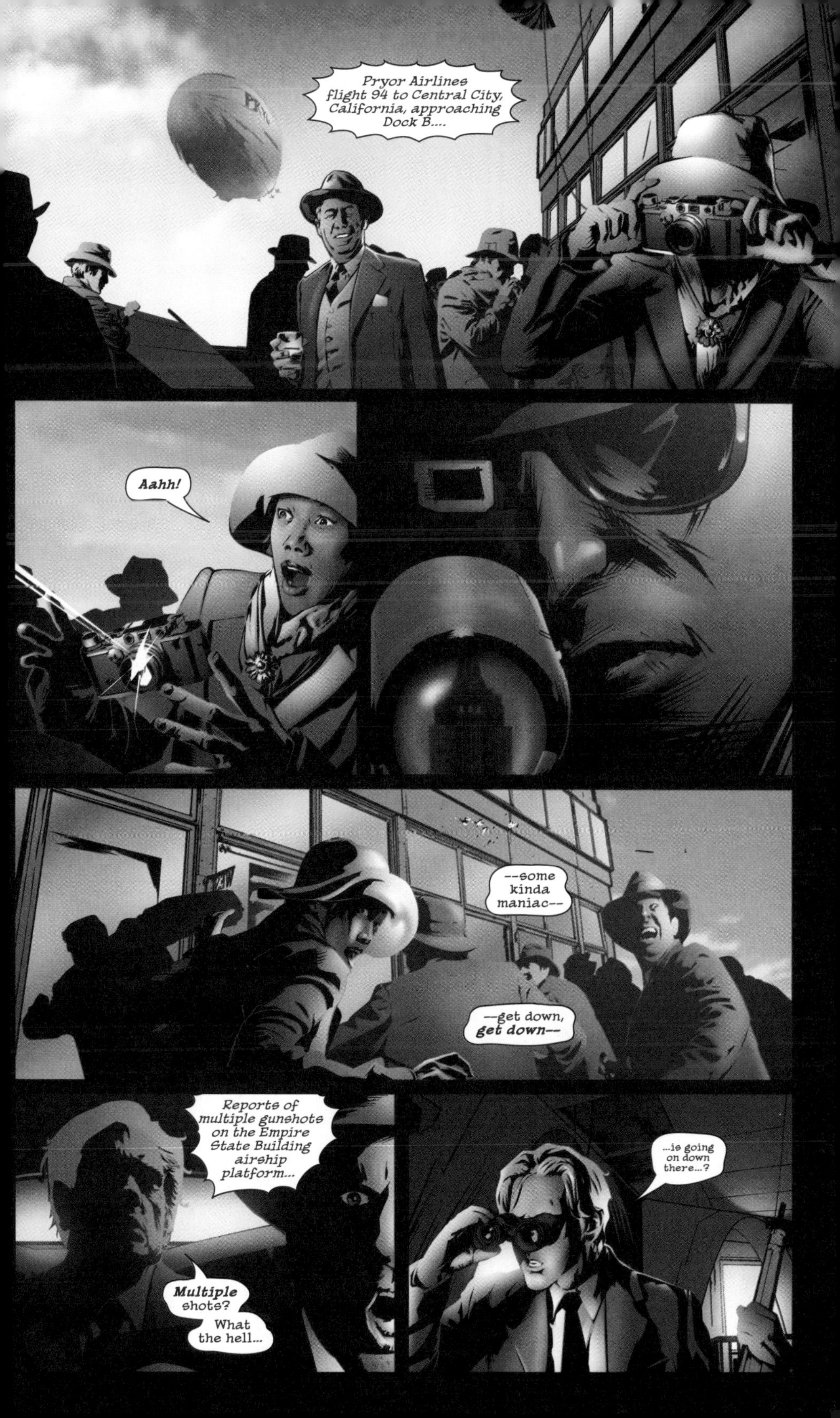
Pryor Airlines flight 94 to Central City, California, approaching Dock B....
Aahh!
--some kinda maniac--
--get down, **get down**--
Reports of multiple gunshots on the Empire State Building airship platform...
Multiple shots?
What the hell...
...is going on down there...?

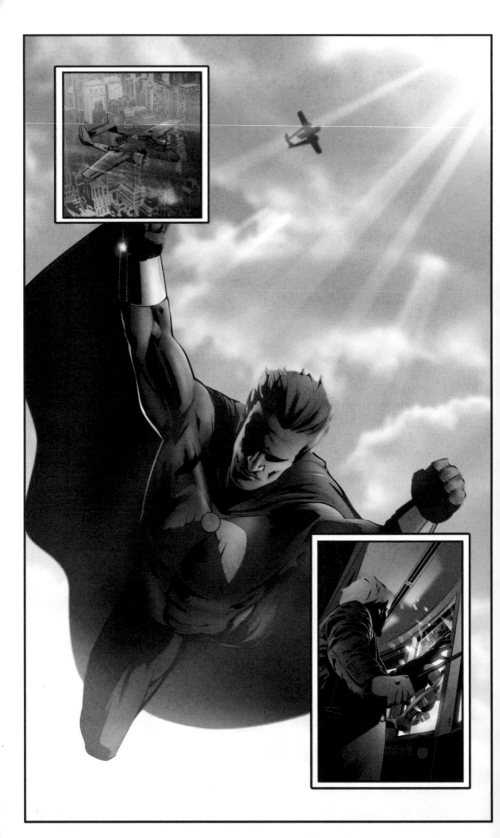

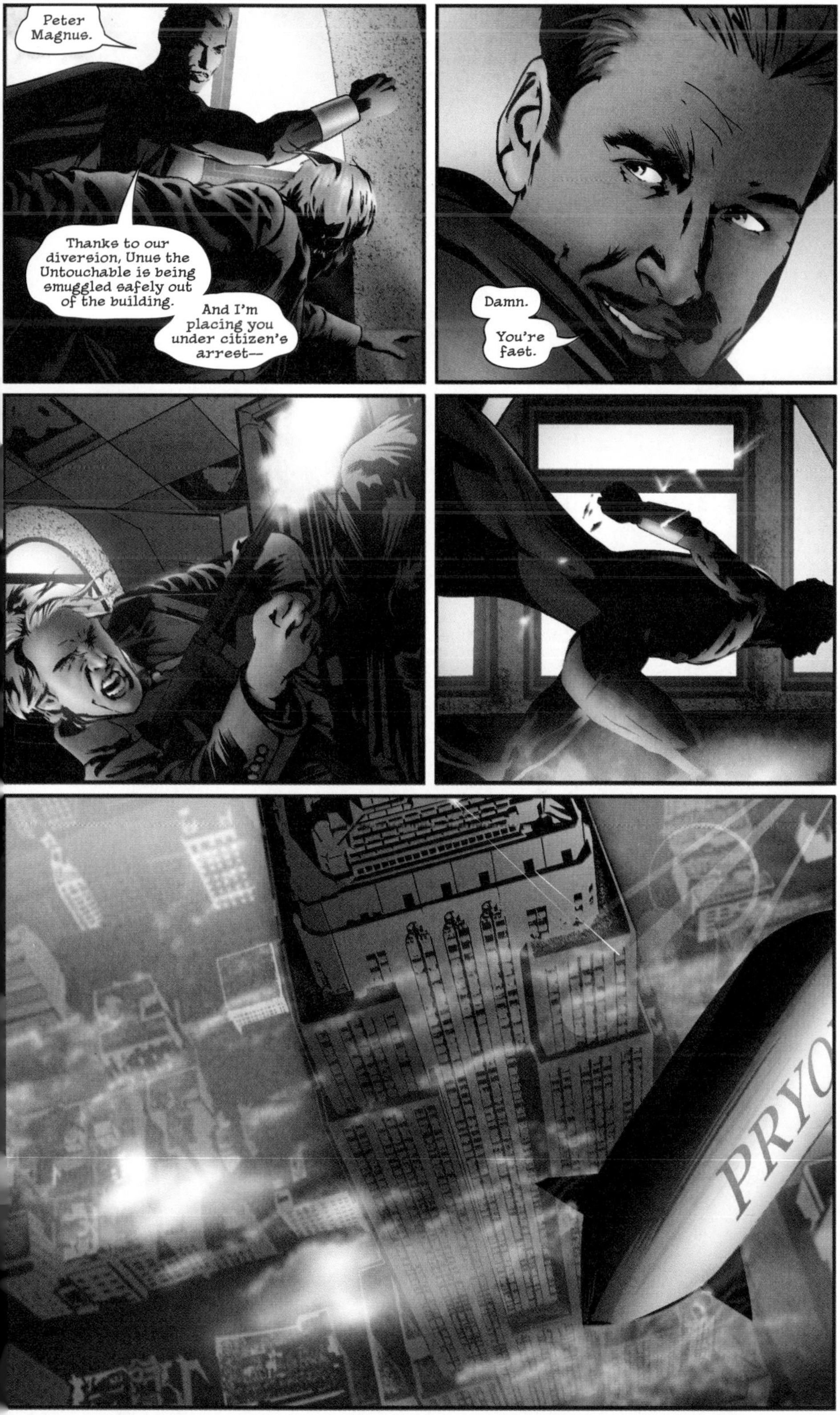
Peter Magnus.
Thanks to our diversion, Unus the Untouchable is being smuggled safely out of the building.
And I'm placing you under citizen's arrest—
Damn.
You're fast.
PRYO

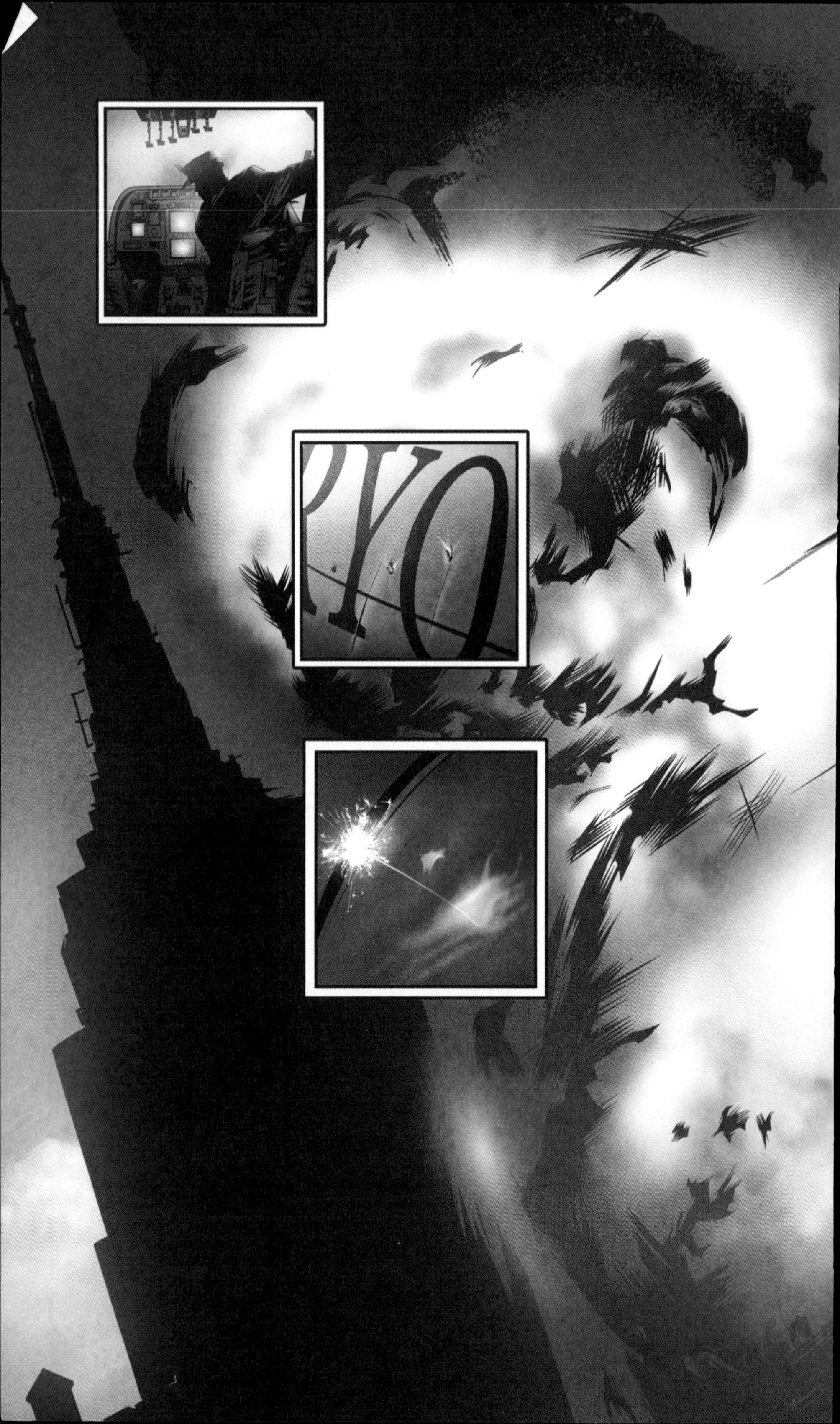

THE SENTINELS

By Bolivar Trask

Racially pure readers of Scienti-Fiction magazine will remember that last month, the genetically perfect Sentinel NIMROD descended into the dank tunnels of the Muties' Queen CALLISTO to rescue his beloved RACHEL – only to discover she really, really likes it there!

Chapter Three: The Age of Apocalypse

Nimrod swiftly unholstered his neutralizer from his belt as Callisto's guards began to advance upon him, virbo-cultasses and laser-blunderbusses raised high!

"Wait!" Rachel cried, leaping off the bed and hurling herself between her beloved and the Muties. "Violence isn't necessary!"

"Violence is always necessary when dealing with dirty, stinking Muties!" Nimrod snarled. "It's the only language they're fluent in!"

"You see, Rachel?" Callisto sneered. "Your male counterpart is not like you – the Breeders Council got to him too soon; his prejudices have calcified into ironclad facts inside his mind. Guards! Continue your seizing of him!"

"No!" the beautiful young Sentinel wailed, pushing the parties apart with lithe muscles spliced from the genes of twelve families of Russian prima donnas. "Please, just listen for a moment, Callisto! I know

Nimrod's mind as well as his heart. If you showed him what I saw when I first arrived here, I have no doubt his super-developed reason will tell him where his true allegiances should lie."

Nimrod thought he could see the knife-fighting scar running across the Mutie queen's cruel face throb red with fury. But with reluctance Callisto ordered her troops back with a single bark.

"This way, Sentinel," Callisto growled. "That is – if your psyche can cope with having its every pillar of faith irreparably shattered."

Nimrod snorted dismissively, but Rachel hooked him by the arm and steered him out the door behind Callisto and her honor guard.

Just beyond lay the long, arched central shaft of the Muties' system of underground trenches, from which all the other tunnels terminated in or branched from. Once an enormous airship raid shelter for the entire population of Manhattan during the dark days of the Cyttorak Gas Wars, it now served as the mass nest for an innumerable horde of Mutie families, which laughed, played, and cooked giant rats on red-hot spits all along its titanic length. Cyclops-eyed children chased their three-legged brothers and sisters, emitting high-pitched sounds that were curious, if not displeasing, to Nimrod's ears.

"What a racket this Mutie spawn makes!" Nimrod whispered to his betrothed. "How can their parents stand idly by while they wallow in such distress?"

"That's just it! It's not distress!" Rachel cried with delight. "They're – I believe Callisto called it 'playing.' It's something you do, well, not for no reason, exactly – but because it's pleasurable. It's fun!"

"'Fun!'" Nimrod blinked in wonderment. "I don't see how that advances the ultimate perfection of the species' genome!"

"It doesn't! And that's kind of the

point, really. And those sounds they're making – they're from joy and excitement! The Muties call it … oh, what's the word … 'Laughter.'"

"Laff-ter." As much as he struggled with the word, Nimrod was having an even more difficult time with its meaning. Already he felt dizzier than the time his propellant pack had malfunctioned high over the New New New New York cityscape. He gripped Rachel's shoulder to walk properly.

The Sentinel duo passed a quartet of Muties engaged in an even more baffling activity. At first his hand flinched toward its neutralizer, for he assumed the weird instruments in their hands were weapons. But then he realized that the brass and wood instruments they blew into and flew their fingers across with such gusto emitted nothing other than sounds – and pleasing ones, at that.

"That sounds nothing like our

synthesized Science Hymns," he breathed in wonder.

Rachel laughed when she saw the smile pass across Nimrod's face. "I know! Wonderful, isn't it?" She gripped Nimrod's hand in hers, spun him out, then pulled him close. "They rescued this music from Old New York – before the mad Egyptian En Sabah Nur dropped his Phoenix Bombs on the city. They call it … 'jass.' And what we're doing now is the traditional response to it: 'dancing!'"

"All right you two, enough of your tomfoolery," Callisto chastised her charges. "He's ready to see you now, and his time is limited."

Callisto led them through a wide, circular cistern mouth into a chamber filled with scientific instruments. For all the strange and wondrous things Nimrod had seen in the Muties' tunnels, this was the most astounding. Standing on its fins before him was a gigantic steel teardrop. It took him a moment to understand what he was looking at, for he had never seen one outside of grainy history-fiches, but soon it dawned on him:

This was a devastating Phoenix Bomb, left over from the Age of Apocalypse!

"By Mendel's beanstalk!" he gasped under his breath to Rachel. "The 'He' must be their god – these primitive Muties worship a bomb!"

"What? No," Callisto snapped peevishly. "He's standing behind the bomb."

From behind the Phoenix Bomb stepped an old man in a lab coat, holding a glass pipette in one hand and a test tube of bubbling liquid in the other. Again, a sense of the familiar washed over Nimrod.

But it wasn't until the old man said, "Nimrod – my greatest creation – I am honored to meet you in the flesh at last" that the Sentinel finally realized he had seen a younger version of this wizened face in the history-fiches as well.

"Doctor Steven Lang!" Nimrod gasped. "The greatest eugenics engineer in history – creator of we Sentinels! But … they told us you have been slain by these repulsive Muties."

Dr. Lang just chuckled kindly. "That is merely what the Hall of Experimental Evolution wanted you to think. In truth, their agents gave me what they thought was a fatal wound with a neutralizer, then dumped me like so much refuse into the Muties' tunnels. Their scheme hinged upon an archeological team 'discovering' me later so the murder could be blamed on Callisto's people."

"But rather, my sweet queen rescued me, and nursed my back to health, and I have been plotting against the Breeders Council ever since. I hope, soon, that all my plans will come to fruition – with your help, noble Nimrod."

Nimrod hardly knew what to think; his mind roared with the revelation, drowning out all other thought; and for

genes here, among the Muties, darling! He wants to reintroduce it into our offspring! Then our sons and daughters truly will be perfect! That's why he captured me, so he could lure you down here!"

Nimrod clutched his head as if it would explode; he feared he was going mad! Could it be possible that every fiche had ever read since the Robo-Womb was a complete and utter falsehood?

At that moment shouts and cries that could not have been mistaken for laughter by even the most naïve listener began reverberating out of the central tunnel

seconds all his mouth could do was gape. "But—why would the Breeders Council desire your assassination?"

"I foolishly warned them I was about to take public my protests against the direction the experimental evolution program was taking," Lang replied. "I had never intended for the pure science of eugenics to be used to control and oppress the common people. The Breeders Council planned not to just retain humanity's best qualities and remove the bad ones – but they would also eradicate every part of us that is spontaneous and unpredictable! The Council, in their mania to perfect humanity, would render us impossible of imperfection – turn us into mere automatons!"

Rachel continued breathlessly to Nimrod: "The doctor found the spontaneity

walls, accompanied by the unmistakable cough and sizzle of neutralizer fire.

One of Callisto's larger guards – the queen had called him "Sunder" – staggered into Dr. Lang's lab, singed all over by scorch marks. He gasped, "Sentinels! Flooding the tunnels! They say … none will leave here … alive!" Then he dropped dead at Nimrod's feet.

"Bastion!" the hero cried. "He must have followed me here!"

NEXT: E IS FOR EXTINCTION!

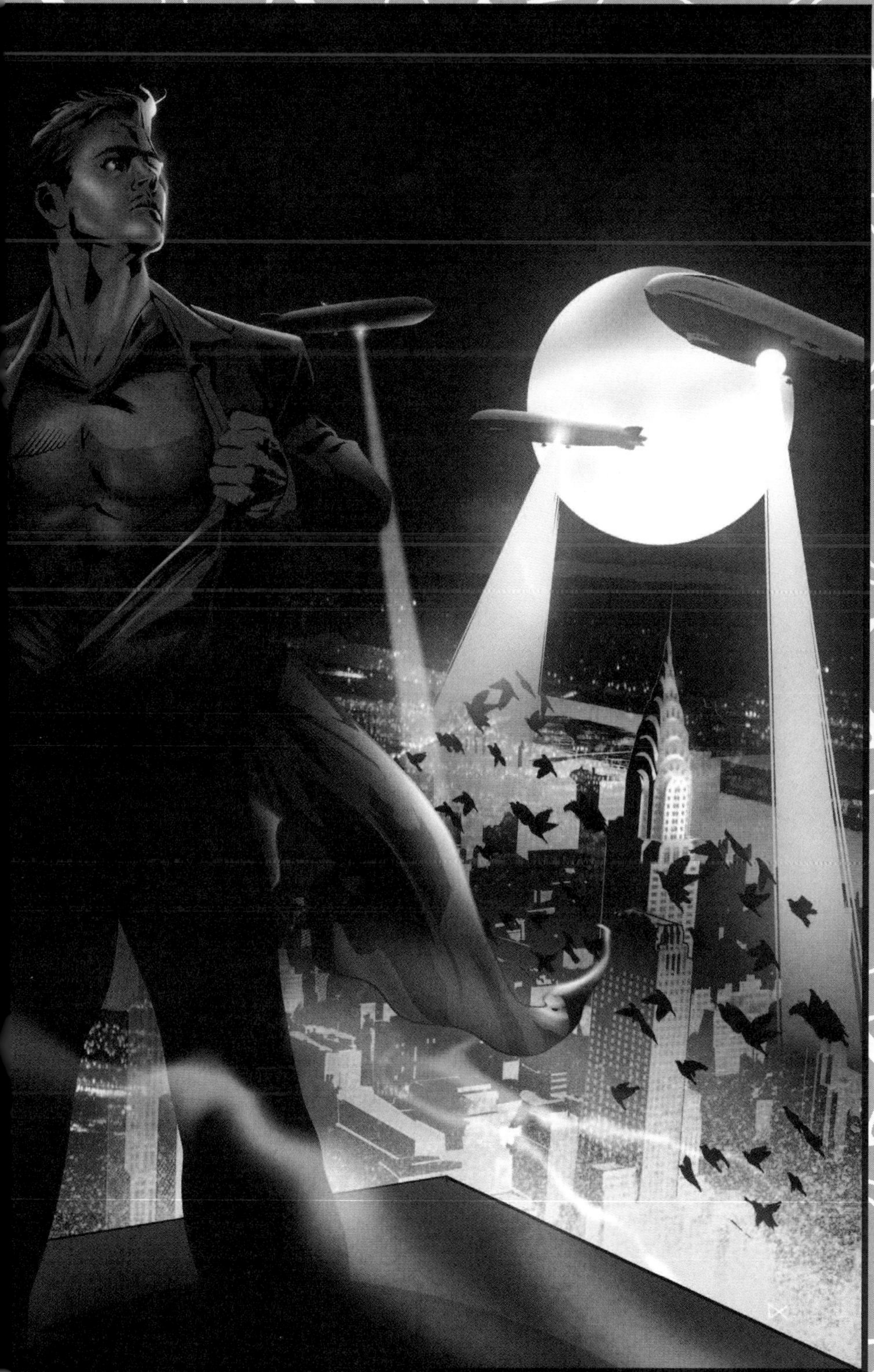

FOUR

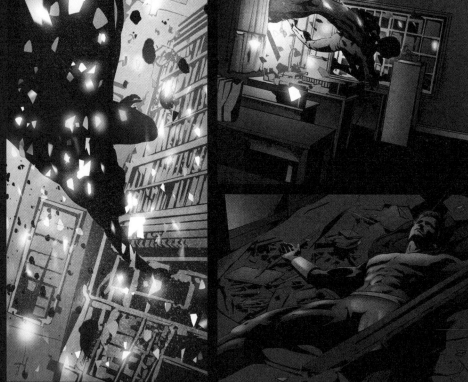

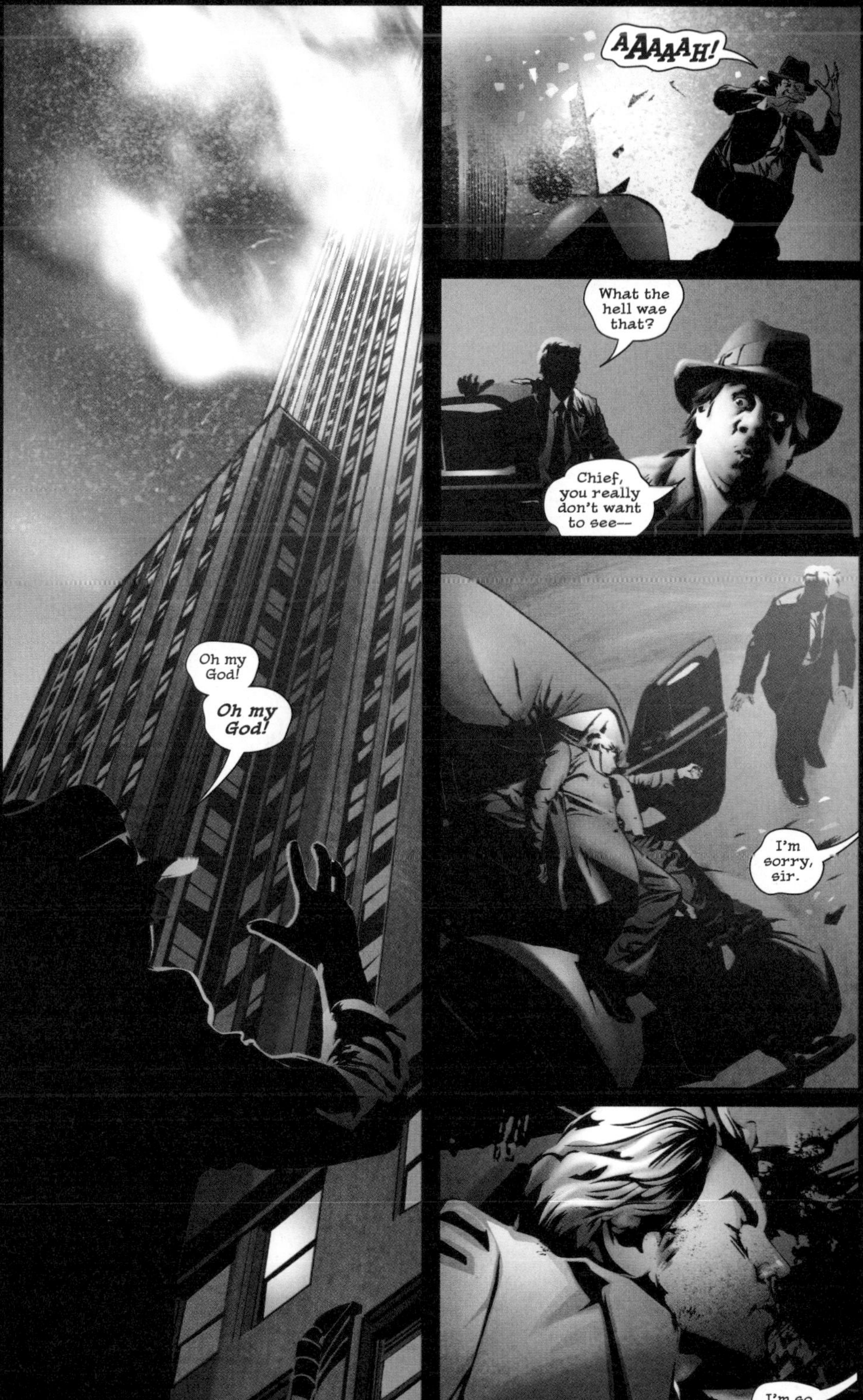
AAAAAH!
What the hell was that?
Chief, you really don't want to see--
Oh my God!
Oh my God!
I'm sorry, sir.
I'm so sorry.

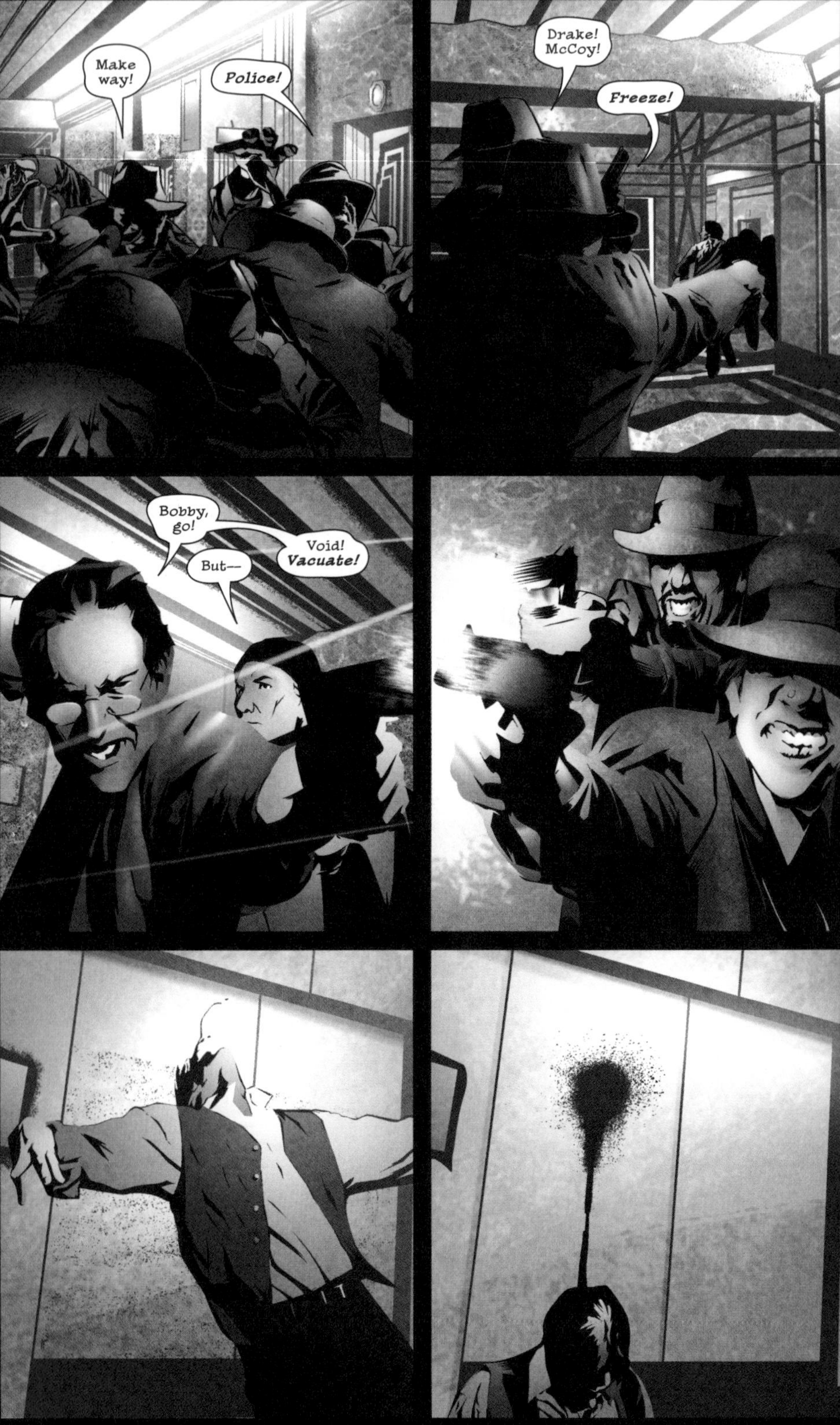

Make way!
Police!
Drake! McCoy!
Freeze!
Bobby, go!
But--
Void! Vacuate!

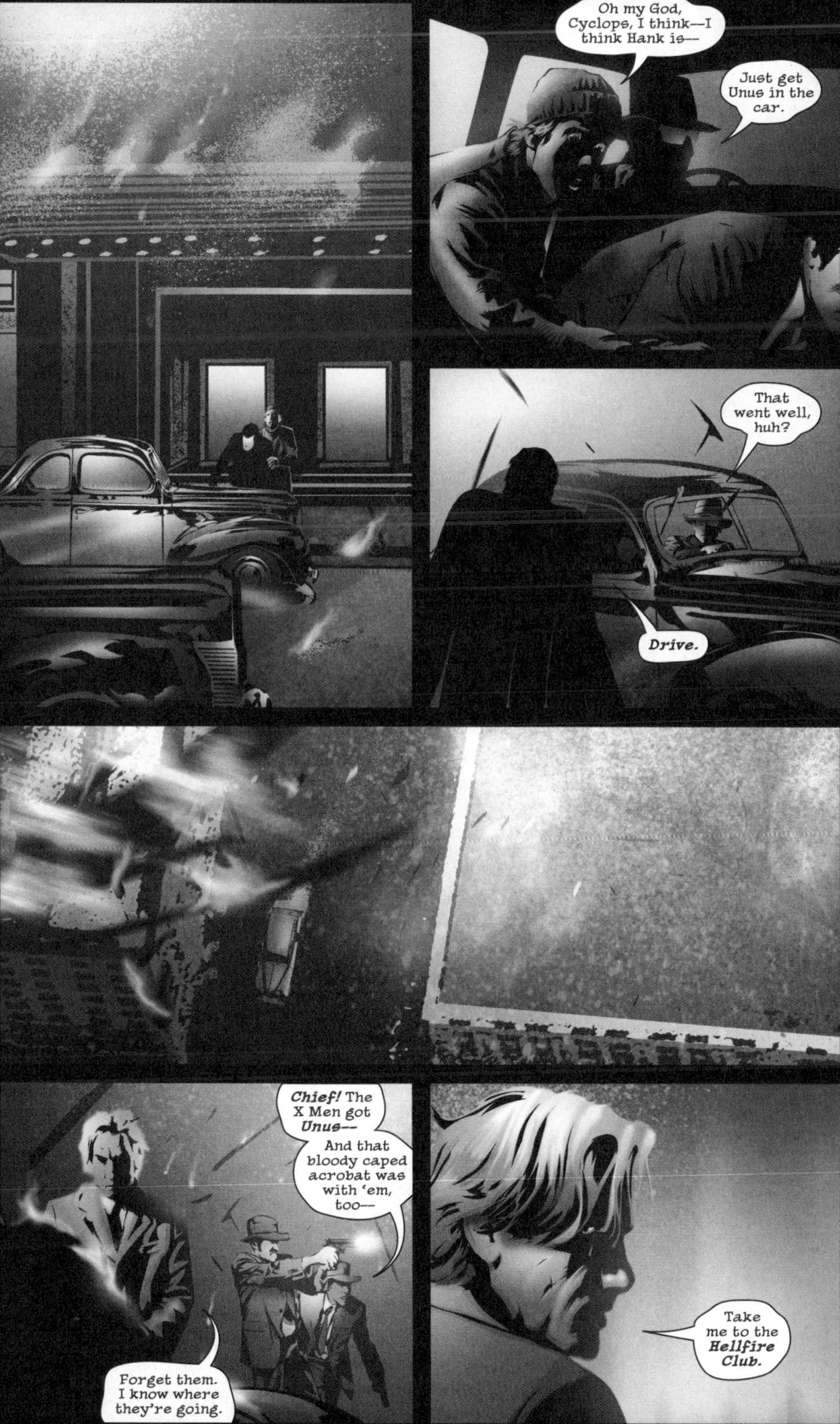
Oh my God, Cyclops, I think--I think Hank is--
Just get Unus in the car.
That went well, huh?
Drive.
Chief! The X Men got ***Unus--***
And that bloody caped acrobat was with 'em, too--
Forget them. I know where they're going.
Take me to the ***Hellfire Club.***

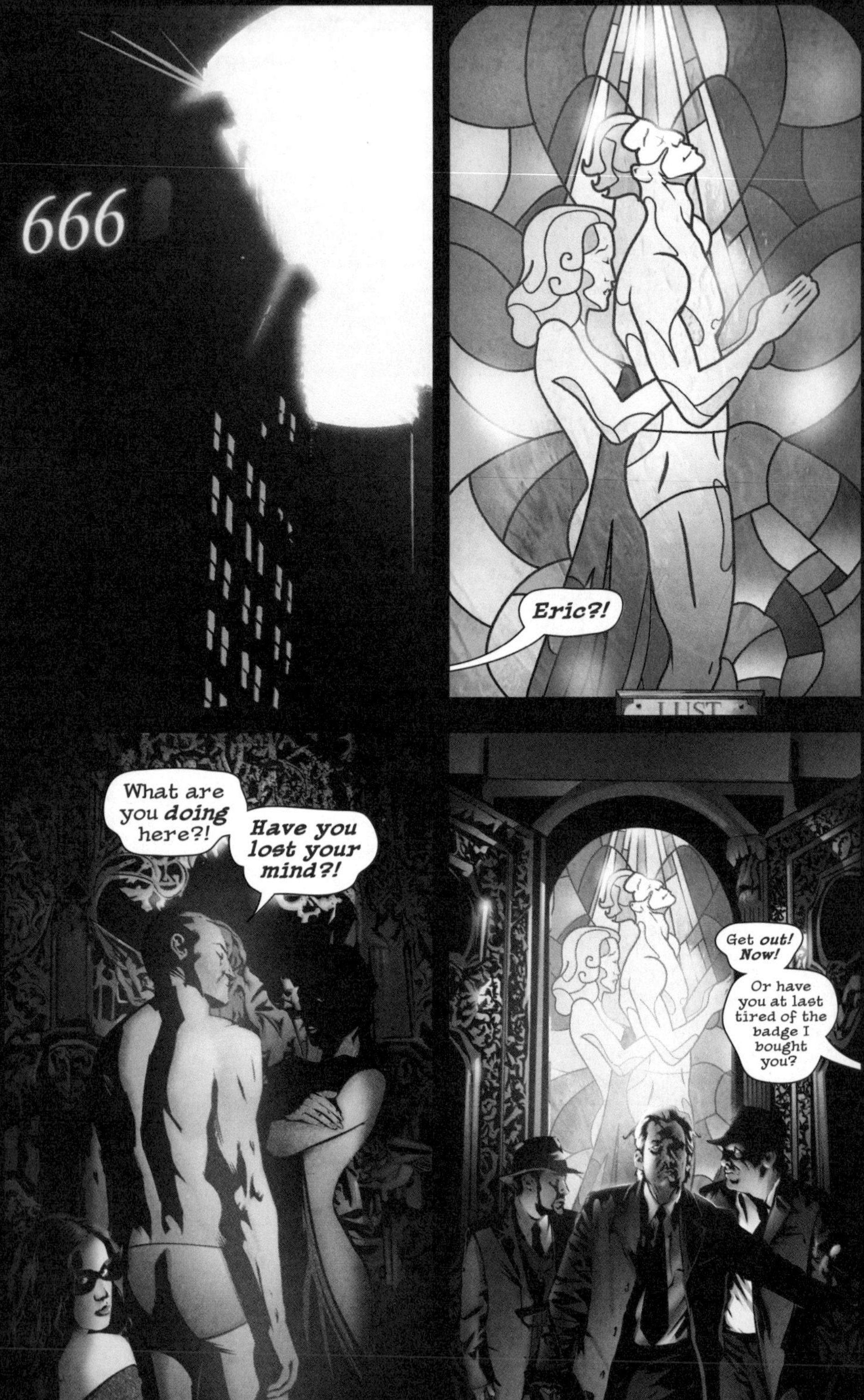
666
Eric?!
What are you *doing* here?!
Have you lost your mind?!
Get ***out! Now!***
Or have you at last tired of the badge I bought you?

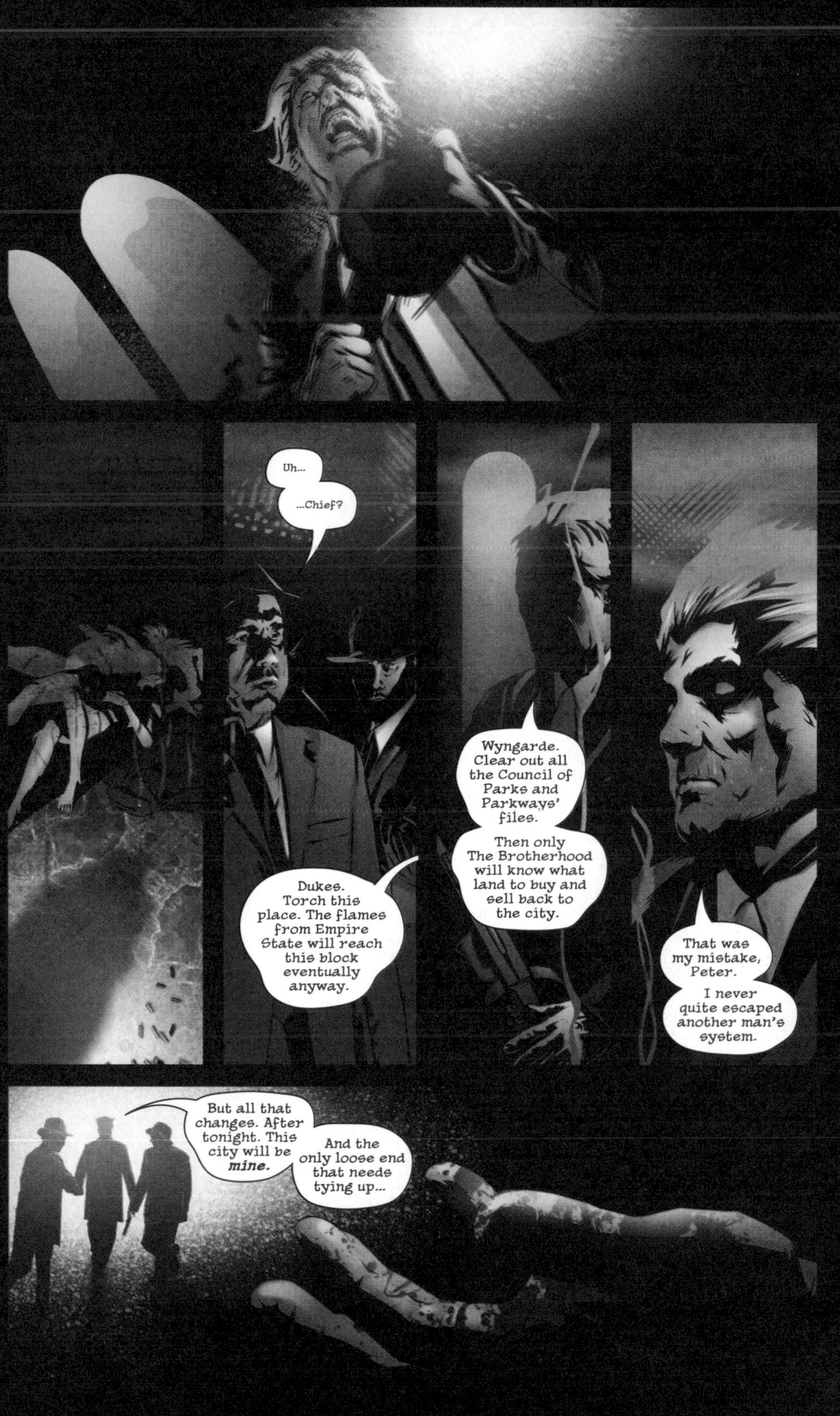
Uh...
...Chief?
Dukes. Torch this place. The flames from Empire State will reach this block eventually anyway.
Wyngarde. Clear out all the Council of Parks and Parkways' files.
Then only The Brotherhood will know what land to buy and sell back to the city.
That was my mistake, Peter.
I never quite escaped another man's system.
But all that changes. After tonight. This city will be *mine.*
And the only loose end that needs tying up...

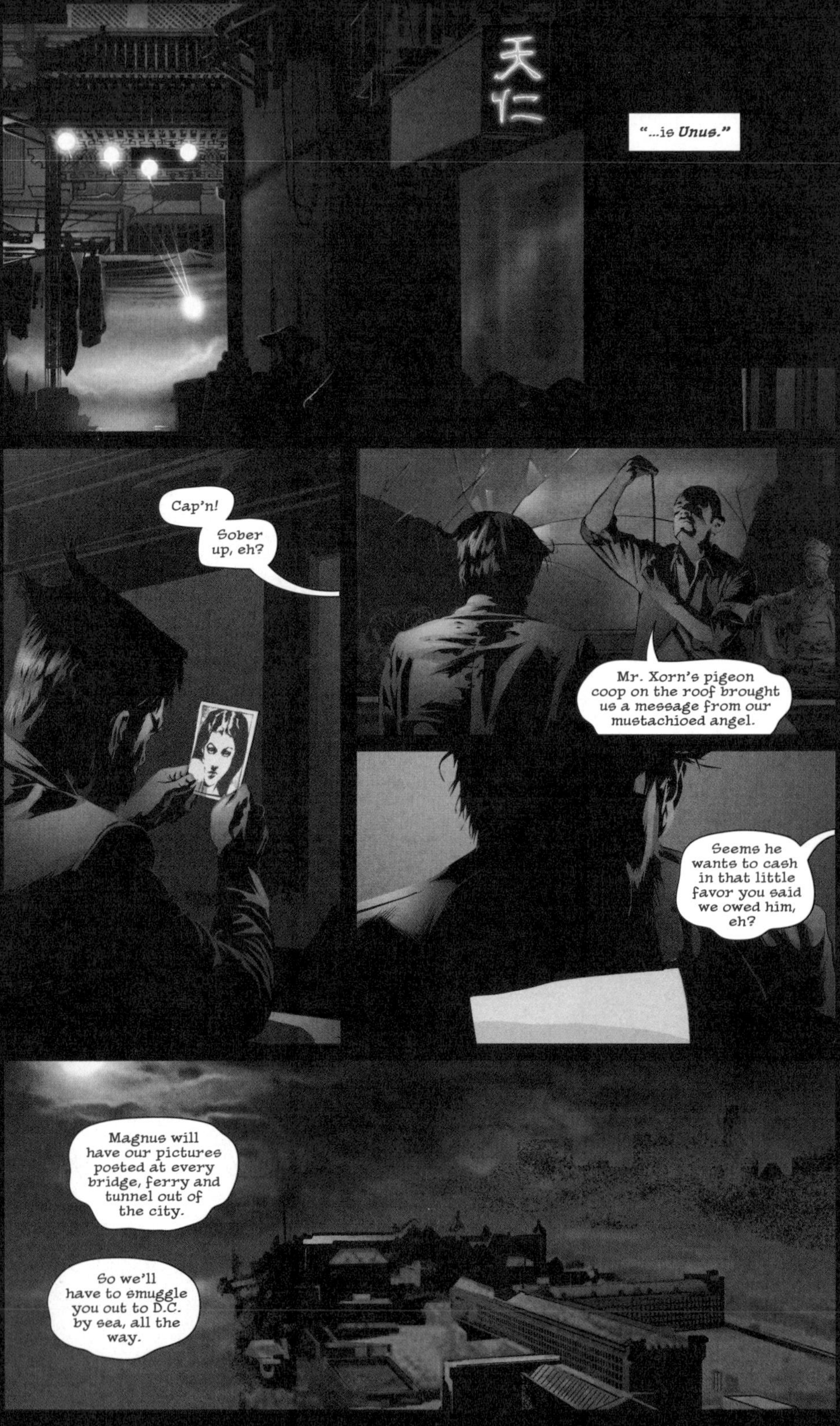
天仁
"...is Unus."
Cap'n!
Sober up, eh?
Mr. Xorn's pigeon coop on the roof brought us a message from our mustachioed angel.
Seems he wants to cash in that little favor you said we owed him, eh?
Magnus will have our pictures posted at every bridge, ferry and tunnel out of the city.
So we'll have to smuggle you out to D.C. by sea, all the way.

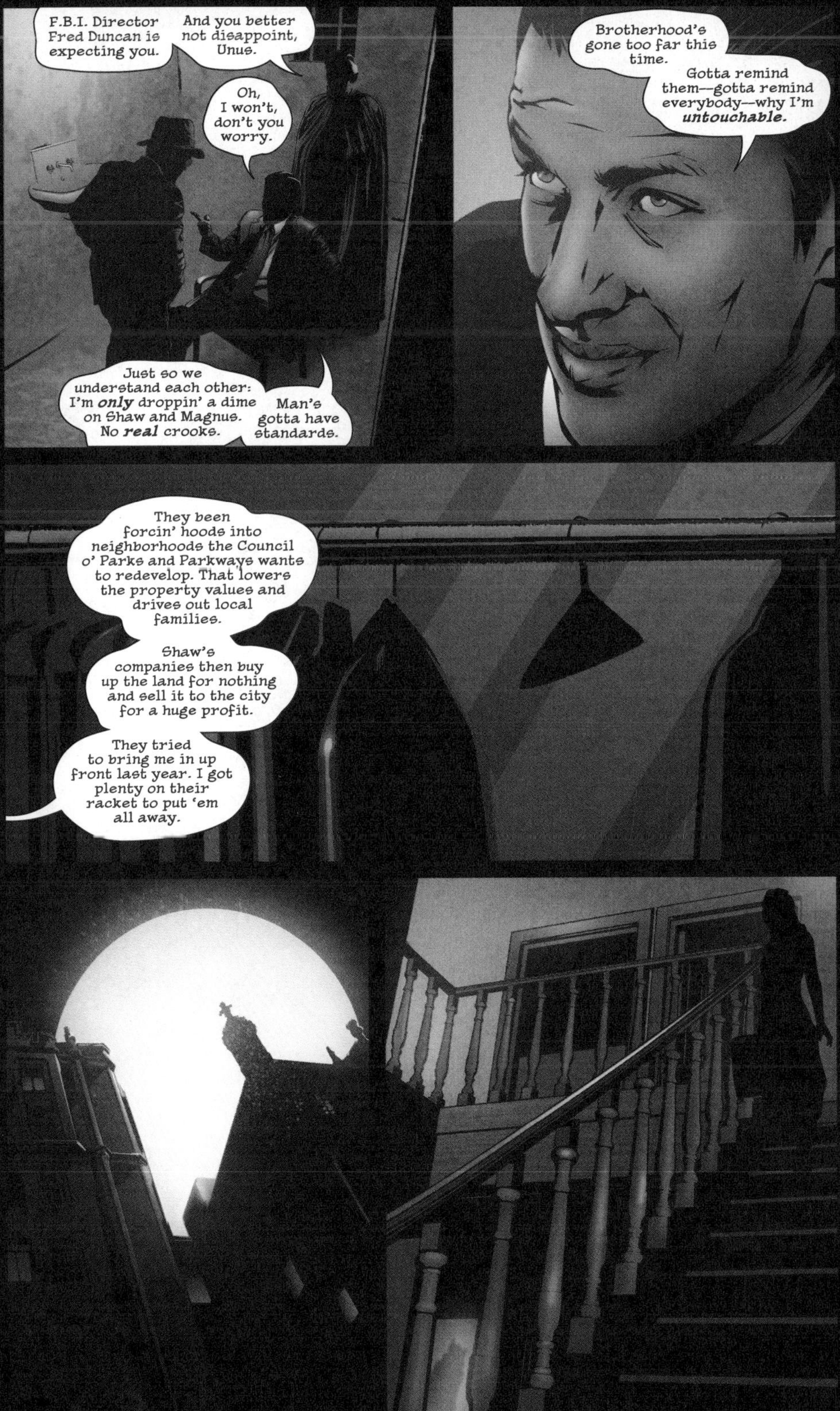
F.B.I. Director Fred Duncan is expecting you.
And you better not disappoint, Unus.
Oh, I won't, don't you worry.
Just so we understand each other: I'm *only* droppin' a dime on Shaw and Magnus. No ***real*** crooks.
Man's gotta have standards.
Brotherhood's gone too far this time.
Gotta remind them––gotta remind everybody––why I'm ***untouchable.***
They been forcin' hoods into neighborhoods the Council o' Parks and Parkways wants to redevelop. That lowers the property values and drives out local families.
Shaw's companies then buy up the land for nothing and sell it to the city for a huge profit.
They tried to bring me in up front last year. I got plenty on their racket to put 'em all away.

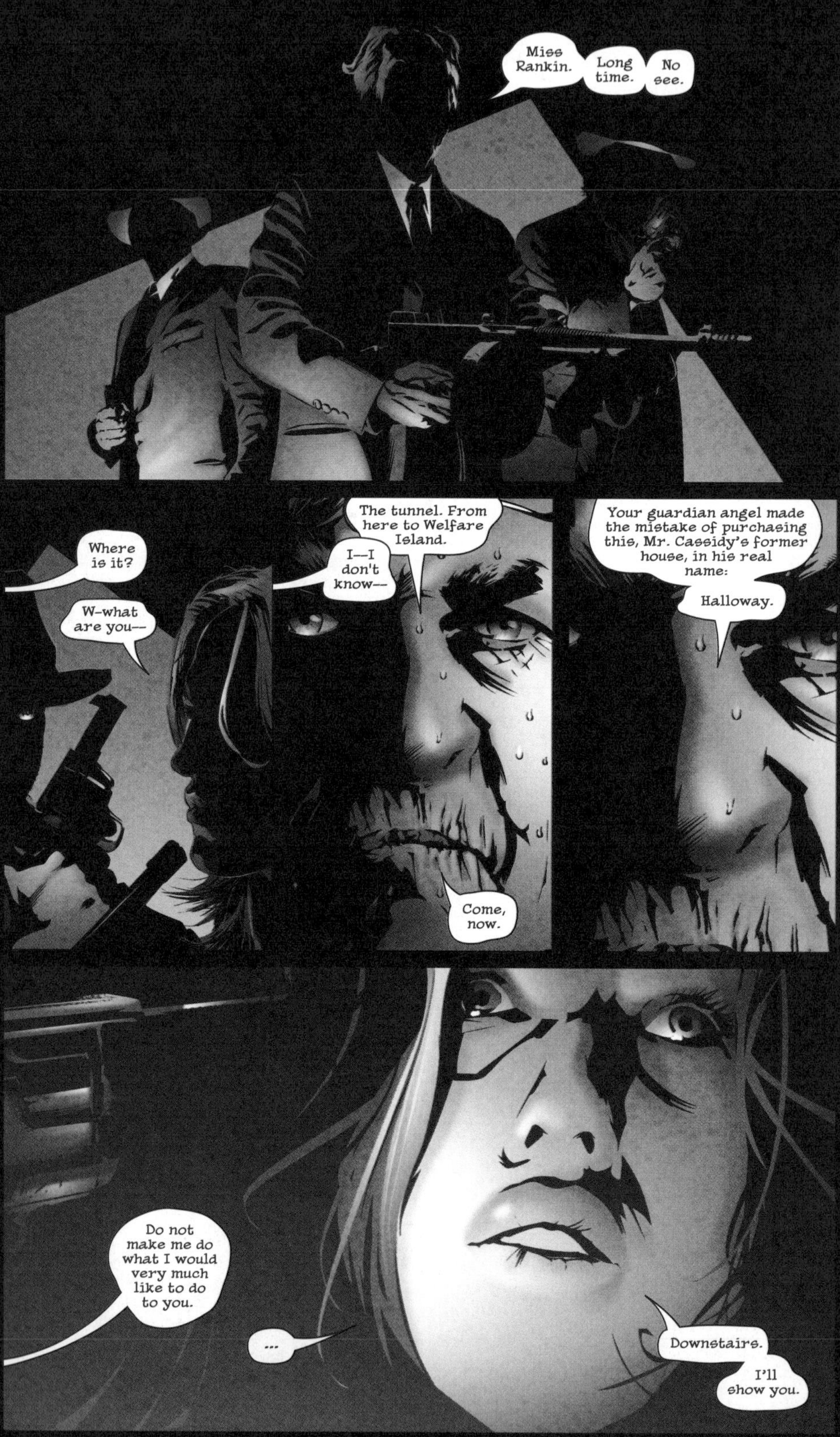
Miss Rankin.
Long time.
No see.
Where is it?
W-what are you--
I--I don't know--
The tunnel. From here to Welfare Island.
Come, now.
Your guardian angel made the mistake of purchasing this, Mr. Cassidy's former house, in his real name:
Halloway.
Do not make me do what I would very much like to do to you.
...
Downstairs.
I'll show you.

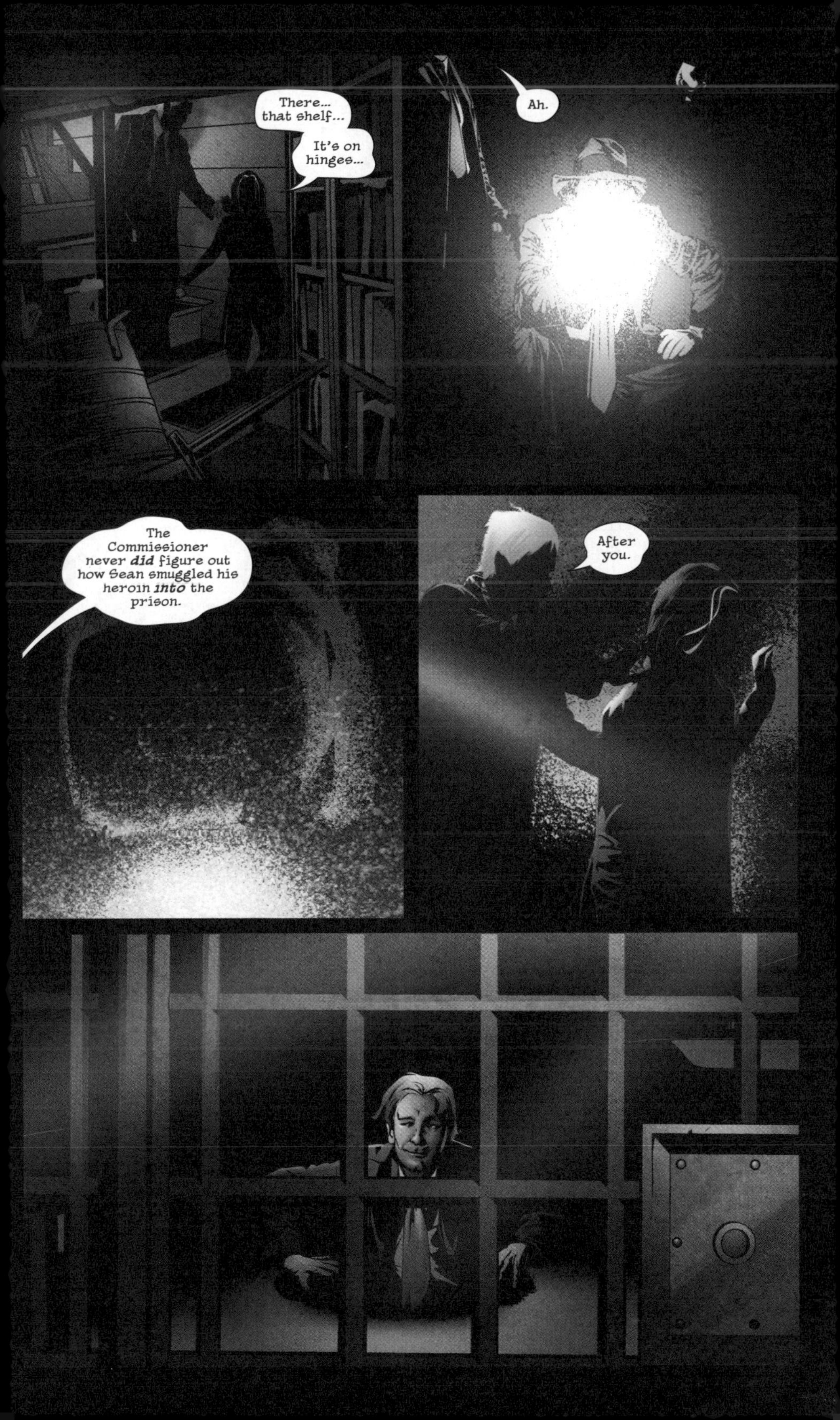
There... that shelf...
It's on hinges...
Ah.
The Commissioner never *did* figure out how Sean smuggled his heroin *into* the prison.
After you.

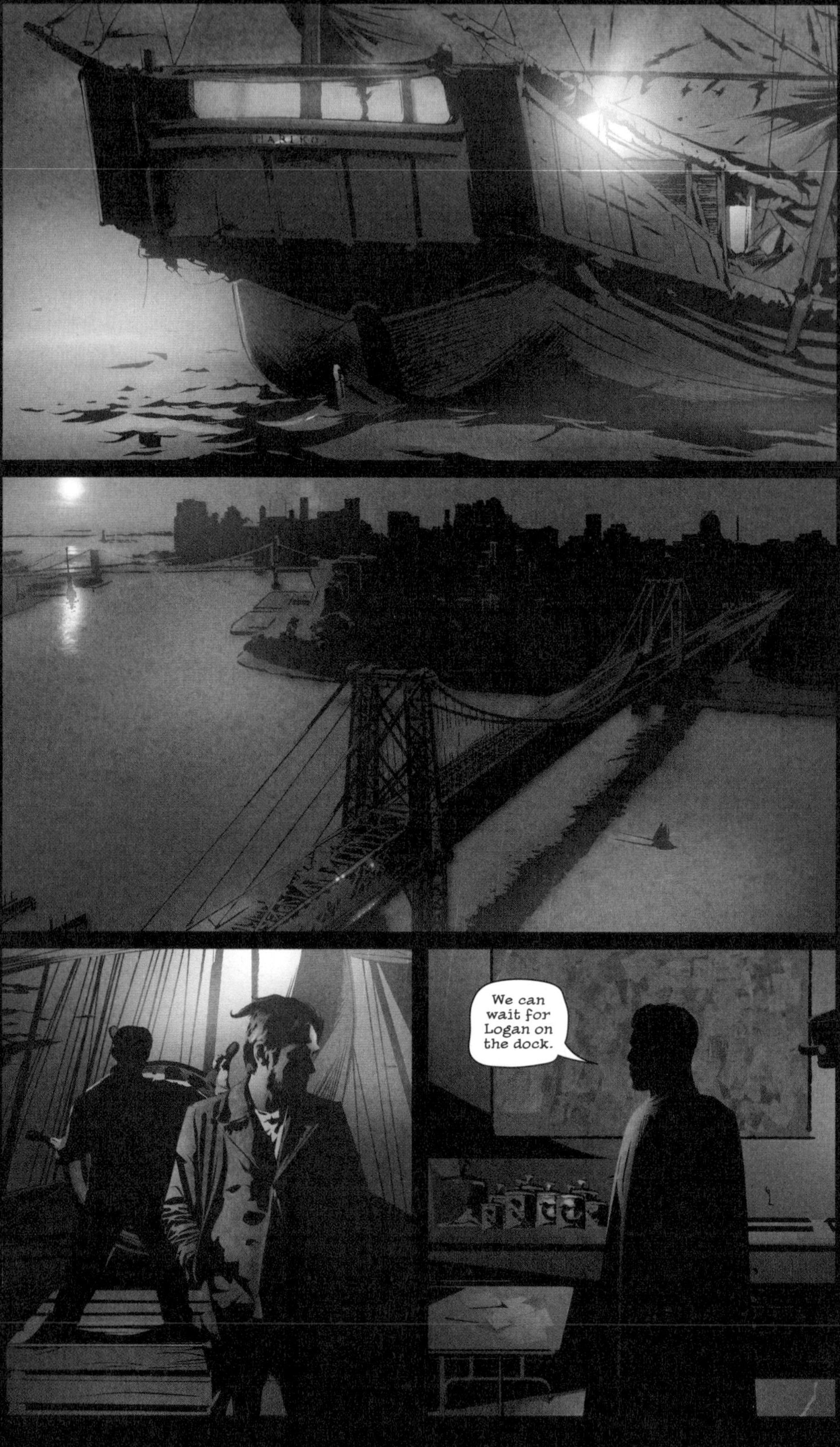
We can wait for Logan on the dock.

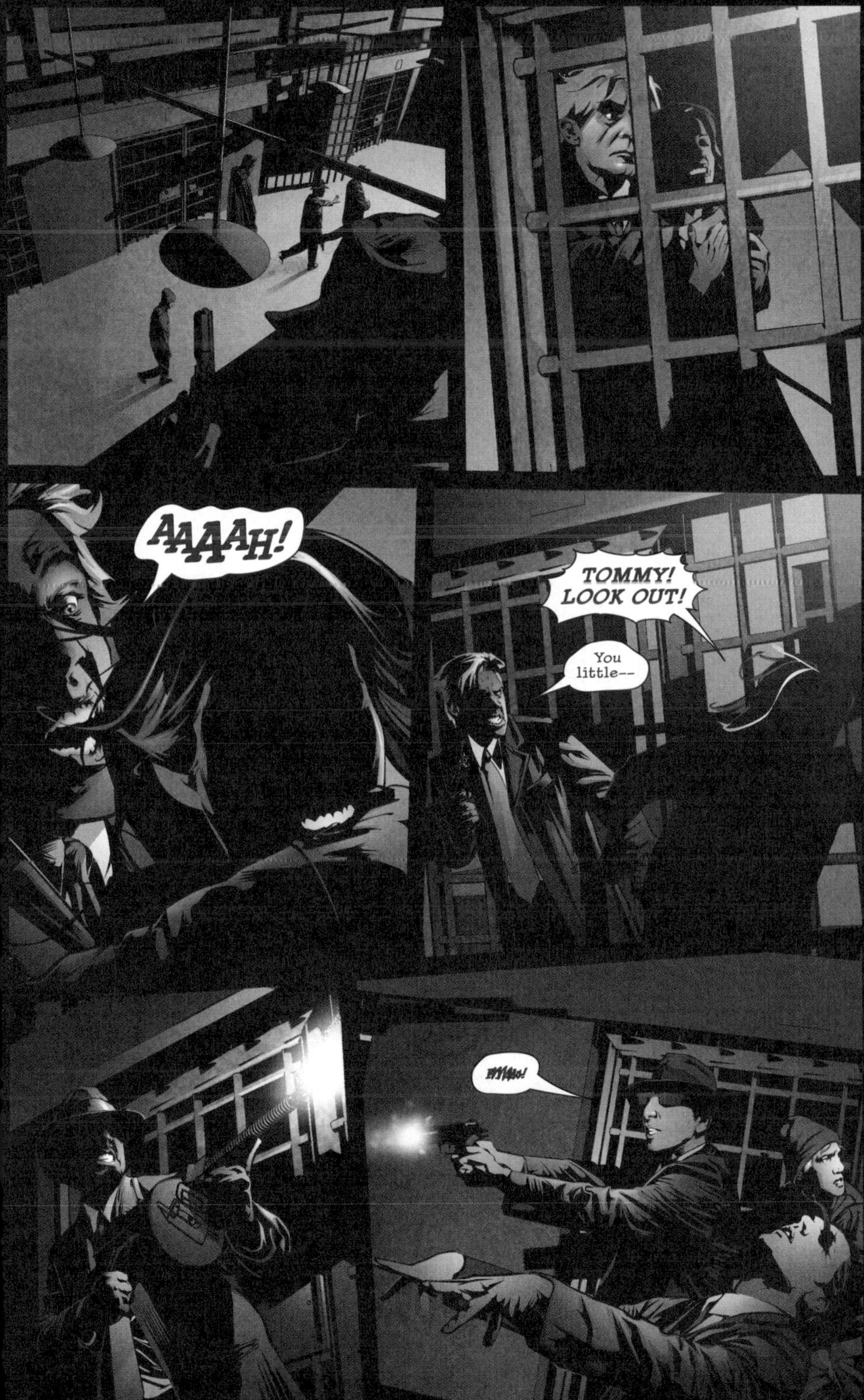
AAAAH!
TOMMY! LOOK OUT!
You little--

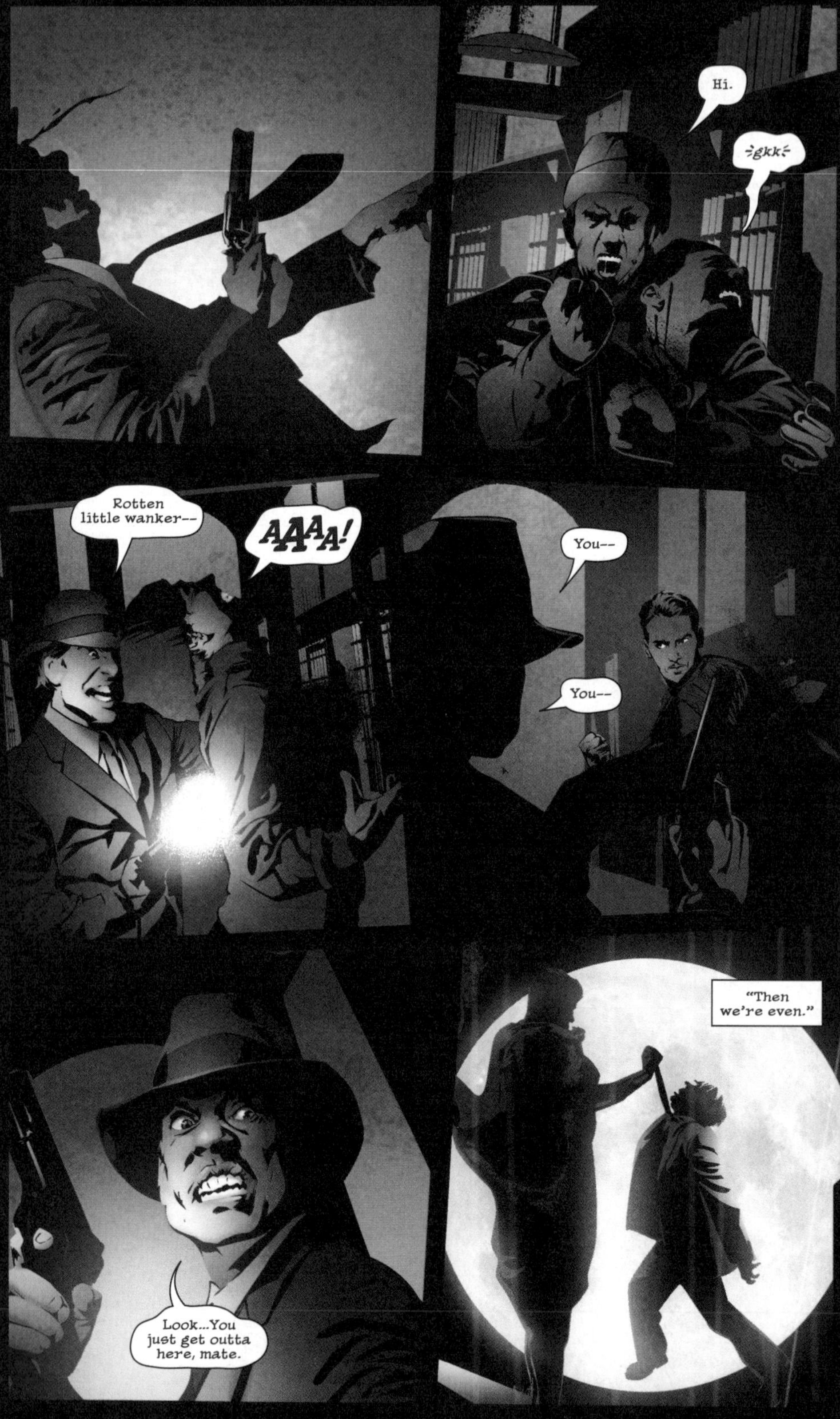
Hi.
gkk
Rotten little wanker--
AAAA!
You--
You--
Look...You just get outta here, mate.
"Then we're even."

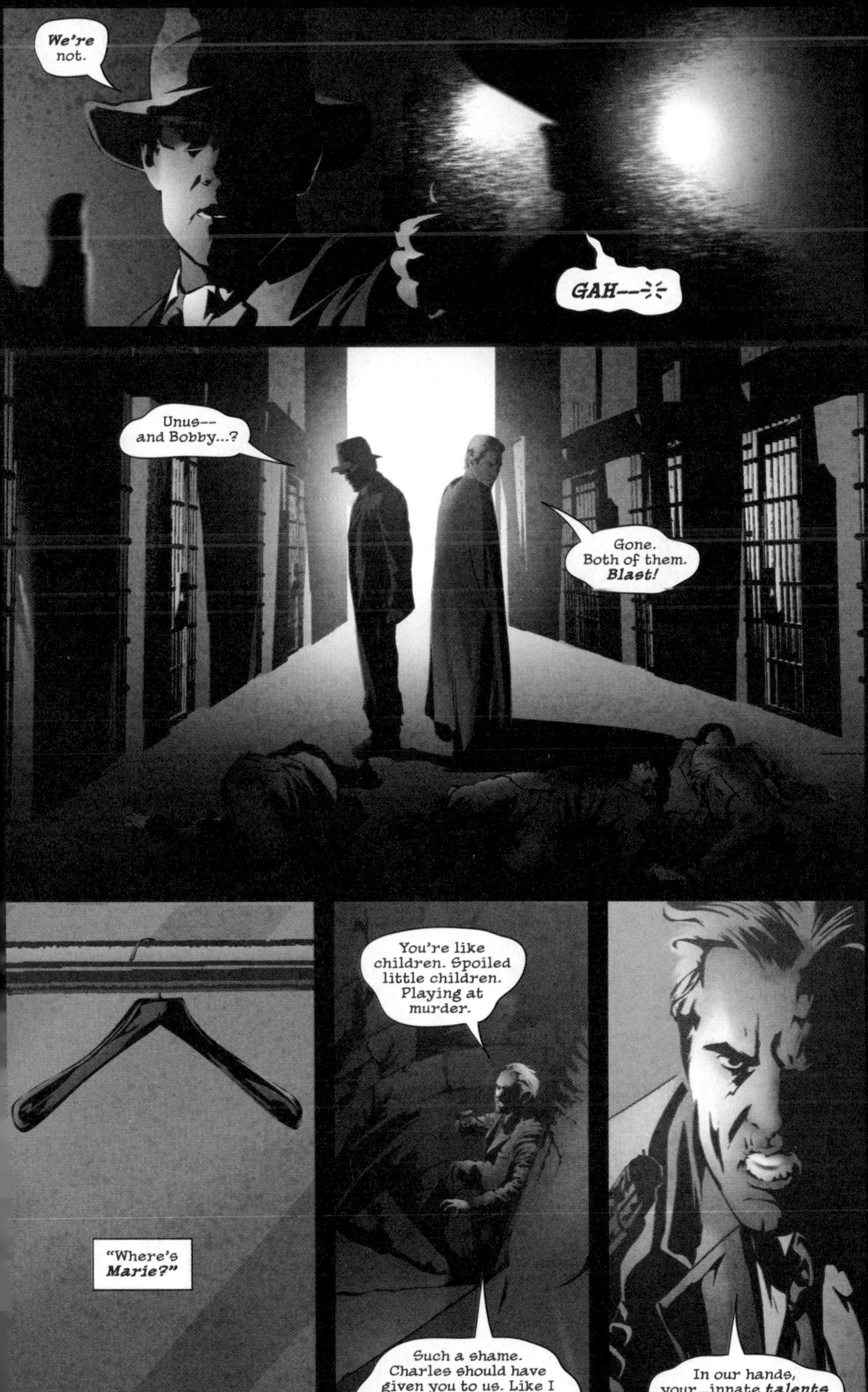

We're not.
GAH--
Unus--and Bobby...?
Gone. Both of them. Blast!
"Where's Marie?"
You're like children. Spoiled little children. Playing at murder.
Such a shame. Charles should have given you to us. Like I asked. The Brotherhood could have used you.
In our hands, your...innate talents could have achieved so much.

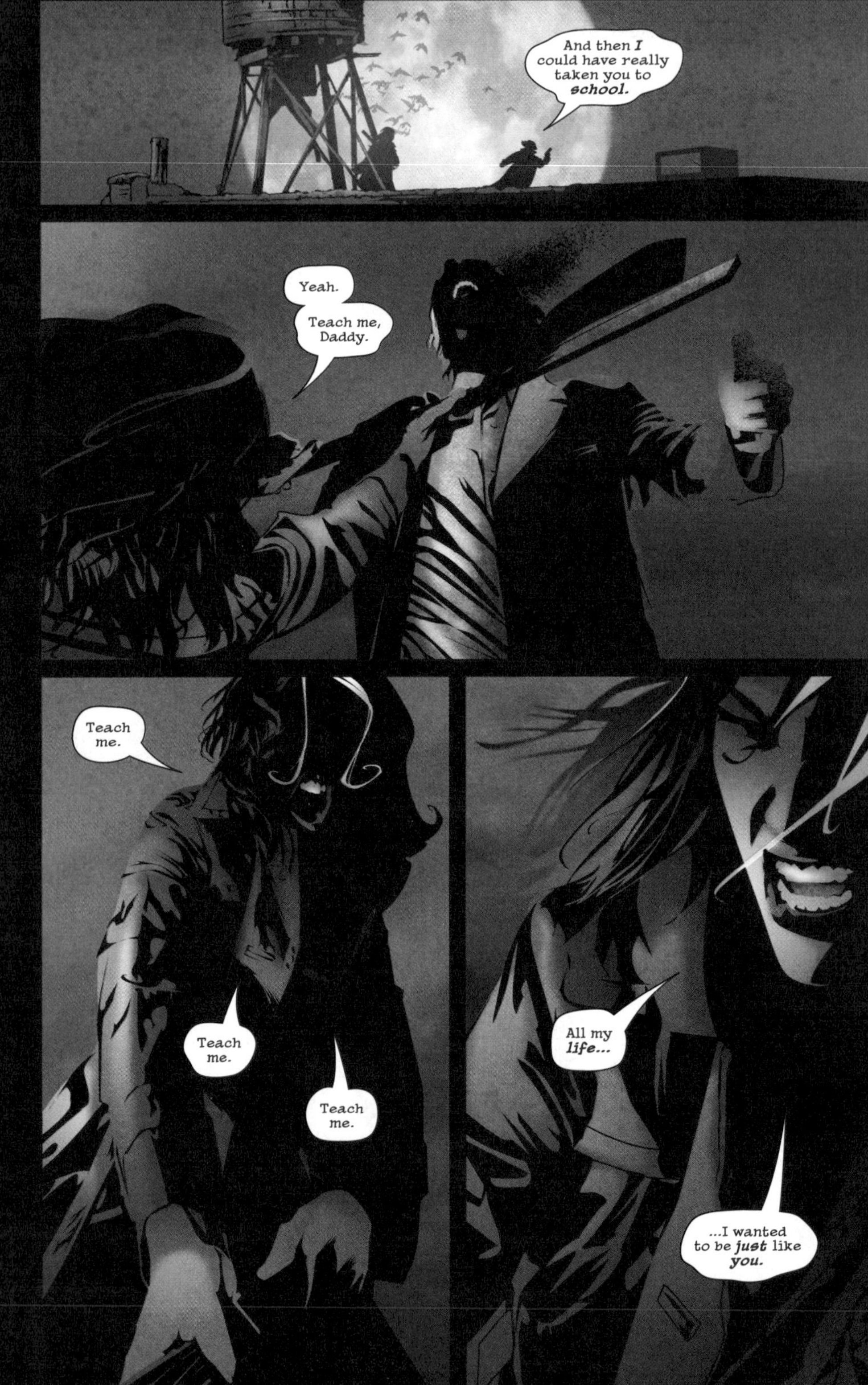
And then *I* could have really taken you to *school.*
Yeah.
Teach me, Daddy.
Teach me.
Teach me.
Teach me.
All my *life...*
...I wanted to be *just* like *you.*

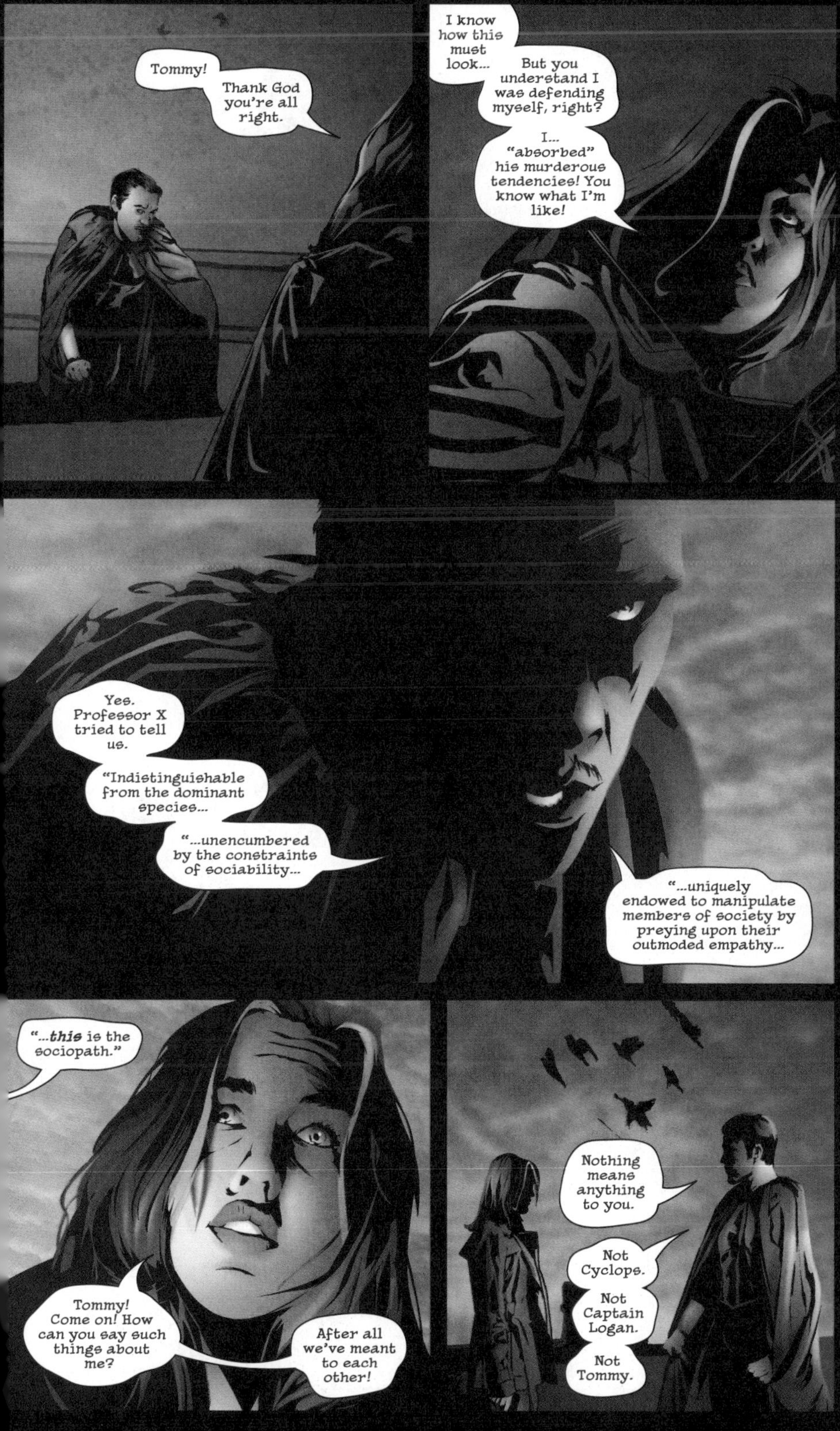
Tommy!
Thank God you're all right.
I know how this must look...
But you understand I was defending myself, right?
I... "absorbed" his murderous tendencies! You know what I'm like!
Yes. Professor X tried to tell us.
"Indistinguishable from the dominant species...
"...unencumbered by the constraints of sociability...
"...uniquely endowed to manipulate members of society by preying upon their outmoded empathy...
"...*this* is the sociopath."
Tommy! Come on! How can you say such things about me?
After all we've meant to each other!
Nothing means anything to you.
Not Cyclops.
Not Captain Logan.
Not Tommy.

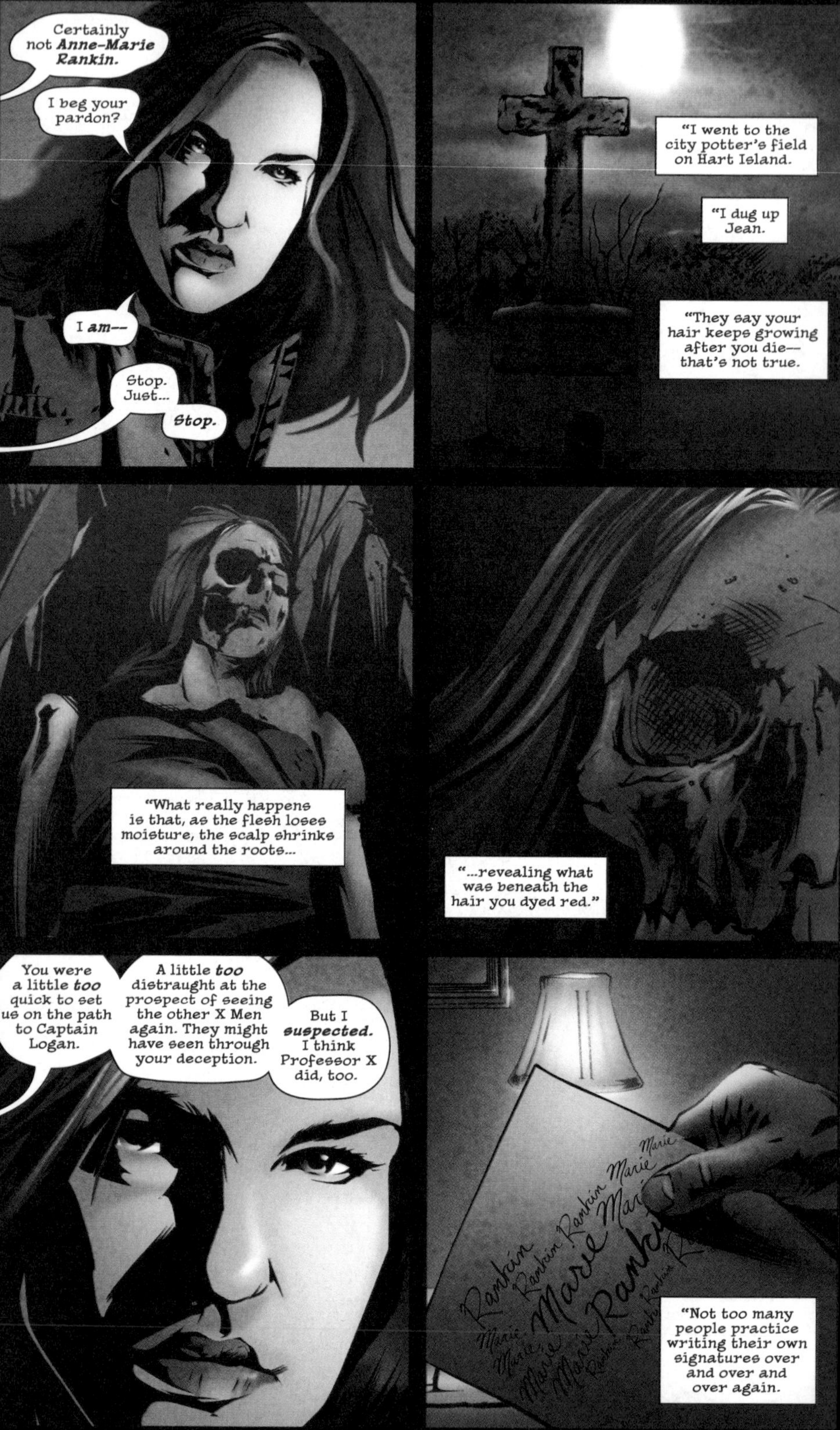
Certainly not *Anne-Marie Rankin.*
I beg your pardon?
I *am*--
Stop. Just...
Stop.
"I went to the city potter's field on Hart Island.
"I dug up Jean.
"They say your hair keeps growing after you die—that's not true.
"What really happens is that, as the flesh loses moisture, the scalp shrinks around the roots...
"...revealing what was beneath the hair you dyed red."
You were a little *too* quick to set us on the path to Captain Logan.
A little *too* distraught at the prospect of seeing the other X Men again. They might have seen through your deception.
But I *suspected.* I think Professor X did, too.
"Not too many people practice writing their own signatures over and over and over again.

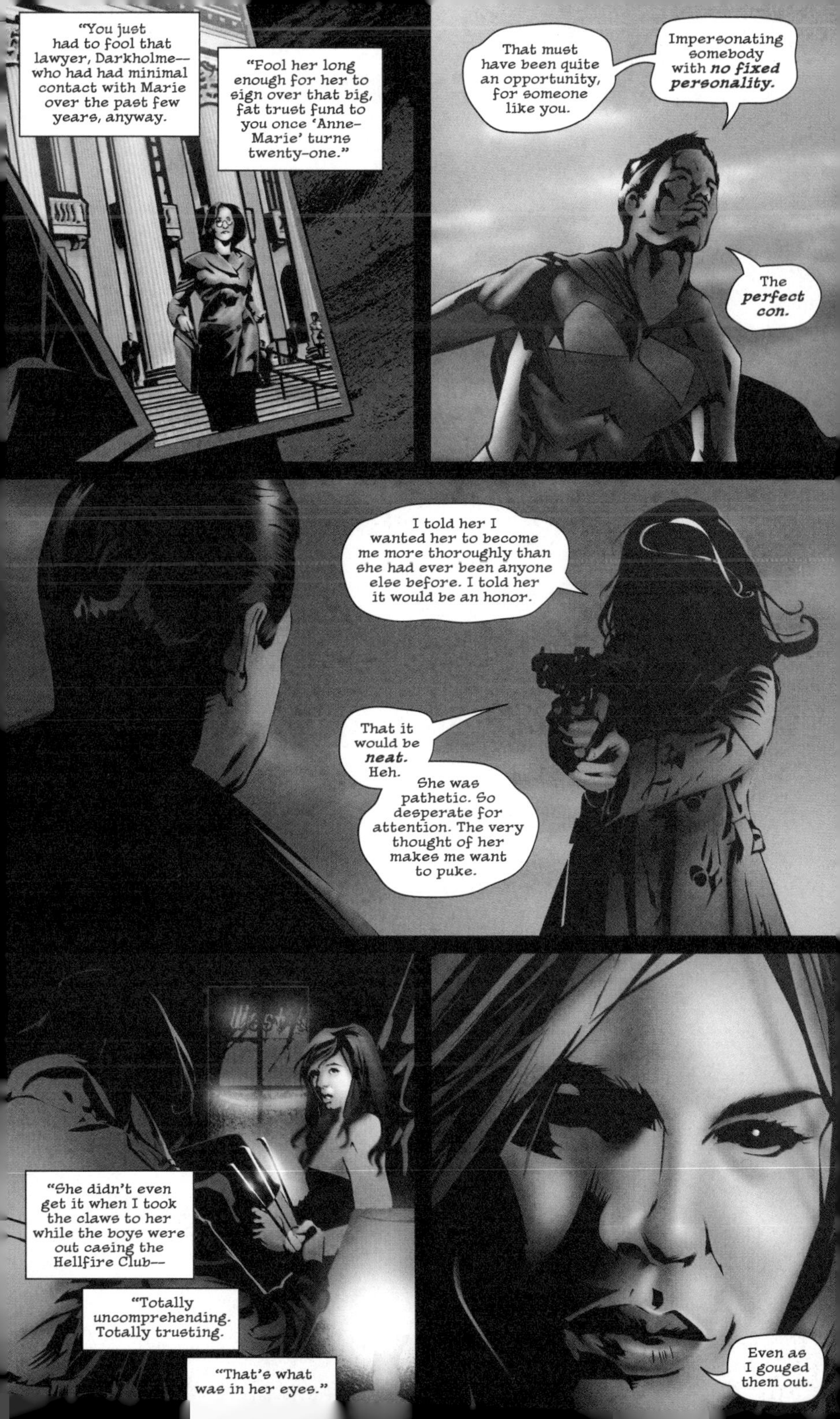
"You just had to fool that lawyer, Darkholme--who had had minimal contact with Marie over the past few years, anyway.
"Fool her long enough for her to sign over that big, fat trust fund to you once 'Anne-Marie' turns twenty-one."
That must have been quite an opportunity, for someone like you.
Impersonating somebody with **no fixed personality.**
The ***perfect con.***
I told her I wanted her to become me more thoroughly than she had ever been anyone else before. I told her it would be an honor.
That it would be ***neat.*** Heh.
She was pathetic. So desperate for attention. The very thought of her makes me want to puke.
"She didn't even get it when I took the claws to her while the boys were out casing the Hellfire Club--
"Totally uncomprehending. Totally trusting.
"That's what was in her eyes."
Even as I gouged them out.

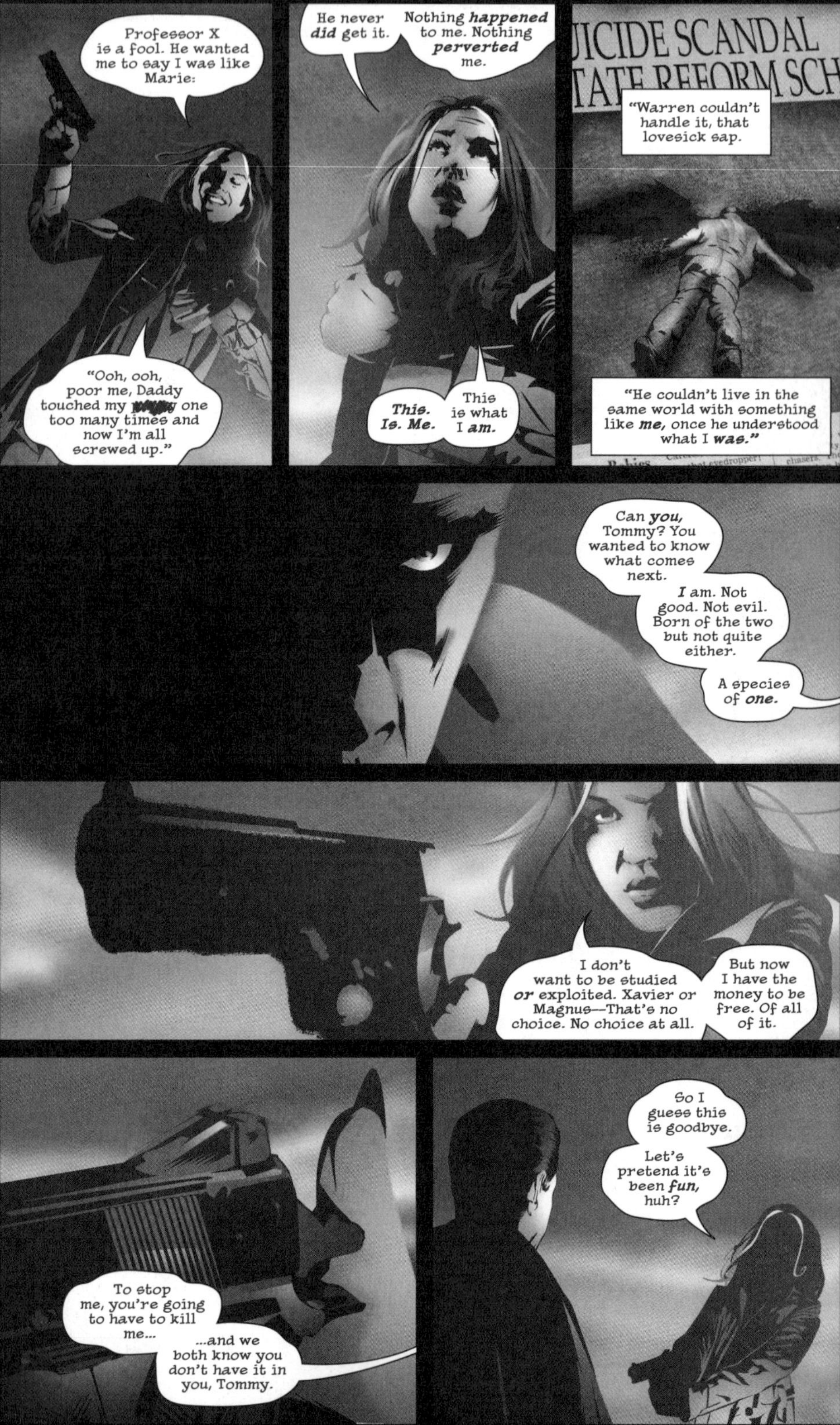
Professor X is a fool. He wanted me to say I was like Marie:
"Ooh, ooh, poor me, Daddy touched my [redacted] one too many times and now I'm all screwed up."
He never did get it.
Nothing happened to me. Nothing perverted me.
This. Is. Me.
This is what I am.
UICIDE SCANDAL
TATE REFORM SCH
"Warren couldn't handle it, that lovesick sap.
"He couldn't live in the same world with something like me, once he understood what I was."
Can you, Tommy? You wanted to know what comes next.
I am. Not good. Not evil. Born of the two but not quite either.
A species of one.
I don't want to be studied or exploited. Xavier or Magnus––That's no choice. No choice at all.
But now I have the money to be free. Of all of it.
To stop me, you're going to have to kill me...
...and we both know you don't have it in you, Tommy.
So I guess this is goodbye.
Let's pretend it's been fun, huh?

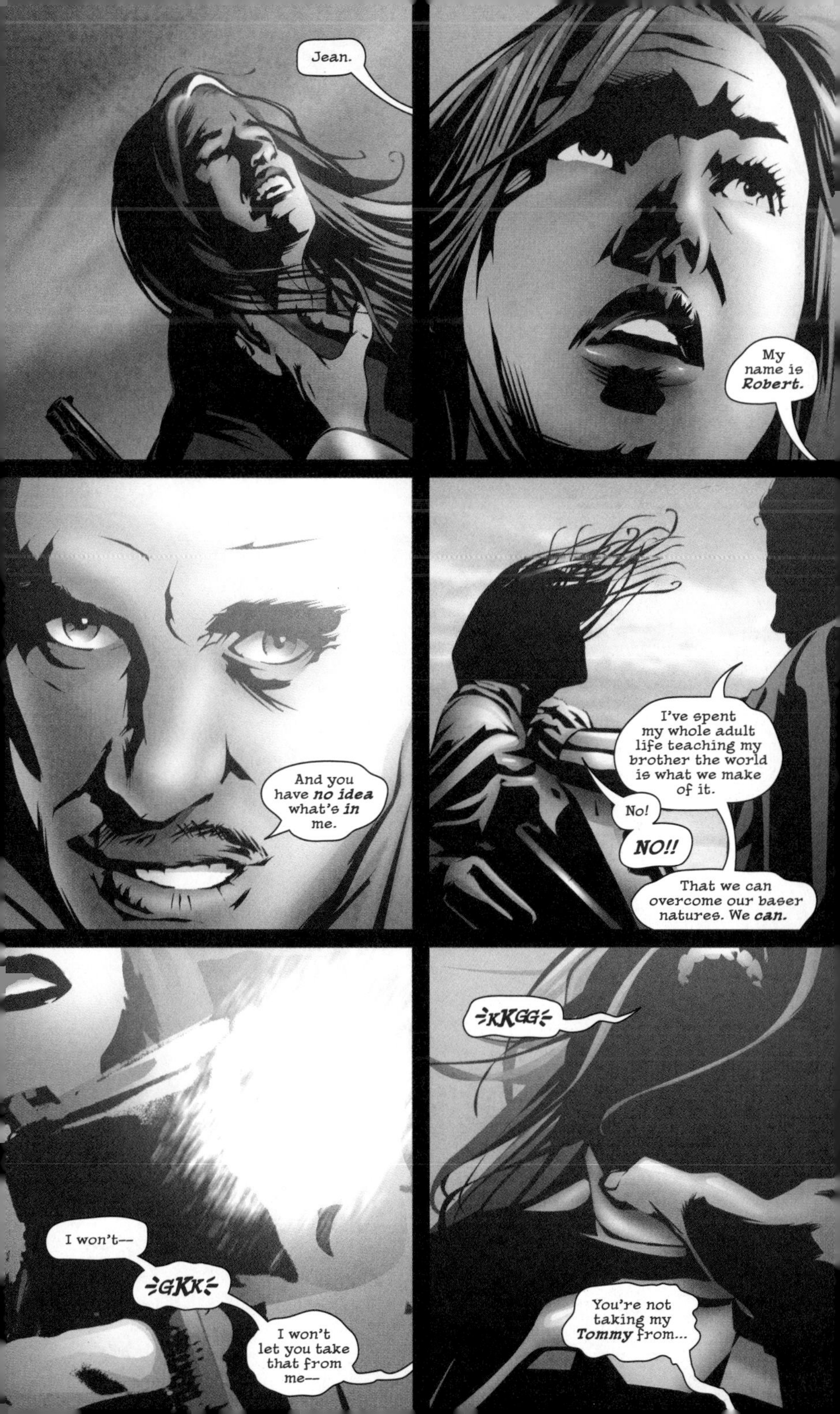
Jean.
My name is *Robert.*
And you have ***no idea*** what's ***in*** me.
I've spent my whole adult life teaching my brother the world is what we make of it.
No!
NO!!
That we can overcome our baser natures. We ***can.***
I won't--
GKK
I won't let you take that from me--
KKGG
You're not taking my ***Tommy*** from...

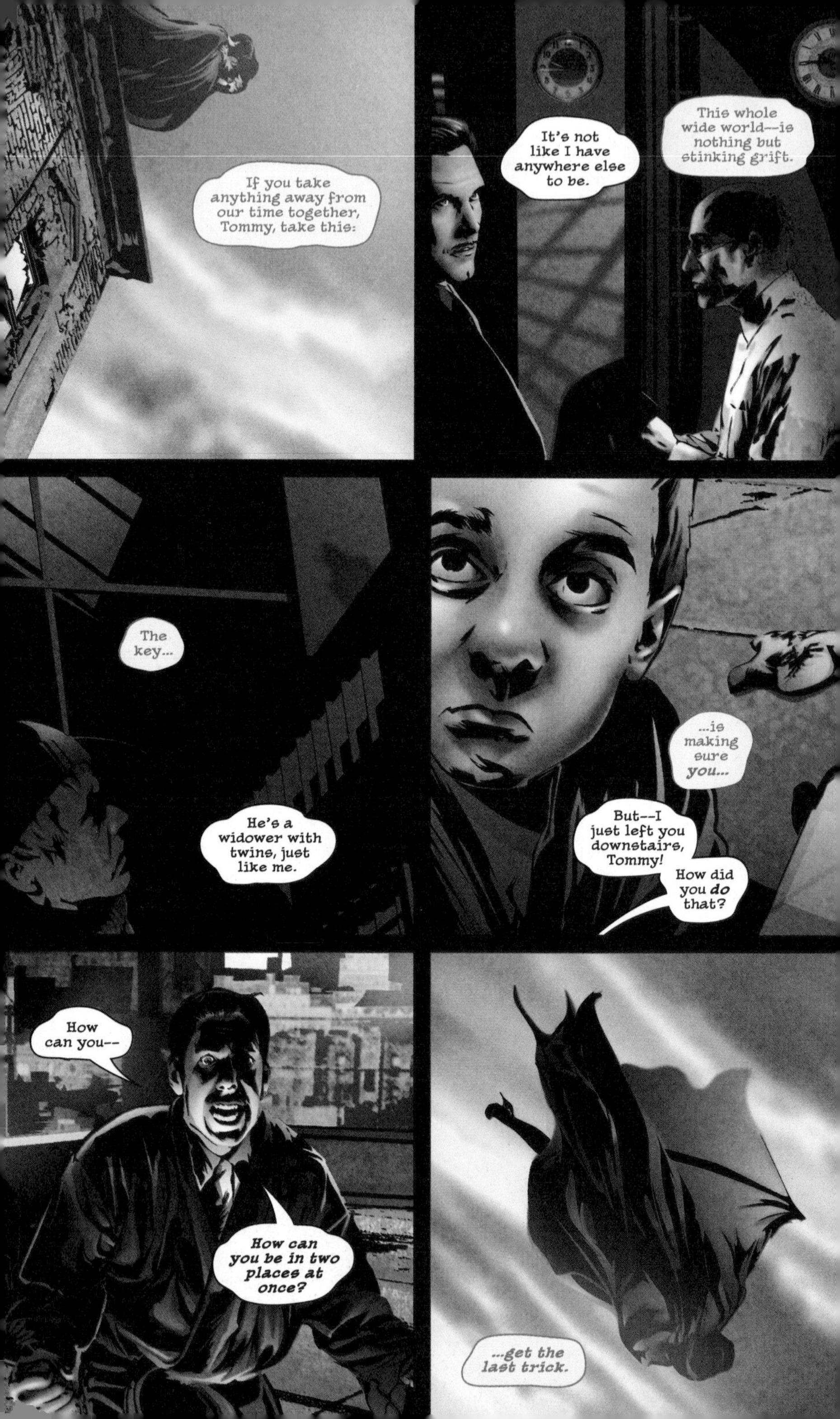
If you take anything away from our time together, Tommy, take this:
It's not like I have anywhere else to be.
This whole wide world--is nothing but stinking grift.
The key...
He's a widower with twins, just like me.
...is making sure *you...*
But--I just left you downstairs, Tommy!
How did you *do* that?
How can you--
How can you be in two places at once?
...get the last trick.

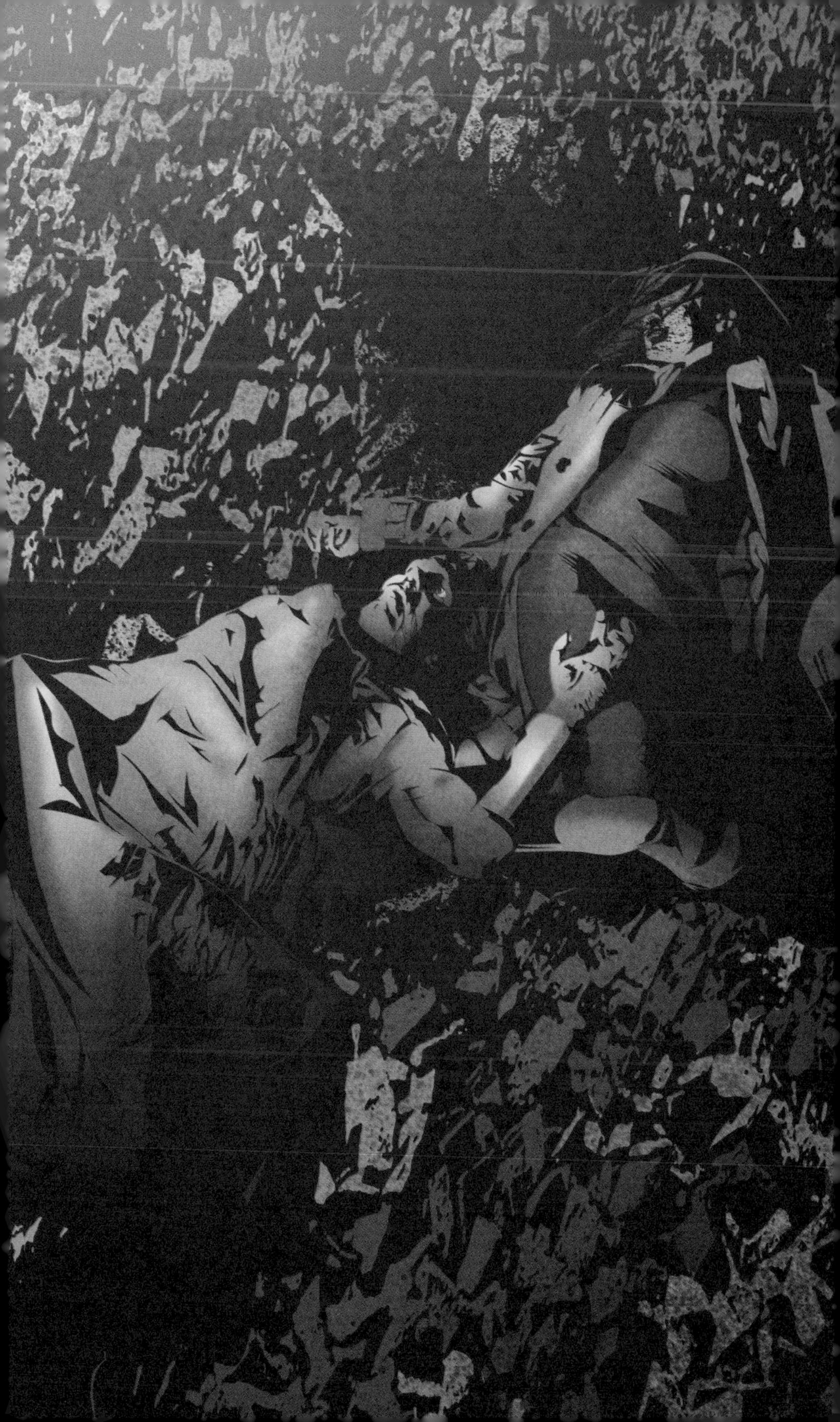

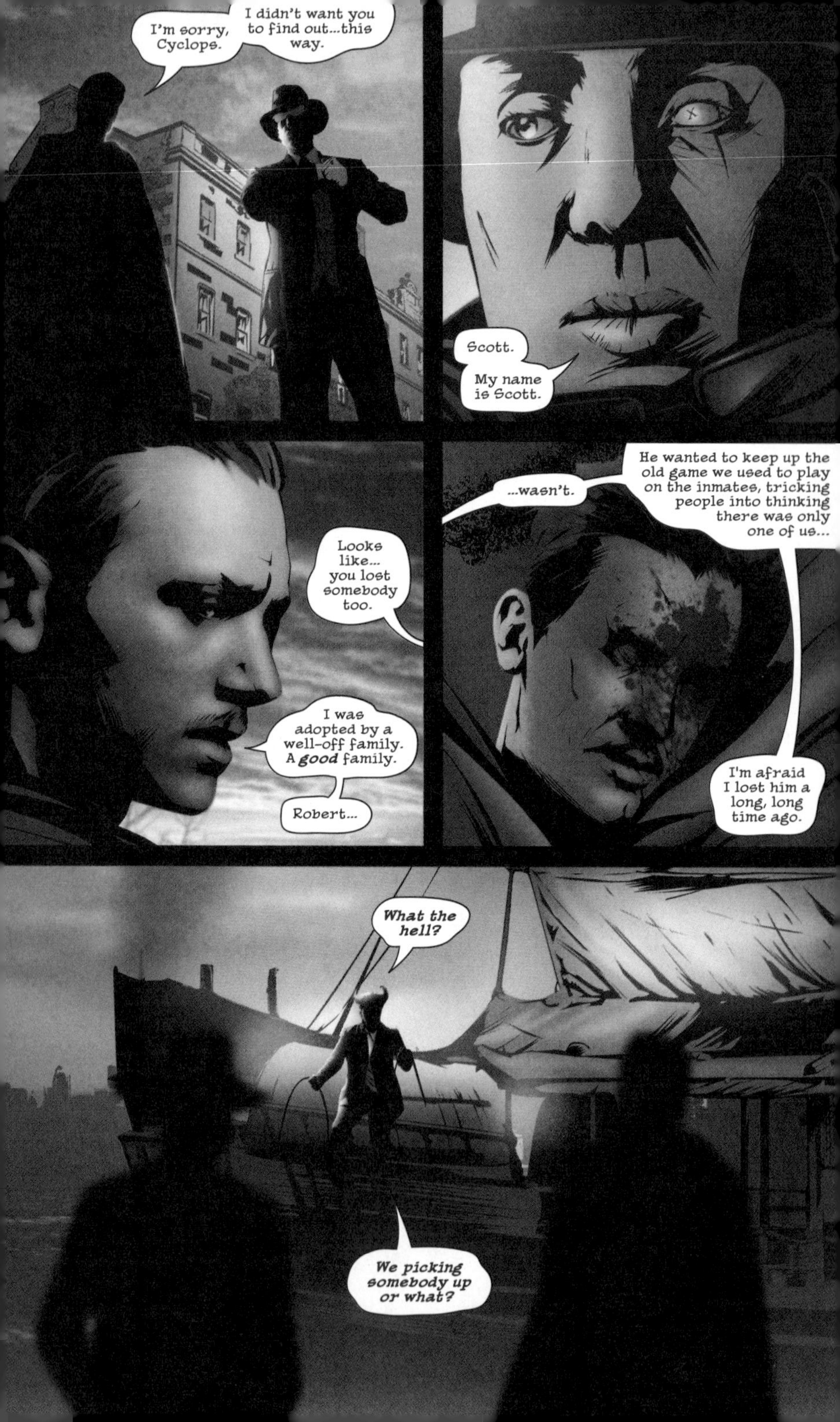

I'm sorry, Cyclops.
I didn't want you to find out...this way.
Scott.
My name is Scott.
Looks like... you lost somebody too.
I was adopted by a well-off family. A *good* family.
Robert...
...wasn't.
He wanted to keep up the old game we used to play on the inmates, tricking people into thinking there was only one of us...
I'm afraid I lost him a long, long time ago.
What the hell?
We picking somebody up or what?

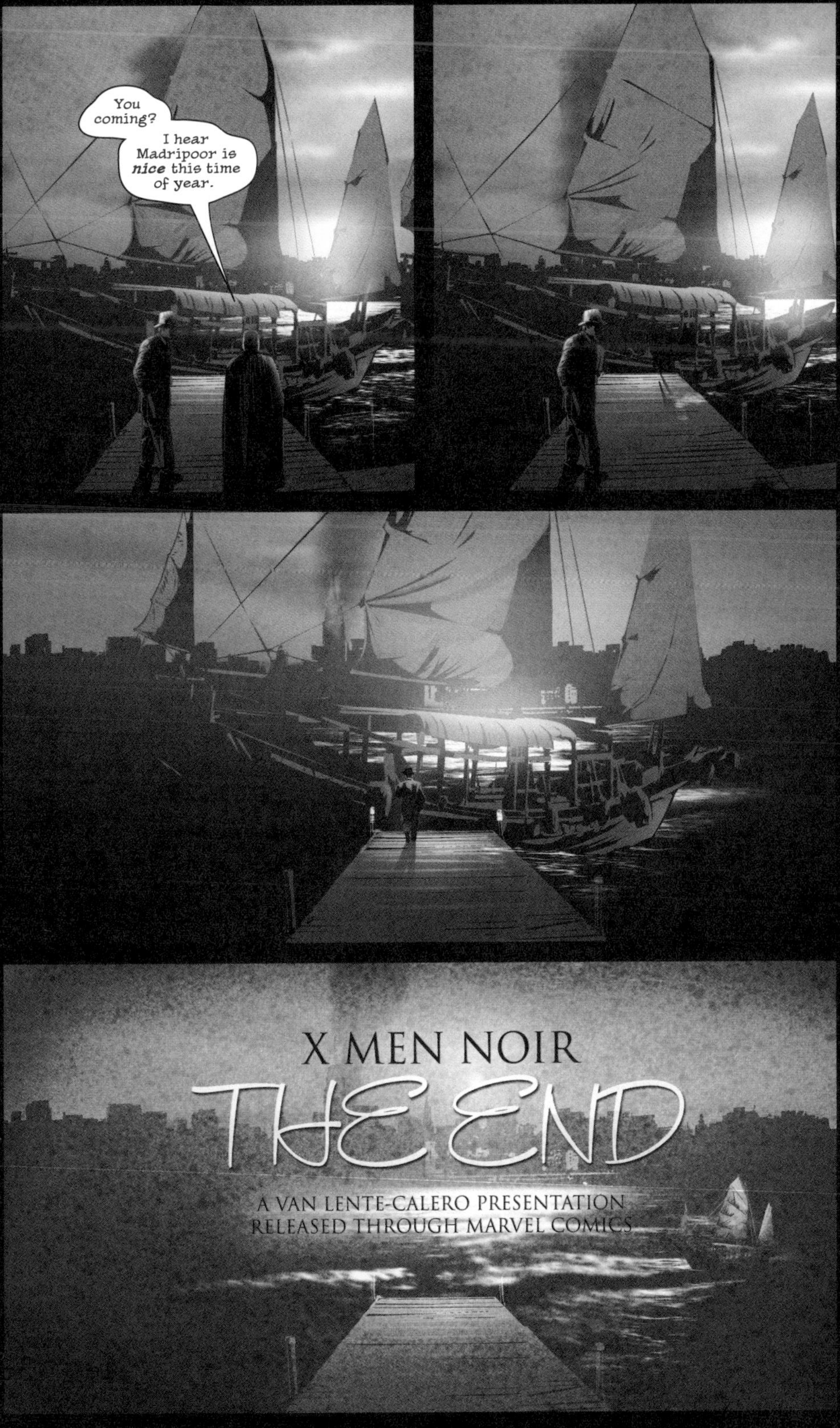
You coming?
I hear Madripoor is *nice* this time of year.
X MEN NOIR
THE END
A VAN LENTE-CALERO PRESENTATION
RELEASED THROUGH MARVEL COMICS

THE SENTINELS
By Bolivar Trask

Chapter Four: E is for Extinction

Nimrod barely had time to react before a crack team of neutralizer-wielding Sentinels burst into Dr. Lang's laboratory, spraying the room with sizzling bioelectric gunfire! One bolt hit the wizened eugenicist right between the eyes, blackening his head like the top of a spent match.

"No!" Rachel screamed, and lunged toward the scientist's plummeting corpse. But this selflessness left her vulnerable to a blast from the rear by one of the invaders.

Time seemed to slow for Nimrod as he watched his beloved collapse to the floor and twitch spasmodically. While Muties and Sentinels clashed all around him, he flew to her and cradled her tight.

Rachel's tenuous hold on the thread of life was fast slipping away. "I… Do not want to leave you… Before we have the chance to pass on… Our perfect genes," she gasped in a weakened voice.

"You *won't* go, Rachel! I won't let you!" Nimrod said, his eyes filling with tears – perfect tears, of course, for the ducts beneath his eyes had been gleaned from the genetic pattern of the most melodramatic starlets of Old Hollywood's silver screen.

"Promise me, won't you, beloved, that no matter who you have children with – you won't let them grow up in a world like this. Save humanity from those who would render it no longer worth saving, Nimrod!"

"I promise, Rachel, I promise!"

Nimrod sobbed, but soon he realized he was making promises to a corpse.

As Nimrod closed his beloved's eyes forever and rose, he found himself looking at the dull iron bulk of that death-dealing remnant of the Age of Apocalypse – one of the mad Egyptian En Sabah Nur's Phoenix Bombs. In the bombardment of shocks that had accompanied his arrival in the Muties' tunnels, he had yet to realize – until now – that the huge explosive rested atop a railway flatbed that itself straddled the subway tracks snaking out of the room and into the underground transit system of Old New York below.

"Callisto!" Nimrod called out to the queen of the Muties, who was running a Sentinel through with her vibro-sword. "Is this ordnance live?"

"It was a dud when we excavated it from one of the old sewer tunnels," came the reply, "but when we rolled it here into Dr. Lang's laboratory he worked his techno-magic on it and reactivated the explosive."

Nimrod's brain raced with a speed equal to or greater than the grey matter of the German philosophers, mathematicians and physicists from which his own mind received its hereditary template. "Do these tracks connect to a subway line that can take us underneath the Hall of Experimental Evolution?" he asked.

Callisto immediately understood the former Sentinel's meaning and grinned raffishly. "I'll drive," she said.

She leapt onto the rear of the railway sidecar coupled to the Phoenix Bomb's side and began pumping the handlebars furiously.

At just that moment a contingent of Sentinels led by none other than Nimrod's duplicitous commander, Bastion, exploded into Dr. Lang's chamber. Nimrod swiftly grabbed dual neutralizers off the fallen ex-comrades lying around him and, twin barrels flashing, kept his enemies at bay long enough to leap on the back of the flatbed as it rolled out of the chamber and into the gloomy, labyrinthine tunnels criss-crossing the barren depths of Old New York.

Nimrod joined his steel-laced muscles to Callisto's and together they pumped the flatbed at incredible speeds, executing a

baffling series of twists and turns, choosing one forking tunnel branch after another. The Mutie queen, who, she claimed, could navigate these tunnels blindfolded since she was but a princess, at last declared they had reached their destination. Nimrod dropped the brake, halting their progress with a loud shriek of metal.

Callisto explained that the Muties had evolved hearing as keen as any dirt-dwelling mole in their long exile underground, and came to this spot to listen to the deliberations of the Breeders Council through the airshafts snaking their way up into the Hall of Experimental Evolution. It amused her people to eavesdrop on the Breeders as they bickered over innumerable sundry schemes for their destruction.

"Well, let's give them something to talk about," Nimrod said, and turned his attentions to the bomb's controls. Beyond the fairly straightforward timer, the only other setting of note was a dial that could point to one of two letters stenciled above its tip: a "D" on the left and an "E" on the right.

"What do these mean?" he asked the Mutie queen.

"Dr. Lang said they indicate the intensity of the Phoenix's blast," she replied. "The 'D' stands for the lesser explosion – 'Destruction.'"

"What about 'E?'"

"'E'…" Callisto looked grimly at her ally. "E is for Extinction."

Nimrod weighed the two options with the wisdom of Solomon, to whom, of course, he was distantly related due to the sheer volume of Israelite blood coursing through his veins.

Before he could reach out and touch the dial, however, a bioelectric blast whined down the tunnel and Callisto cried out in agony as her shoulder was singed coal-black!

Nimrod whirled to see Bastion holding a smoking neutralizer, standing atop his own railway flatbed, powered by a dozen desperately pumping Sentinels. The perfect men and women's combined horsepower allowed them to catch up to the Phoenix Bomb much faster than Nimrod could have guessed.

"It's over, traitor," Bastion snarled. He and the other Sentinels disembarked from the flatbed and advanced upon their former comrade, neutralizers drawn and pointed at him. "This is your last chance to surrender. If you're lucky, the Breeders Council will have mercy on you. They might not sentence you to death – just sterilize you. Clearly, somehow, your otherwise perfect genome has been accidentally polluted by criminal chromosomes that simply cannot be passed on to the next generation."

Nimrod hopped down from the Phoenix Bomb and stood on the tracks, holding his hands – one still gripping his drawn neutralizer – in the air. "That seems a little optimistic to me, Bastion, old boy," Nimrod chuckled. "The Council will never let me live, not with what I know now."

"Go on, set your gun down on the ground." Bastion prompted Nimrod with the barrel of his own weapon. "What do you know, exactly? That the Breeders Council is trying to help humanity reach its greatest potential? To eradicate all doubt, all fear, all prejudice? Has your mind been so fully and so swiftly infected by these Inadequates? Don't you want to be perfect?"

"No." Nimrod was in the process of crouching down, preparing to place the neutralizer on the ground. He paused however, to look up, into Bastion's eyes. "I just want to be human."

With that, Nimrod pressed the barrel of the neutralizer to the old metal track and pulled the trigger before Bastion or the other Sentinels could stop him. The neuro-electrical blast from the gun coursed down the length of the tracks and into the bodies of the gathered lawmen who had foolishly chosen to stand on them. Within moments their bodies were all jerking and smoking, and the fetid air of the tunnel was worsened by the stench of burning flesh and hair. Nimrod himself, of course, took pains to stand on the wooden cross-planks of the tracks and stood up with nary a singe as

The bomb detonated just as Nimrod beached their skiff on the irradiated shores of Old New Old New Jersey. The massive explosion leveled the glittering spires of New New New York in a brilliant fireball that from a distance appeared to take the form of a great majestic orange bird spreading its blinding wings wide and taking flight.

"We have ended a civilization – two civilizations – today," Callisto noted. "My Muties' tunnels won't survive the collapse of the city, either."

"Indeed, and I take no joy in it," Nimrod replied. "But sometimes, before

the other Sentinels dropped dead to the tunnel floor.

Nimrod leapt back up onto the Phoenix Bomb and found Callisto clinging to life. With a quick inspection of her injuries, however, Nimrod was confident he could effortlessly nurse her back to health with his own medicinal skills and herbal remedies, gleaned from the cultural memory of 5,000 years of Chinese doctors' closely-guarded secrets.

"The tunnel … to our left … lets out near the river …" Callisto gasped. "There are boats there…"

Nimrod nodded, gently silencing her by placing his fingers to her lips. He slung her over his shoulder and ran down the tunnel after setting the Phoenix Bomb for a two-hour timer, and turning the intensity dial to "E."

there can be a new beginning, there must be an ending. Humanity has rebuilt after apocalypses–twice, now. We can do it again. And we'll get it right this time."

"True. But without Dr. Lang's science wizardry how will we mix the Sentinel and Mutie genomes together?"

"Well." Nimrod winked at the Mutie queen. "There is always the old fashioned way."

The man and the woman linked hands and helped each other away from the crumbling ruins of the past, toward the future – and their Destiny.

THE END.

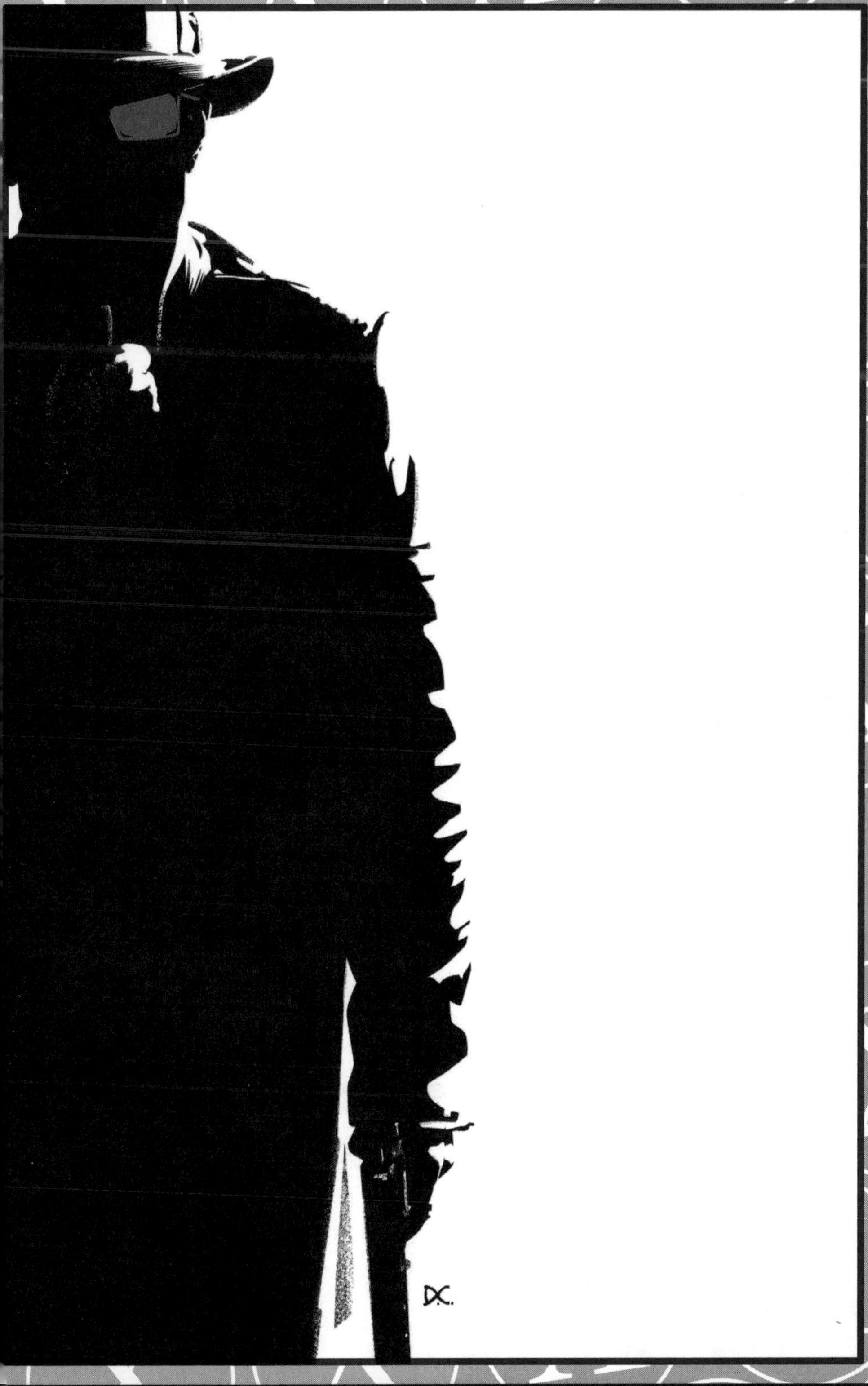

#1 VARIANT

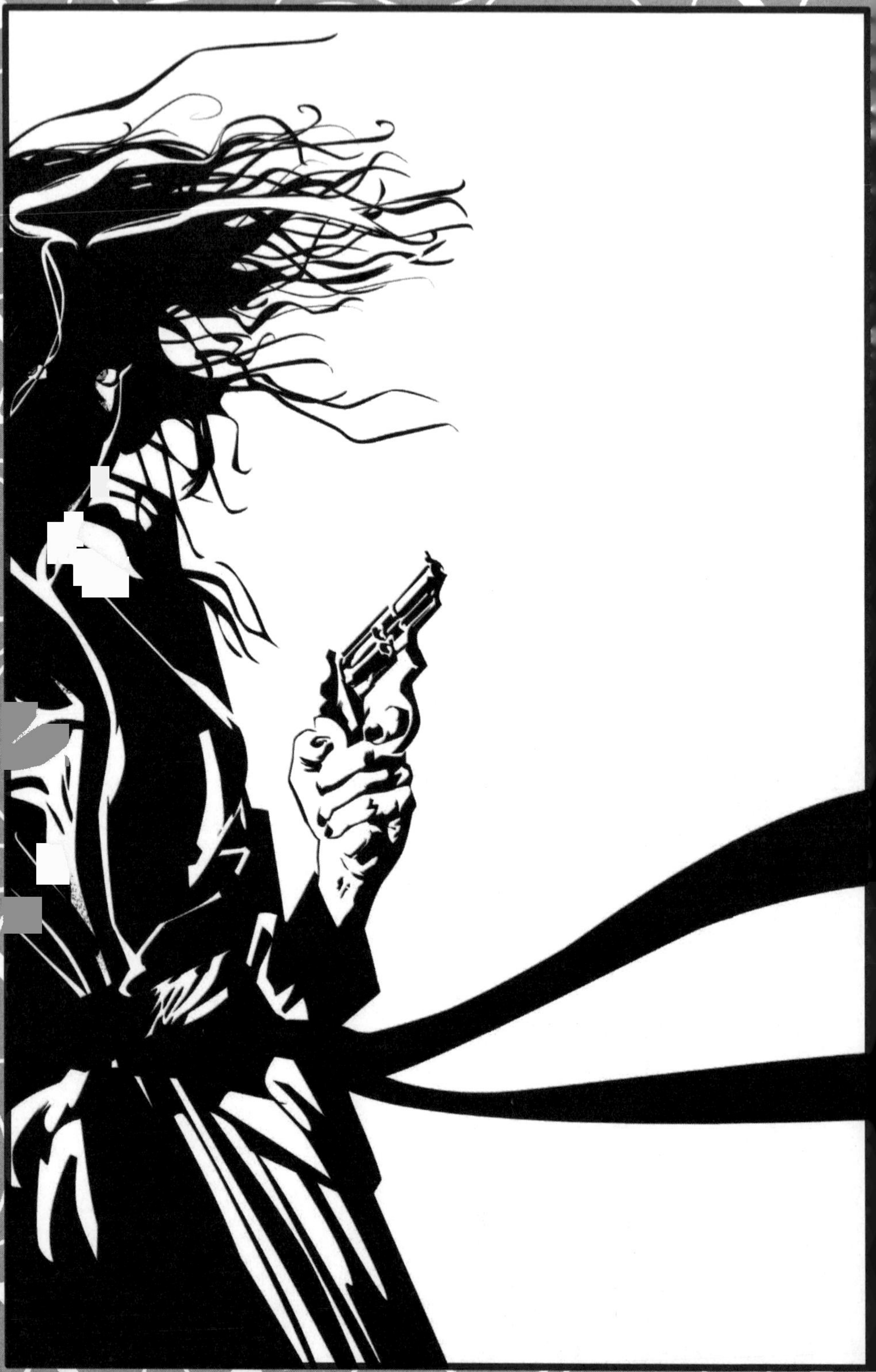

#2 VARIANT

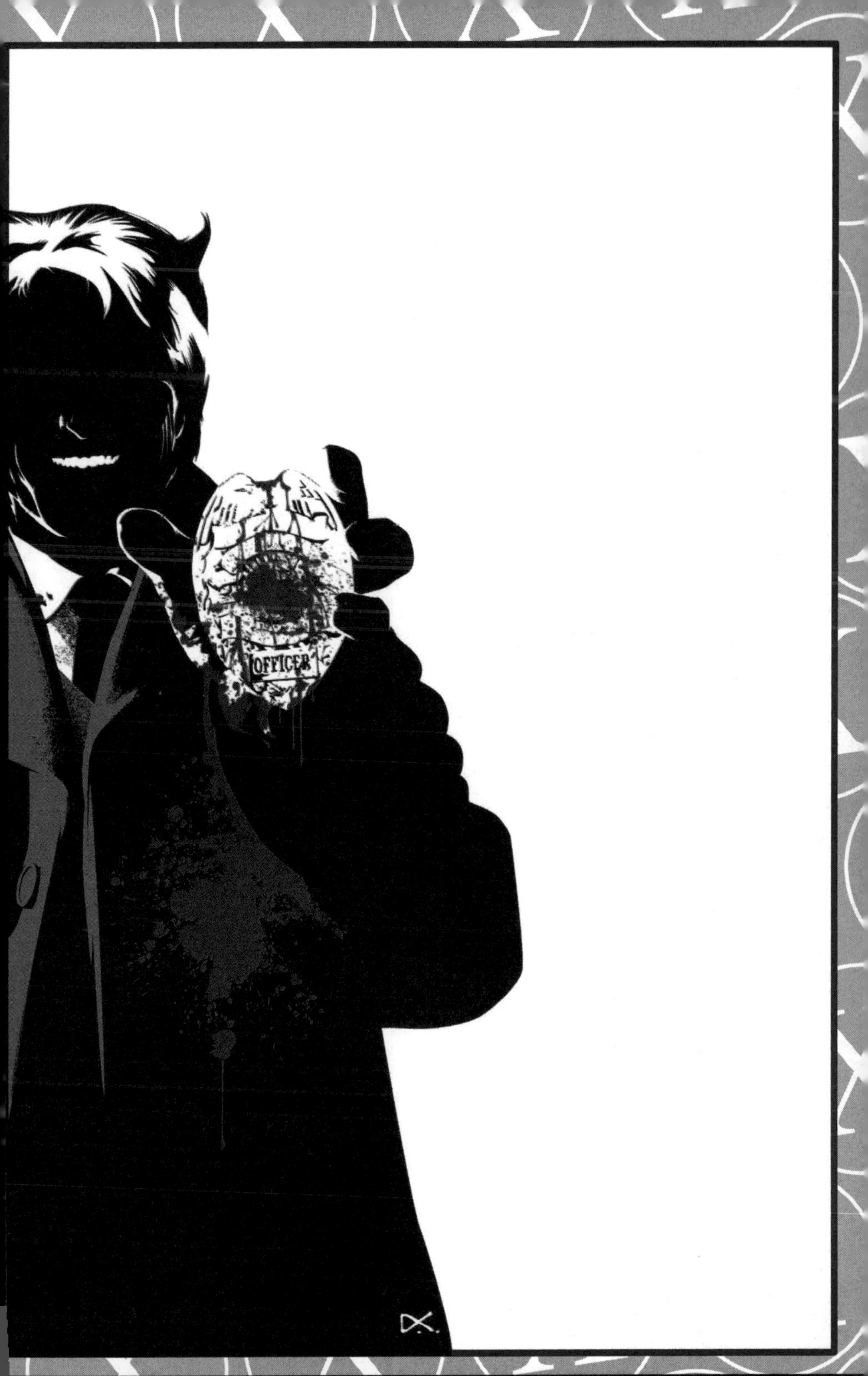
OFFICER

#3 VARIANT

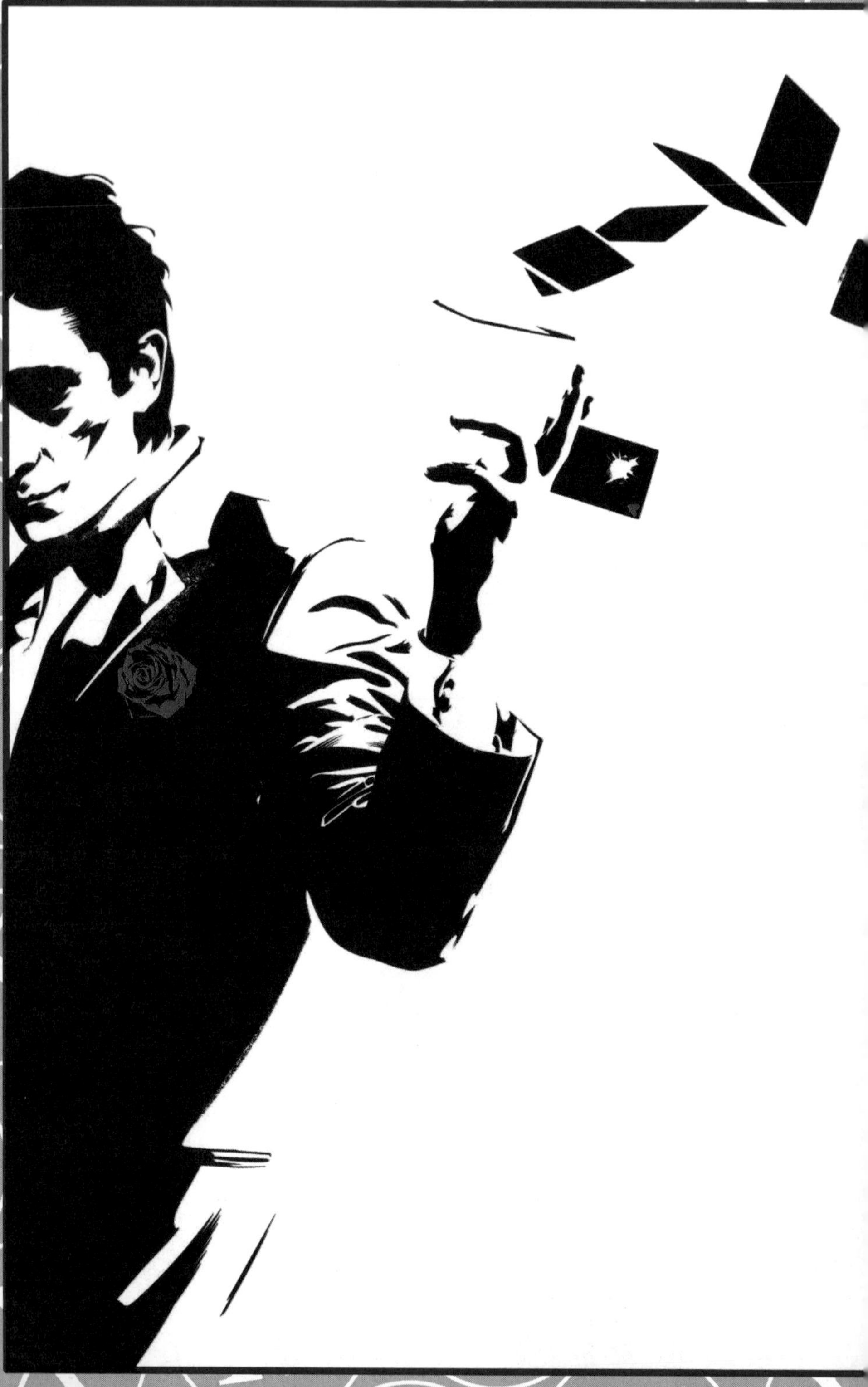

#4 VARIANT

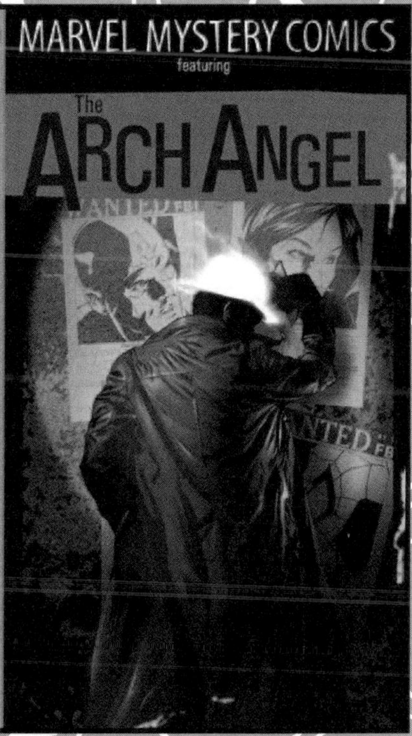
MARVEL MYSTERY COMICS
featuring
The
ARCH ANGEL
WANTED FBI
WANTED FBI

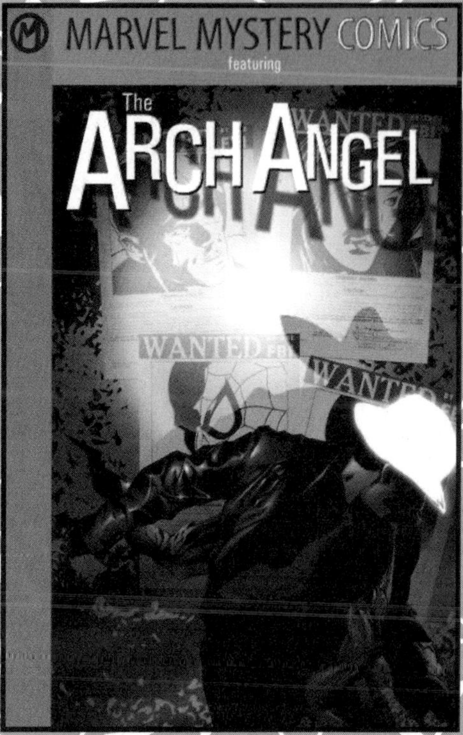
MARVEL MYSTERY COMICS
featuring
The
ARCH ANGEL
WANTED FBI
WANTED FBI
WANTED

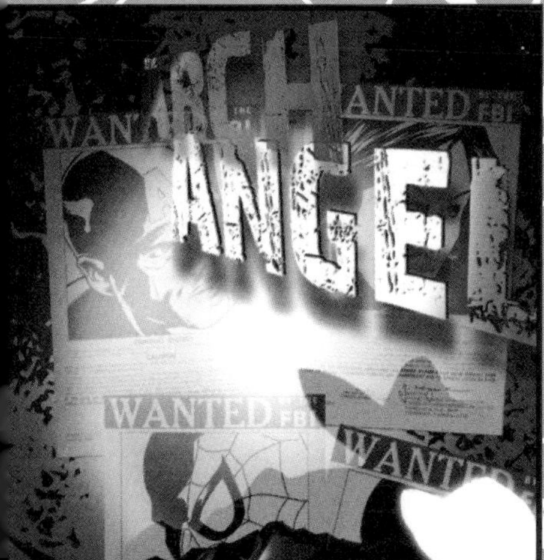
ANGEL
WANTED
WANTED FBI
WANTED FBI
WANTED

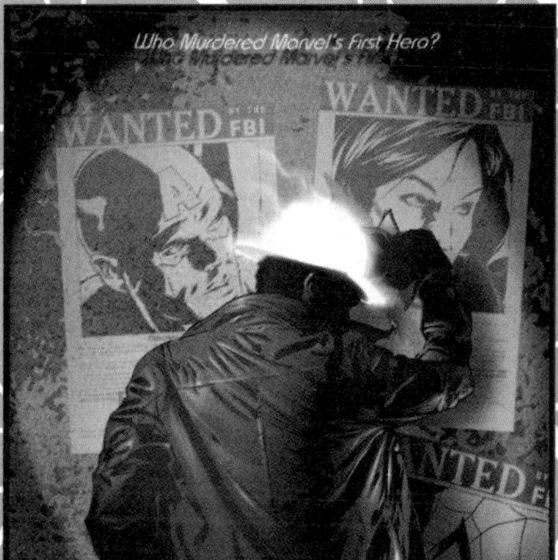
Who Murdered Marvel's First Hero?
WANTED BY THE FBI
WANTED FBI
WANTED
ANGEL

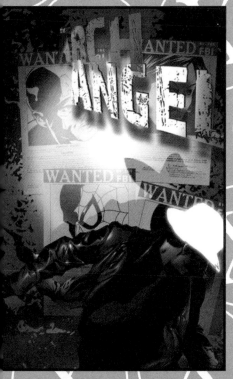

ORIGINAL CONCEPT ART

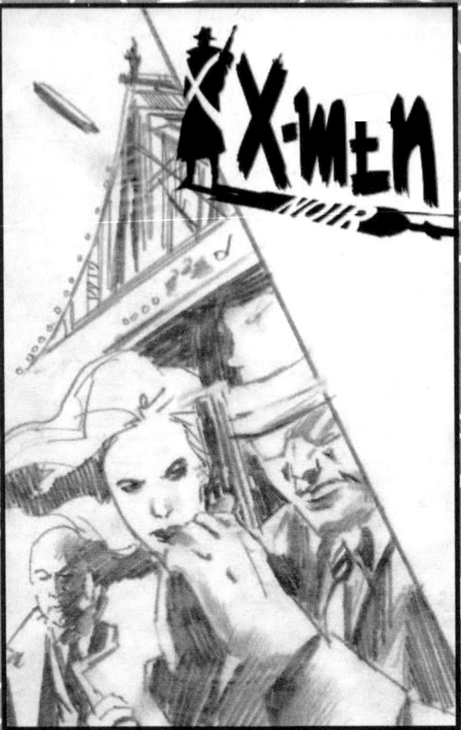
X-MEN
NOIR

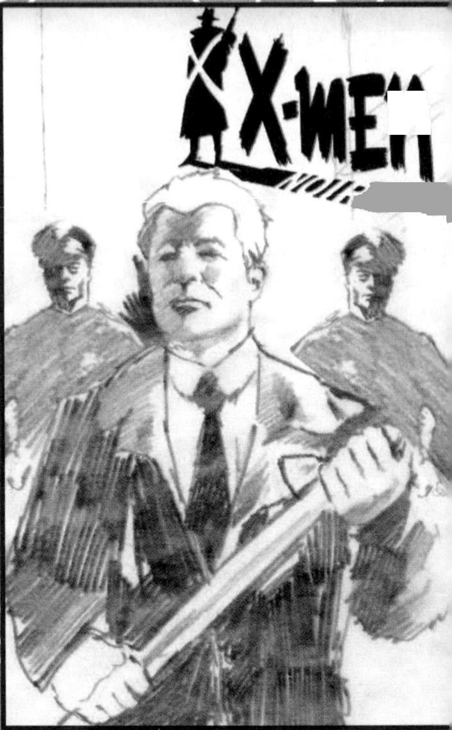
X-MEN
NOIR

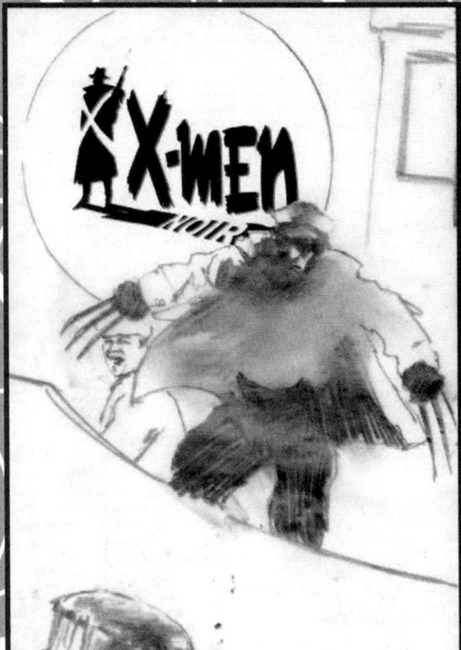
X-MEN
NOIR

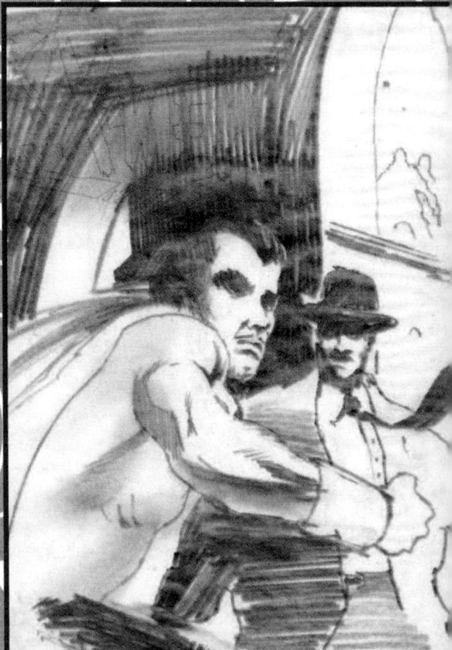

COVER SKETCHES

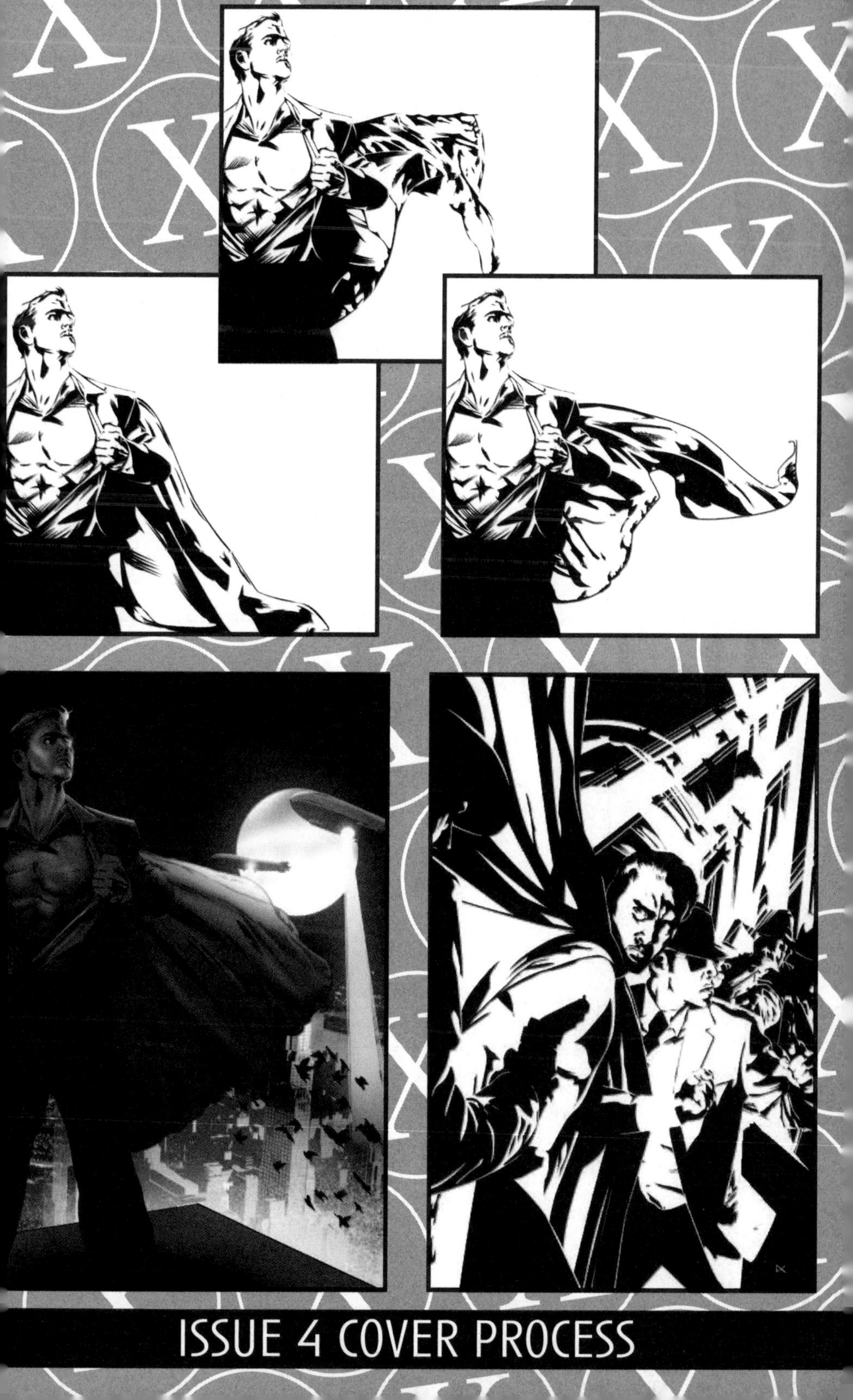

ISSUE 4 COVER PROCESS

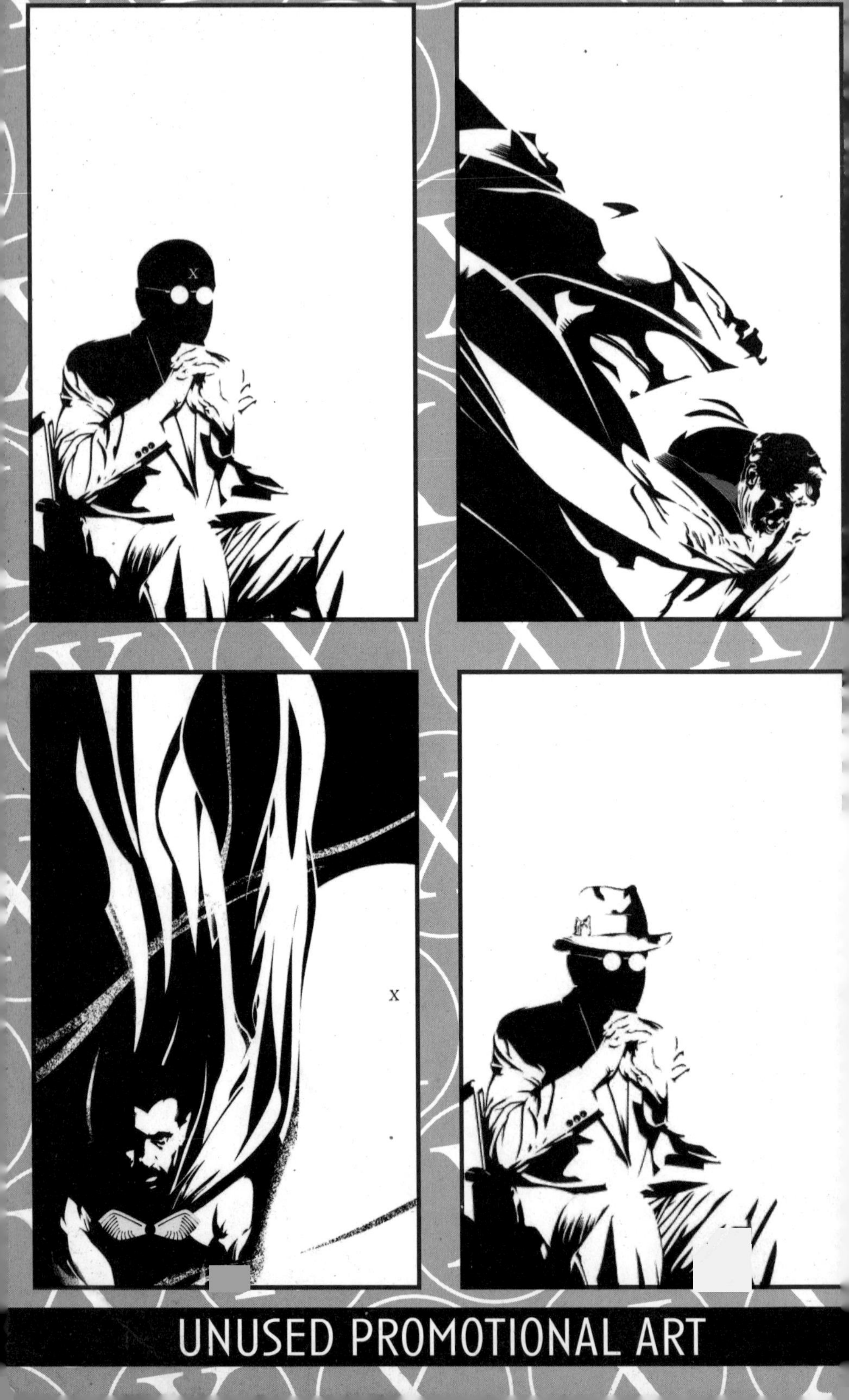

UNUSED PROMOTIONAL ART